# Back of the Big House

The University of North Carolina Press    Chapel Hill and London

The Fred W. Morrison Series in Southern Studies

# Back of the Big House

## The Architecture of Plantation Slavery

### John Michael Vlach

Manufactured in the United States of America

The paper in this book meets the guidelines for permanence and

durability of the Committee on Production Guidelines for Book

Longevity of the Council on Library Resources.

Library of Congress Cataloging-in-Publication Data

Vlach, John Michael, 1948–

   Back of the big house : the architecture of plantation slavery /

by John Michael Vlach.

     p.   cm.—(The Fred W. Morrison series in Southern studies)

   Includes bibliographical references and index.

   ISBN 0-8078-2085-7 (cloth : alk. paper).—ISBN 0-8078-4412-8

(pbk. : alk. paper)

   1. Slaves—Southern States—Social conditions.   2. Space

(Architecture)—Southern States—History—19th century.

3. Vernacular architecture—Southern States—History—19th century.

4. Plantation life—Southern States—History—19th century.

5. Southern States—Social conditions.  I. Title.  II. Series.

E443.V58   1993

975′.00496—dc20       92-34579

                   CIP

97  96  95  94  93     5  4  3  2  1

For Beverly

# Contents

# Preface

In 1865 an officer of the Freedmen's Bureau stationed in South Carolina was confounded by the behavior of his black clients. He wrote to his superiors in Washington, D.C., that former slaves from coastal plantations who had been relocated during the Civil War to inland sites "were crazy to get back to their native flats of ague and country fever." Similar reports came in from Mississippi and Louisiana as well.

One South Carolina freedman, after several years of service in the Union Army, did, in fact, return to take charge of a section of the plantation where he had previously lived and worked. Ignoring the protests of Thomas Pinckney, his former owner, he marched back to his old cabin and from its porch, rifle in hand, he declared, "Yes, I gwi wuk right here. I'd like tuh see any man put me outer dis house." Among emancipated slaves, freedom was presumed to go hand in hand with the right to own land, particularly the land they had worked for so many years. In a collective petition to President Andrew Johnson, a group of former slaves living on Edisto Island, South Carolina, clearly made this point when they protested the restoration of plantation lands to their former owners, declaring, "This is our home. We have made these lands what they are." Over and over again, newly emancipated blacks expressed a surprisingly intense connection to their former places of servitude.[1]

Some observers dismissed these attachments simply as expressions of homesickness and considered them to be indications of the former slaves' need for white supervision. But for years black people had kept their own mental account books in which they reckoned the value of their uncompensated toil, and, with the North's victory in the Civil War, they tried to take advantage of a fleeting opportunity to obtain what they considered their justly deserved payment. Freedman Bayley Wyat of Yorktown, Virginia, in a speech given in 1865, was most explicit about his people's claims: "We has a right to the land where we are located. For why? I tell you. Our wives, our children, our husbands, has been sold over and over again to purchase the lands we now locates upon; that the reason we have a divine right to the land. . . . And den didn't we clear the land, and raise de crops ob corn, ob cotton, ob tobacco, ob rice, ob sugar, ob everything?"[2] Blacks had made similar statements even while still enslaved, although they were usually cloaked with gestures of indirection. Aware of his slaves' claims to his estate, Alabama cotton planter J. W. DuBose wrote that the typical slave on his place "was proud of the beautiful cotton growing under his toil, proud of the majestic corn he cultivated, proud of the colts he broke to bridle, of fat hogs he slaughtered for 'our' people. . . . It was to him all 'ours.'"[3] By using the possessive pronoun, DuBose's unnamed slaves clearly indicated that they considered themselves at times to be on equal footing with him. J. Motte Alston, master of Woodbourne plantation in South Carolina, encountered the same assumption in the behavior of Cudjoe, his slave foreman, who, Alston said, "looked upon my property as belonging to him."[4]

Thus at the outbreak of the Civil War, when slaves sang songs of jubilation that included lines like "De whip is lost, de han'cuff broken" and "The darkies gonna occupy the land," these were not new sentiments. They were only the most recent and most forceful expressions of a decidedly African American view of land tenure, a view rooted in a firm sense of place. Former slaves did not want just any land; they wanted land that was familiar to them, plantation land with which they had developed a personal bond.

The sudden declaration of claims to land among southern blacks in 1865 points up the fact that, hidden within the official, ordered landscapes established by planters, there was another system of definitions developed by slaves. Almost without their owners' even being aware of it, over the course of several generations—but particularly during the first half of the nineteenth century—slaves carved out landscapes of their own. My main objectives here are first to describe, in broad terms, the architectural settings of plantation slavery and then to suggest some of the ways in which black people may have transformed those architectural settings into places that best served their social needs. Beyond the houses to which they were confined, slaves were able to influence the ways that planters chose to live as well. How slaveowners laid out their estates, where they placed their homes, what types of buildings they chose to erect, and many other matters that determined the look of the landscape were all contingent to some degree on their involvement with chattel slavery and thus ultimately were affected by the slaves themselves.

Although black carpenters and masons made an obvious imprint on the cultural landscape with their skilled labor, greater impact was achieved by more basic means. So vast was the demographic dominance of black people across the South that many places were unavoidably seen as black places. In the counties of coastal Georgia, for example, slaves made up almost three-fourths of the population.[5] In such situations, the spaces assigned to slaves were often left to them as well. When the population balance of a southern community favored the enslaved segment—as it certainly did on the more than two thousand large plantations where hundreds of slaves outnumbered the handful of white residents—the simple act of occupying a space was tantamount to appropriating it.

Slaves took a more active role in defining and claiming their territorial domains than their owners suspected, and they employed a variety of means that historian Rhys Isaac has collectively labeled "slave opportunism."[6] According to Isaac, black territorial definitions were often made in subtle or clandestine ways and probably went unrecognized by most slaveowners. The notion of slave opportunism, then, offers an important insight into the understory of plantation architecture, for it reminds us that appearances can be deceiving and that an apparent order on the land may not be the only order present. If the slaves' sense of place was different from that of the slaveholders, the differences were likely to be manifested as much by thought as by deed, as much by speech as by physical act. Well before their official emancipation, slaves were already laying claims to portions of the plantation landscape, even to spaces not specifically ceded to them. Through acts that ran the gamut from courage to accommodation, slaves defined landscapes that were uniquely theirs.

Images from the Historic American Buildings Survey (HABS) provide most of the evidence for this study of plantation buildings and spaces. The HABS, originally founded in 1933, is still operating as a division of the National Park Service. The survey collections, which are housed in the Prints and Photographs Division of the Library of Congress, currently contain information on approximately 23,000 buildings. Because slightly more than one third of these structures are located in the South, a review of the HABS is an indispensable first step for any architectural investigation of the region.

What I found most surprising about the HABS collection—and what spurred me to write this book—was my discovery that it documented such a large number of slave buildings and associated spaces. HABS teams have, over the last fifty-plus years, made more than five hundred photographs and executed more than one hundred sheets of measured drawings of slave cabins, kitchens, barns, stables, and other slave workplaces at nearly three hundred different sites. Although some of this architectural evidence, dealing with a few states, has been reported, the survey has never been analyzed as a unit for what it might reveal about the entire region. It is my aim to use these records to recover the dimensions of southern architectural history that have, like these archival images, been too long overlooked and unreported.

A regional survey of the architectural contents of southern plantations—and I use the term *survey* loosely, as there are notable gaps in the HABS coverage—is possible because the HABS images are so wide ranging. Although not every building type found on old plantations appears in this collection, examples of more than twenty different types of structures are included. The HABS documented plantations across fourteen southern states, but Alabama, Virginia, and South Carolina are the most thoroughly covered—these three being states that represent the lower, upper, and coastal sections of the region.

But what is most useful about the HABS collection is the quality of its images. Made by professional architects, draftsmen, and photographers expressly as aids to architectural research, these images are an invaluable resource. HABS researchers noted specific locations for properties, along with the names of former or current owners. In addition to full-frame photographs that reveal a structure's essential features, they quite often also made supplementary, close-up photographs of important details. A building considered particularly interesting would prompt a series of scaled drawings that might include floor plans, sectional views, and elevations, along with specific renderings of trim moldings, fireplace mantles, and various items of hardware like hinges and door handles. A number of sites were even mapped to indicate the spatial relationships of different buildings. HABS teams set high standards for architectural documentation that remain unsurpassed by even the most rigorous contemporary scholars. Although there is no substitute for firsthand fieldwork, a HABS record can sometimes provide nearly as much information as a personal site visit.

The majority of the slightly more than two hundred images analyzed in this book were made during the 1930s. In many instances, that was the last time some of the structures could have been studied. More than seventy years had passed since the end of the Civil War, and former slave cabins and related buildings were, as many of the photographs show, fast falling into ruins. The value of the HABS as a rescue mission, then, is incalculable; it preserved, in paper form, hundreds of buildings destined to vanish without a trace. Now, armed with its copious documentation, one can—while still in the library—not only move across the countryside to "visit" buildings in many different places but also occasionally travel back in time to experience structures that are now destroyed. There are many other troves of images housed at various libraries, archives, and historical societies that could be used to recapture the visual history of plantations. However, few of these collections can provide an encounter with architecture equal to the HABS.

Given the fact that most of the HABS fieldworkers were decidedly antiquarian in orientation and were primarily concerned with high-style architecture, their attention to slave structures is fortuitous, if not unanticipated. But they were given orders to document "*any* kind of structure of which there are good specimens extant," and obviously they followed these directions from time to time.[7] Although there apparently was no planned effort to record the tangible vestiges of slavery that were still standing, what emerged from the survey (albeit unintentionally), by virtue of repeated forays into the countryside, was a sizable record of slave buildings.

Look at the pictures. Pore over the drawings. Check their details. Do it carefully, and you can develop almost a tangible sense of the buildings that once sheltered the everyday routines of slaves. But knowledge of slave structures alone is not enough. Some understanding of the human dimensions of old buildings is also required for a complete description of the lives they enclosed. What the enslaved occupants of these buildings and spaces thought and felt remains hidden in the images, but their feelings and attitudes, fortunately, were preserved elsewhere.

At the same time that HABS teams were moving across the South to record old buildings, a second set of government employees, interviewers working for the Federal Writers' Project, was collecting life histories from former slaves. They visited thousands of aged black men and women during the late 1930s and early 1940s and recorded what these people could still remember about slavery times. Enough such reminiscences were gathered to eventually fill forty thick volumes. Although their recollections after so many years were limited by physical infirmities or the passage of time or were inhibited by the fact that most of the interviewers were white, many of these informants still had specific and detailed memories of the buildings in which they had once lived and worked. I have matched selected testimonies with the HABS images in order to "people" the photographs and drawings. Former slaves were certainly the people best able to explain what those places were like. My description of the architecture of slavery thus meshes information from two archival projects that have been separated for more than half a century. Some might label the results "historical ethnography"; put more simply, I have used, wherever possible, the old words of old black people to interpret their old buildings.[8]

Because the testimonies of former slaves make no mention of many plantation buildings (probably because interviewers never thought to ask), I have turned as well to conventional sorts of evidence, such as planters' correspondence, diaries, ledgers, travel accounts, newspaper stories, and other similar materials as further sources for period comments on slave buildings. Some visitors to the South—Frederick Law Olmsted perhaps being one of the most noteworthy—were very careful, even studious, observers of local architectural practices. Consequently, even a thoroughly digested source like Olmsted's travel memoirs can be of great value in recapturing the story of black builders. So-called standard references, when viewed with new purposes, can spur new insights. The range of these sources is indicated in the notes.

My analysis of plantation architecture is further undergirded by personal field research on southern vernacular architecture. In a series of projects carried out over the past two decades, focusing primarily on African American building traditions, I have studied over a hundred black buildings in both urban and rural contexts and visited plantation sites in eight different states. Although I do not explicitly discuss those experiences here, they have helped me develop the skills needed to interpret with confidence the archival data in the HABS collection.

As the title *Back of the Big House* suggests, this volume moves away from the domains of the slaveholders toward the places claimed in some way by their slaves. Given that the black presence has been generally ignored in architectural histories written about the South, this focus on African Americans is altogether necessary. Before we can present a revised portrayal of southern architecture to correct this deficit, we must first ascertain the black contributions to the built environment. It is with these concerns in mind that this book provides a descriptive sampling of the range of buildings in which slaves lived and worked.

In addition to a physical analysis of the buildings, I also consider how these structures and spaces were linked by the slaves', as well as by the slaveowners', sense of place. As these perceptions evolved over the course of several generations, the spatial domains defined by slaves developed cognitive boundaries that abutted and overlapped with the domains of their owners. Both Big House and slave quarter, although they were distinct places, were still elements of single landscape—one helped to define the other. A master's house was "big" only if it had smaller buildings nearby, and, conversely, a small cabin was defined as a slave cabin because it was unquestionably linked to a particular owner's residence. These points are elaborated in Chapter 1, which outlines the historical development of the southern plantation as a landscape shaped and occupied by two different groups of people.

The book's subsequent chapters move the reader from the back door of the planter's house—a building commonly referred to by slaves as the Big House—toward the quarters of the field slaves. In order to see both of these sites on a large plantation, a visitor might have to travel a distance of two or three miles and, along the way, would probably encounter the quarters for house slaves, the kitchen, a smokehouse and other outbuildings, barns and stables, pieces of plantation machinery, and an overseer's house before reaching the gathering of cabins reserved for the field hands. Each of these places is examined in its own chapter. Chapter 12 describes several sets of buildings that constitute what I call "plantation landscape ensembles." Included in this sample are plantations located all across the South, from Maryland to Texas. The ensembles help illustrate the sense of place that can arise from the way that individual structures are grouped together.

The rationale for my chapter divisions comes principally from the content of the HABS collection. If the HABS researchers documented a significant number of buildings of a single type—say smokehouses—then I examine those buildings in a separate chapter. Where there are only a few examples, I have grouped them with buildings that share similar functions. By following the HABS patterns, I found that I could both replicate a tour across a model estate and examine numerous variations within the plantation ideal.

In this book, I stress images over verbal description. I therefore encourage readers to look first at the photographs and drawings and then read the accompanying text. My words are intended to serve essentially as a running commentary that will guide the reader through a visual encounter with the architecture of plantation slavery. I hope that the reader will look, read, and then look again with greater understanding and insight.

For some years now, historians of the South have pointed out that the region's most distinctive features are probably owed to the centuries of interaction between blacks and whites. C. Vann Woodward was most explicit on this point when he wrote that black and white southerners "have shaped each other's destiny, determined each other's isolation, shared and molded a common culture." So bonded are they by their shared fate, says Woodward, that "it is, in fact, impossible to imagine the one without the other and quite futile to try."[9] It follows, then, that any meaningful study of domestic architecture in the South must take this interaction into account.

The plantation landscapes that I consider here were first laid out by slaveholders and then incrementally marked by slave reactions. Though I acknowledge that plantations were the products of an interaction between their black and white residents, my study forgoes a detailed discussion of planters' Big Houses to concentrate on the buildings and spaces assigned to slaves. To attempt a full synthesis of the cultural history of plantation architecture would be premature at this time. The task is too large and the evidence too diffuse. Instead, I have focused mainly on the slave end of the topic, because it is the dimension most often ignored. But I also entertain the hope that others will be encouraged by this study to undertake companion projects that will, in concert with mine, more fully summarize the whole saga of the southern plantation, a primary emblem of region's identity.

# Acknowledgments

One rarely travels the winding road of book publishing without accruing a certain amount of indebtedness for kindnesses and encouragements received along the way, and the journey that led to this volume is no exception to this rule. Recognizing that I have many "bills" to pay, I want to take this opportunity to thank all those who have helped in one way or another over the past five years as I coerced an idea into a manuscript and the manuscript into this present work.

To begin, I want to thank The George Washington University for granting me a sabbatical leave so I could work full time on my proposed study of plantation architecture and for generously providing funds to pay for the reproduction of drawings and photographs as the project neared completion. During my seemingly countless visits to the Prints and Photographs Division of the Library of Congress to study the holdings of the Historic American Buildings Survey, I could always count on the efficient courtesies of Mary Ison, George Hobart, Marilyn Ibach, Maya Keech, Sam Daniel, and Jerry Kearns. Amazed by the images I found there, before long I was eager to show off my discoveries. Although many friends humored my enthusiasm, I especially recall the encouragement I received from Simon Bronner, Steve Ohrn, Gene Metcalf, Mike Jones, Richard Longstreth, Archie Green, Larry Levine, Catherine Bishir, John Moe, Joey Brackner, Dell Upton, and Iris Hill.

It was, in fact, Iris Hill who smoothed my entry into the University of North Carolina Press "stable" as my research phase blended into the writing phase. Even though she was soon to move on, she left me in the capable hands of a terrific publication crew, including David Perry, Rich Hendel, and Pam Upton. Their commitment to this book and the editing and design services they have provided are much appreciated.

As chunks of this book started to take shape, I was given a number of opportunities to test my findings in front of various audiences. I want, therefore, to thank Camille Wells for her invitation to speak at Mary Washington College, Phillipe Oszusick for inviting me to provide a keynote speech for the Pioneer America Society, and Ted Ownby for asking me to participate in the Chancellor's Symposium at Ole Miss.

Some of the ideas in this book were tested in an essay entitled "Plantation Landscapes of the Antebellum South," commissioned by the Museum of the Confederacy in Richmond, Virginia. I also want to acknowledge the feedback received from students in various classes at The George Washington University and from my fellow colleagues of the Vernacular Architecture Forum and the American Folklore Society. The more I was able to work through my ideas out loud, the better I was able to write them down.

Dell Upton, Catherine Bishir, and Daniel C. Littlefield all gave this book a thorough reading while it was still in manuscript (Dell twice). Their collective proddings and challenges forced me to rethink, reorganize, and recast what I had written, and the book is certainly better because of their contributions.

Finally, I want to note that this book is dedicated to my wife, Beverly W. Brannan. Although she says that she would rather have a "book about people" dedicated to her, she deserves this volume, too.

# Back of the
# Big House

# ONE

# The Plantation Landscape

Beyond the white master's residence, back of and beyond the Big House, was a world of work dominated by black people. The inhabitants of this world knew it intimately, and they gave to it, by thought and deed, their own definition of place. Slaveowners set up the contexts of servitude, but they did not control those contexts absolutely. There were many chinks in the armor of the "peculiar institution." Taking advantage of numerous opportunities to assert counterclaims over the spaces and buildings to which they were confined, slaves found that they could blunt some of the harsh edges of slavery's brutality. The creation of slave landscapes was one of the strategies employed by blacks to make slavery survivable. It is now widely accepted that blacks and whites both played important roles in shaping everyday life in the South. Many expressions of southern folklore—tales, proverbs, sayings, dance steps, tunes, recipes, beliefs, quilt patterns, house types, and the like—are known equally well by both races. Consequently, we can expect to accurately understand southern plantation landscapes only if the contributions of slaves are acknowledged and included. To study these places without including the slaves' perspectives would not only be inadequate, it would be futile.

The creation of a slaves' landscape was a reactive expression, a response to the plans enacted by white landowners. To mark their dominance over both nature and other men, planters acquired acreage, set out the boundaries of their holdings, had their fields cleared, selected building sites, and supervised the construction of dwellings and other structures. The design of a plantation estate was an expression of the owner's tastes, values, and attitudes. To appreciate what slaves eventually did with the realms fashioned by planters and to more fully understand the choices available to them, it is necessary first to consider the world the slaveholders made. The achievements of the planter class provided the social context that slaves would manipulate for their own ends. Ultimately, the slaveholders' world would become the raw material with which slaves would attempt to satisfy some of their own social aspirations.

## The Planter's Landscape

A plantation was not always understood to be a large agricultural estate. Indeed, in its earliest usage, the word *plantation* referred simply to an "act of planting." Any farm, even a garden or a clump of trees, might be called a plantation. It was only after England's conquest of Ireland in the sixteenth century that the meaning of the word was expanded to signify a large holding, namely "a settlement in a new or conquered country," like the newly formed Plantation of Ulster and later the Plimoth Plantation in Massachusetts. Not until 1706, according to the *Oxford English Dictionary*, was there written evidence that the word indicated "an estate or farm producing a crop with servile labor," the connotation generally intended by contemporary usage.

For most of the seventeenth century, a southern planter was a poor farmer who held claim to about a hundred acres and owned no slaves.[1] His house was, according to British traveler J. F. D. Smyth, likely to be a tumbledown dwelling built "almost all of wood, covered with the same; the roof with shingles, the sides and ends with thin boards, and not always lathed and plastered within; only those of the better sort are finished in that manner, and painted on the outside. The chimneys are sometimes of brick, but more commonly of wood, coated on the inside with clay. The windows of the best sort have glass in them; the rest have none, and only wooden shutters."[2] English revenue agent Edward Randolph reported in 1696 that when Virginia planters laid claim to new lands, they would merely "clear one Acre of that land, and . . . plant and tend it one year . . . but take no care of their Crop, nor make any further use of their land."[3] Generally, a common planter's fields were haphazardly tended; crops were raised in odd-shaped plots scattered about his holdings. Hills of tobacco and corn were scratched up with hoes between dead trees and the remnants of charred stumps, while livestock foraged freely, without supervision, across unfenced woodlands, marshes, and pastures. Ground that was worn out by too many seasons of planting a single crop was allowed to grow up in briars and bushes. These scraggly holdings, although productive enough to support their owners, were denounced by many visitors, who saw in the increasingly gullied and eroded farms only ruin and waste.[4]

By the last quarter of the seventeenth century, this apparent disregard for the look of the land was effectively countered by a small group of well-off planters, those who were able to assemble large holdings extending over thousands of acres.[5] Among this rising group of fashion-conscious social elites, which included no more than two dozen family lines, neatness and order were considered important attributes of landscape management. According to the new dictates of the Georgian mode, a proper gentleman's house was not only substantially constructed but was, in plan, symmetrically balanced. The predictable order of a house's facade and of its spatial arrangement was extended to the surrounding gardens and, as far as was reasonable, to the layout of the entire estate.

Bacon's Castle in Surry County, Virginia, built about 1665, was among the earliest of these new, imposing estates. Although the house was modest in size, it was constructed in brick at a time when almost all of the houses in Virginia were wooden frames sheathed with thin skins of riven boards, and therefore it was no doubt seen as a mansion. Standing two-and-a-half stories high, Bacon's Castle was also distinguished from the houses of the common folk by its fashionable curved gables, triple diamond-set chimney stacks, and full-height porch and stair towers. Another expression of status was the large, formal pleasure garden, enclosed by walls and hedges, that stretched out in front of the building. Divided into eight rectangular units by graveled paths, the garden also contained several secluded nooks equipped with built-in benches where visitors might take their ease.[6]

The inspiration for estates like Bacon's Castle and the others that followed it was provided by English manorial estates, which usually consisted of a "smaller Georgian house set in a park of modest proportions—a warmth of red brick, a flash of stucco, among luxuriant trees." The parklands surrounding these manor houses were, writes landscape historian W. G. Hoskins, their most impressive feature: "Parks grew yet more extensive during the eighteenth century, in the age of the territorial aristocracy. Building themselves magnificent houses, they needed (or thought they needed) more square miles of conspicuous waste to set them off."[7] It was quite understandable, then, that the estates developed by the Virginia gentry would remind British visitor William Hugh Grove of the pleasant parks and manor houses of the English midlands.[8] The members of this upper class, too, had made themselves into a "territorial aristocracy," and they, too, quickly put as much distance as possible between themselves and the rest of the population.

The resemblances between the aristocratic estates of England and the American colonies were more than coincidental. Frances Carter, wife of Robert Carter of Nomini Hall, informed her husband that she would not feel comfortable in Virginia until he had "made her a park and stock'd it."[9] Some Virginia planters either patterned their houses upon specific English country houses or availed themselves of architectural guidebooks published in London to ensure that their homes would conform to the latest British fashions. William Byrd II, for example, is believed to have based the design of Westover, the great house overlooking the James that he built in 1735, on Drayton Court, the Northamptonshire seat of the Earl of Peterborough.[10] Almost a decade earlier, Mann Page had fashioned his mansion at Rosewell after Cound Hall in Shropshire.[11] English influences were also conveyed by such books as William Lawson's *A New Orchard and Garden* (1618), which contained detailed diagrams and instructions for laying out formal gardens, or Walter Blith's *English Improver; or, a New Survey of Husbandry* (1649). The new Virginia plantations were so thoroughly linked to British antecedents that, even two decades after the American Revolution, a Polish visitor to Washington's Mount Vernon would remark: "The General has never left America, but when one sees his house and his garden it seems as if he had copied the best samples of the grand old homesteads of England."[12]

Similar developments were also visible during the early eighteenth century in the Carolina lowcountry. In the hinterlands of Charleston, for example, members of the Middleton family established two impressive estates. The house at Crowfield, the plantation built by William Middleton in 1730, was approached by a long, ramrod-straight avenue, and its grounds were ornamented with numerous "garden contrivances" including basins, fishponds, canals, elegant parterres, and a bowling green. The whole estate was laid out symmetrically along a north-south axis extending from the road through the house and gardens to the rice fields beyond. Ten years later, Henry Middleton acquired a large plantation tract along the Ashley River, one of twenty he was to own in his lifetime. By 1755 his Middleton Place was as sumptuous as his brother William's plantation. Both were thoroughly British in character; Crowfield was, in fact, named for an English holding belonging to the family. The gardens on the two plantations are readily compared with the detailed views of the landscaping of English country estates found in J. Kip's *Britannia Illustrata* (1709), a book that may have guided the Middleton brothers.[13]

These grand estates in the Carolinas and the Chesapeake region were extraordinary places. Vast beyond comprehension in size and elaborately designed and decorated, they were atypical, showplace plantations. Yet, their very exceptionalism made them so impressive that, by the middle of the eighteenth century, the definition of *plantation* would change once more. No longer just a large farm run with supervised captive labor, from the middle of the eighteenth century onward the ideal plantation was a large, tastefully appointed country estate belonging to a prominent gentleman.

The tangible glory of manorial estates served as the most persuasive propaganda for the celebration of the plantation ideal. Implicit in the structured layout of Georgian houses, formal gardens, and extensive stretches of fenced and cultivated fields was a strong sense of the planter's dominance over both nature and society. The wide gap between the material condition of a great planter and that of even his closest local rival was underscored by the way in which his house was approached. Access was achieved by moving along a route marked by a series of threshold devices—gates, drives, forecourts, steps, terraces, porches, passageways, doors—all of which were intended to make the house, and its owner, appear more impressive.[14] At Thomas Lee's Stratford Hall, for example, a low wall stretched across the forecourt of the building, effectively stopping visitors from riding their horses up to the steps. Only a "humbling pedestrian access" to the house was allowed.[15]

Guiding these planters in setting up their estates was a highly rational formalism. The world was, in their view, suitably improved only after it was transformed from its chaotic natural condition into a scene marked by a strict, hierarchical order. The planters' landscapes were laid out with straight lines, right-angle corners, and axes of symmetry, their mathematical precision being considered as a proof of individual superiority.

Although the aloofness and reserve signaled by this rigid imposition of order was intended chiefly to ensure that the plantation owner received the respect he felt was his due, ironically such expressions of social hierarchy actually made the new plantation ideal appealing to "middlin'" yeomen. The commoners who were effectively put in their place upon visiting a Westover or a Stratford Hall were anxious to have their own turn to exercise a similar social authority. It is not too surprising, then, that when new plantations were created in interior portions of the South during the nineteenth century, the old manorial model served as their inspiration. This new generation of planters, often young Virginians or Carolinians gone west to seek their fortunes, hoped to attain at last the prominent social rank that their foreparents had sought. As they moved first to the frontiers of Georgia and Kentucky and later as far west as Texas, they carried an eighteenth-century idea with them as an important item of cultural baggage. Architectural historian Roger G. Kennedy aptly observes that this "New South was the Old Tidewater South transported across the Piedmont."[16]

Certainly the plantation established by Benjamin Grey in central Kentucky was as impressive as any back in old Virginia. A journalist visiting Grey's estate in 1843 wrote that his house "stands near the centre of the domain on rising ground, and commands a fine view of the country around. . . . A pretty yard of smooth greensward, decked with shrubbery and evergreens, is enclosed around with pointed white palings, and adjoining this is a noble park." Grey's neighbor Nicholas Hart, in an attempt to imitate the ancient ways of the English nobility, stocked his own park with a herd of elk.[17] The conspicuous grandeur of Oak Valley, a plantation located in Yazoo County, Mississippi, as described by private tutor DePuy Van Buren, once again suggests manorial aspirations: "In the front ground, you see magnificent China-trees. The orange myrtle, with its glossy green foliage, trimmed in the shape of a huge strawberry; the crape myrtle with its top hanging thick with long cone shaped flowers of a peach-blow color; the cape jasmine, with its rich polished foliage spangled all over with white starry blossoms . . . and that richest and sweetest blossom of tropical shrubs— the japonica."[18]

Further evidence of the westward diffusion of the Tidewater plantation form is provided by some of the sugar plantations in southern Louisiana. Along the shores of Bayou Teche, plantations developed by Anglo-Americans were laid out in what geographer John B. Rehder calls a "block plan." On these estates, the planter's mansion, farm buildings, and slave houses were all clustered closely together in a gridlike pattern. Plantations of this type were easily distinguished from the estates of French planters, who employed a linear format. While the block plan probably stems from the formal geometry first used in the design of gentry estates in Virginia and Carolina, mid-nineteenth-century visitor Thomas Bangs Thorpe thought he recognized along the shores of the Teche "expressions so often witnessed in the lordly parks of England."[19]

Although plantations were established all over the South, by 1860 the largest, and therefore the most lavishly developed, estates tended to be concentrated in three distinct areas (fig. 1.1). The oldest and generally most prominent plantations were located in a coastal region extending from the Chesapeake Bay to northern Florida and not more than a hundred miles inland from the Atlantic. A second concentration of large plantation estates occupied a fifty-mile-wide arc of cotton lands running

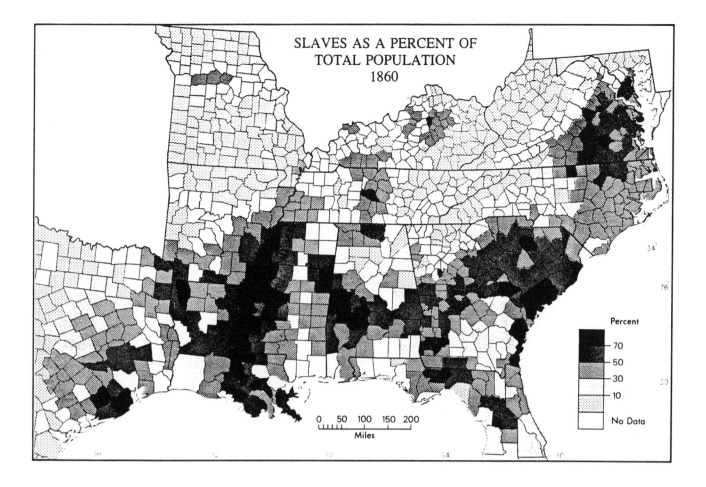

SLAVES AS A PERCENT OF
TOTAL POPULATION
1860

Percent

70
50
30
10
No Data

0  50  100  150  200
Miles

through the middle portions of South Carolina, Georgia, and Alabama, terminating in eastern Mississippi. A third plantation zone consisted of the fertile bottomlands of the lower Mississippi Valley, from just above Memphis to below New Orleans. There were also noteworthy plantation zones in the Florida Panhandle, northwestern Alabama, and along the Gulf Coast of Texas, but these were smaller enclaves rather than major regions.

Large plantations dotted the southern countryside fairly evenly from Maryland to Texas, signaling to all passersby the financial and social rewards of the plantation system. However, well into the nineteenth century, those benefits were still only realized by a few families. Historians have usually granted planter status to those men and women who owned at least twenty slaves. Thus in 1860, when plantation agriculture had reached its furthest extent, there were only 46,274 plantations in the entire South. Though this the figure may seem large, it represents only 12 percent of all slaveholding families, who in turn made up only 24 percent of all white southerners.[20] The greatest proportion of these estates—some 20,789—were run with between twenty and thirty slaves and though considered small plantations, they were, in fact, only slightly larger

1.1

Map indicating the number of slaves per county in the South in 1860. The areas with the largest concentrations of slave population are also those characterized by the presence of plantation estates. From Sam Bowers Hilliard, *Atlas of Antebellum Southern Agriculture* (Baton Rouge: Louisiana State University Press, 1984).

than slaveholding farms and not very different in character. Only the plantations that were run with large numbers of slaves, a hundred or more, approached the manorial ideal. By this measure, there were in 1860 only about 2,300 truly large-scale plantations, and perhaps only half of those were developed to the state of elegance promoted by the widespread southern mythology.[21] By the middle of the nineteenth century, less than 1 percent of all slaveholding families fit the plantation stereotype, a percentage that had remained constant since the middle of the eighteenth century.[22]

How such an unrepresentative place as the great plantation estate came to dominate the self-perception of the South is a matter about which there has been considerable discussion. It is enough to say here that both those farmers who owned only a few slaves and those who owned none were impressed by the lavish plantations inhabited by the gentry, and they looked upon them with a mixture of admiration and envy. The deference with which the few great planters in any county were regarded is related no doubt to the messages that were visually conveyed by the design of their estates, crystal-clear indications of a landlord's dominance that required the submission of black laborer and white visitor alike.

According to architectural historian Dell Upton, the highly formalized layout of showplace plantations constituted an "articulated processional landscape," a spatial system designed to indicate the centrality of the planters and to keep them aloof from any visitors behind a series of physical barriers that simultaneously functioned as social buffers.[23] A yeoman farmer entering a planter's estate would follow a prescribed, formal route that led to the planter's parlor or office. Although the intricate sequence of gates, terraces, pathways, and other threshold markers was intended to emphasize the yeoman's lack of standing in relation to the planter, it could just as easily have indicated whether the yeoman's social position was improving. In other words, a visitor's status was measured by how far into the planter's world he or she was allowed. The plantation ideal remained pervasive in the South for more than a century because the will of the elite was matched by the acquiescence of those who could only dream of owning such a grand place.

Even though ownership of a lavish plantation estate was beyond the reach most southerners, planters of more modest means still tried to make their homes and gardens fashionable by incorporating some formal qualities of design or decoration. A Greek Revival porch, for example, complete with columns and entablature, might be grafted awkwardly onto a humble log cabin as a statement of presumed sophistication. Self-proclaimed arbiters of taste promoted the formal plantation style, usually by berating struggling would-be planters for their failures. In 1857 a Georgia newspaper editor wrote that, on plantations in his locale, there was "the singular want of elegance and comfort about the domestic arrangements of those who are able to provide them. . . . A log house half decayed with age, or a frame house without paint, and . . . a yard with out a shrub or a flower . . . are too frequently the insignia of a planter's premises."[24] Even more shrill was the attack launched by John Forsyth in an address to an Alabama horticultural society in 1851. He directed his listeners to "Go to the homestead of a Southern farmer and tell me what you see." Making no pause for an answer, he thundered, "The planter's home is generally a rude ungainly structure, made of logs, rough hewn from the forest; rail fences and rickety gates guard its enclosures. And why? . . . We murder our soil with wasteful culture because there is plenty of fresh land West—and we live in tents and huts when we might live in rural palaces."[25] The plantation ideal established such high architectural expectations that most planters were doomed to fail; the only acceptable level of success was great success.

In the second quarter of the nineteenth century, the most representative planters owned between twenty and thirty slaves and devoted the larger portion of their four or five hundred acres to cotton, probably on recently cleared "newgrounds." In 1853 Frederick Law Olmsted visited just such a plantation in northern Louisiana. He found that the owner's house was but a "small square log cabin, with a broad open shed or piazza in front, and a chimney, made of sticks and mud, leaning against one end." Nearby was "a smaller detached cabin, twenty feet in the rear . . . used for a kitchen." The spaces surrounding this cabin suggested an obvious concern with workaday routine that was relieved only slightly by a few ornamental shrubs:

About the house was a large yard, in which were two or three China trees, and two fine Cherokee roses; half a dozen hounds; several negro babies; turkeys and chickens, and a pet sow, teaching a fine litter of pigs how to root and wallow. Three hundred yards from the house was a gin-house and stable, and in the interval between were two rows of comfortable negro cabins. Between the house and the cabins was a large post, on which was a bell to call the negroes. A rack for fastening horses stood near it. On the bell-post and on each of the rack-posts were nailed the antlers of a buck, as well as on a large oak-tree near by. On the logs of the kitchen a fresh deer skin was drying. On the railing of the piazza lay a saddle. The house had but one door and no window, nor was there a pane of glass on the plantation.[26]

Plantation life, particularly in the western portion of the cotton belt, was essentially a Spartan pioneer experience on the edge of a constantly advancing frontier.[27] Settlements like the one visited by Olmsted were carved out of the wilderness in the optimistic hope that a substantial upgrading would follow after a few harvests. More often, however, these temporary homes were abandoned altogether as the cycle of planting was started again on a new, more promising tract of land. The common planter might follow the model of a large plantation estate and create an ensemble of buildings including a separate kitchen, a string of slave houses, and several barns and storage cribs, but these were, as Forsyth had complained, only "rude ungainly structures," and no one would ever have mistaken such a house for a "rural palace."

That plantations existed along a spectrum ranging from superbly appointed mansions set amidst well-tilled fields to expedient shelters thrown together in slash-and-burn clearings is certainly borne out by the testimony of former slaves. Martha Colquitt from Lexington, Georgia, recalled: "Our Big House sure was one grand fine place. Why, it must have been as big as de Mill Stone Baptist Church. It was all painted white with green blinds and had a big old high porch dat went nigh all 'round de house." This dwelling presents a marked contrast to the house of Mary Ella Grandberry's master in Barton, Alabama, which she described in the 1930s as "a li'l old frame building like a ordinary house is now. He was a single man and didn't have so terrible much, it seem . . . just to look at him you'd think he was a poor white man."[28]

The appearance of a plantation certainly varied with the crop that its owner attempted to grow. The cultivation of tobacco, cotton, rice, and sugar, the primary staples of the plantation economy, each followed different schedules and work routines and used different equipment and storage structures. One type of plantation could be distinguished from another by its barns, mills, and other gear. The identity of a tobacco plantation was marked by the distinctive tobacco barns used to cure the leaves before they were packed into huge barrels. Standing in the yards of most cotton plantations were both a gin house and a press for compacting processed lint into bales. By the second quarter of the nineteenth century, rice plantations often had large steam-powered mills to complement the older threshing platforms and winnowing houses where slaves had previously refined the rice by hand. The mills located on Louisiana's sugar plantations were large sheds, sometimes as much as three hundred feet long, containing boilers, engines, conveyor belts, rollers, and evaporators. Because these mills spewed clouds of smoke and steam as the cane juice was transformed first into syrup and then into raw sugar, it is not surprising that sugar plantations were said to resemble New England factory towns.[29]

The appearances of plantation fields also varied with the crop that was grown. The rice fields of South Carolina and Georgia, for example, stood out prominently because they were developed on reclaimed wetlands. Rice paddies were diked off from the surrounding marshes, leveled, and then irrigated ingeniously by means of a system of sluice gates and canals. The landscape resulting from these efforts was, according to Olmsted, "Holland-like."[30] The sugar fields of Louisiana, laid out in rectangular units marked off by ditches and cross-drains, also had an engineered appearance. British observer William H. Russell thought John Burnside's sugar plantation was impressive in part because his fields were judged to be "as level as a billiard-table."[31] Because the crop did not require any specialized techniques of cultivation, a cotton planter's acres did not look very different from any other farm. And because cotton planters tended to specialize only in their single cash crop, their fields showed the viewer little more than continuous furrows pushing up the same plant, often right up to the door of the planter's house. Contemporary visitors, hoping for more diversity, denounced the monotonous rows of cotton as drab.[32]

Other variables affecting the visual appearance of a plantation included the size and organization of the available work force, the condition of the soil, and the willingness of its owner to embrace up-to-date methods of cultivation, harvest, and processing. There were also inevitable subregional differences within an area as large as the South, a geographic zone reaching from the Atlantic Ocean to the prairies of central Texas and from the Gulf of Mexico to the Ohio River Valley.

Any plantation reflected not only the local ecology and climate, but the consequences of a particular settlement history as well. Finding it difficult, if not impractical, to ignore the customs of the cultural region in which their estates were located, planters frequently used the same designs for houses, barns, and outbuildings as did their yeoman neighbors. In the Tidewater South, where single-pen barns were favored, for example, planters also used single-crib barns. Similarly, the planters in the Piedmont and upland South showed their regional allegiances by selecting double-crib barns over other possible barn types. Maryland plantation estates closely resembled mid-Atlantic farmsteads both in their layout and in their selection of buildings. It is apparent that so-called plantation architecture was often nothing more than a particular expression of whatever vernacular tradition happened to be dominant in a given region. It is difficult, then, to refer with confidence to a single "plantation style" of architecture, for these regional variations in building customs affected the design of houses as well as service structures.

## The African American Plantation Landscape

The experiences of plantation slaves were quite different from those of plantation owners, not only because of their status as captive laborers, but because so many of them were held on the larger and therefore less typical plantations. Historian John B. Boles demonstrates how so many slaves came to live on large-scale manorial holdings.

Imagine a universe of ten slaveholders, eight owning two slaves apiece, one owning twenty-four, and the tenth possessing sixty. Obviously most slaveholders (80 percent) would own fewer than five slaves, but most slaves (84 out of 100) would reside in units of more than twenty. Such an imaginary model suggests what the numbers reveal. In 1850 . . . over half [of the slaves], 51.6 percent, resided on plantations of more than twenty bondsmen. The figures were more pronounced in the Deep South, and still more so in 1860, when fully 62 percent of the slaves in the Deep South lived in plantation units.[33]

Plantations, albeit unintentionally, served as the primary sites at which a distinctive black American culture matured. By 1860 over 800,000 slaves were living mostly in the company of other slaves, in groups of fifty or more. On almost 11,000 plantations, consequently, slave settlements were big enough to resemble, in the words of former slave occupants, "little towns."[34] No doubt their quarters did resemble villages. A group of fifty slaves probably contained about ten families housed in as many as ten but no fewer than five cabins, depending on the type of buildings used as quarters. Slave settlements containing larger populations obviously required more houses and thus were even more townlike. Bill Homer, a former slave from Shreveport, Louisiana, described a large grid pattern of slave houses when he recalled that the quarters on his plantation "was fifty one-room cabins and dey was ten in a row and dere was five rows."[35] A map of the Stapleton plantation on St. Helena Island, South Carolina, drawn up in 1789, shows that the slave quarter, containing eighteen cabins, was set out in a block pattern three rows deep and six rows wide.[36]

Although slaves had no legal power, they were often able nonetheless to use their marginal status to their advantage. Kept for the most part in small frame or log houses, slaves knew that they were being humbled by their master, who owned a big mansion—or at least a bigger house—that often was located on the highest ground available. However, because their more modestly constructed slave quarters frequently were located some considerable distance from the planter's residence, slaves also had ample opportunity to take control of many domestic concerns. Beyond their master's immediate scrutiny, at the margins of the plantation and in the thickets beyond its boundary lines, slaves created their own landscape. This was a domain that generally escaped much notice, mainly because it was marked in ways that planters either considered insignificant or could not recognize.

Rhys Isaac has suggested that paths and trails into the countryside were the central elements of the slave landscape in Virginia. Some of these secret tracks led to clandestine meeting places in the woods, used sometimes for ritual purposes and at other times for festive parties at which fiddles were played and stolen pigs barbecued. Paths also led from the slave quarters across the fields to a particular corn house or to some other food store that was known to have a conveniently loose board in its gable. A shortcut through the woods or marshlands that surrounded the fields may have allowed slaves from different plantations to rendezvous more conveniently and to return to their assigned tasks with less chance of detection. On those plantations located near navigable streams and rivers, the waterways were yet another domain over which slaves exercised particular control by means of their boating skills.[37] The whole ensemble of sites and pathways constituted, in Isaac's terms, "an alternative territorial system."[38]

This system, used wherever large groups of African Americans were gathered together, encouraged racial solidarity and provided slaves with a means to escape, at least temporarily, from their masters' control. Moreover, the informal qualities of this type of landscape, one established more by a set of behavioral associations than by specific material indications, may also have reflected an ethnic choice. The loose, ad hoc scheme of preferred paths and gathering places was created incrementally by a series of improvisational responses to the given landscape rules of white masters. Because similar improvisational responses by black people to Anglo-American culture are known to have resulted in the creation of distinctive African American forms of speech, music, and dance, it is not too farfetched to suggest a parallel development in their responses to their assigned environments.[39]

Some slaves are known to have countered the geometrically circumscribed order imposed by their masters' logic with what seemed like chaos. For example, the forty-one slaves at Mount Vernon who were assigned to the so-called Muddy Hole Farm, where they worked under the supervision of a black overseer, located their cabins randomly among the trees at the edge of the cleared fields. Those slaves living on the plantation's other "farms," where they were supervised by white overseers, had their cabins set in straight lines at regular intervals along the edge of a road.[40] One observer of Georgia rice plantations similarly noted that when slaves were given the chance to build their own houses, "they wanted their cabins in some secluded place, down in the hollow, or amid the trees, with only a path to their abode."[41] In one of the slave villages at J. J. Smith's cotton plantation near Beaufort, South Carolina—apparently located far away from his central processing area—although the cabins consisted of a row of boxy frame buildings, all were set at odd, irregular angles to one another.[42]

If the black system of place definition positively embraced the random and meandering givens of the natural world, their spaces would naturally strike white observers as sloppy and poorly maintained. British visitor Edward Kimber, in fact, went so far as to certify that slave settlements located on the backlands of plantations (those fields beyond their owners' immediate scrutiny) produced "Indolence and Nastiness."[43] What white people were prone to criticize as sloppy (or worse, as "nasty") was the slave preference for a landscape marked by few overt boundaries and fixed sites, an environment open to and characterized by movement. Planters who wanted their places clearly and certainly defined could only be annoyed at the way slaves acted. In an 1833 issue of the *Southern Agriculturist*, a South Carolina planter wrote: "A plantation might be considered as a piece of machinery; to operate successfully all of its parts should be uniform and exact and the impelling force regular and steady."[44] Clearly slave actions went against this advice, countering its suggestions with behavior that seemed deliberately careless. In the light of what is known about life within various slave communities, the inhabitants' actions were indeed deliberate, for they hoped thereby to carve out a domain of their own and thus improve, however slightly, the conditions of their captivity.

Within their settlements, slaves established strong family identities, created distinctive art forms, and developed meaningful religious rituals.[45] To the furthest degree possible, they took charge of their lives. Among the many tangible signs of black initiative and autonomy, the foremost spatial statements were the extensive vegetable gardens, sometimes as big as half an acre per person, in which slaves raised much of their own food. Such self-sufficiency was undergirded by other demonstrations of slave skill. Frances Anne Kemble, who in the late 1830s lived on a plantation in coastal Georgia with a slave population approaching five hundred, observed that slaves who had woodworking abilities built furniture and boats, which they sold for considerable sums in the nearby town of Darien.[46] On other plantations, slaves developed similar entrepreneurial enterprises, selling chickens, ducks, and pigs that they raised, and even a horse or two. Others were able to improve their material conditions by offering their blacksmithing, tailoring, or coopering skills for hire.[47] Frederick Law Olmsted noted that at one particularly large slave village, again in Georgia, the slaves daily secured their homes and possessions under lock and key, asserting their right to personal space and property.[48] By acting as if they owned the quarters, these slaves had overturned the declared order of the plantation. Although everything they had could be taken away in a moment if the master so desired, few planters wanted to disturb the inner workings of large slave villages. As long as the slaves performed their assigned tasks with reasonable efficiency, planters concerned themselves neither with the routines of the slave quarters nor the domestic claims being exercised there.

Once they were able to establish a level of proprietorship in the quarters, some slaves felt emboldened enough to exert a claim over their work spaces as well. Philip Fithian, a tutor in Lancaster County, Virginia, during the late eighteenth century, found that the slaves at Nomini Hall regularly took over the stables as a place in which to hold their private entertainments. From his frequent complaints that his pupil, Henry Carter, spent too much time in the kitchen or in the various craft shops, we can infer that these buildings, too, were regarded as black spaces and therefore off limits to white boys who hoped to become well schooled in the refined ways of gentlemen.[49] The cook at the Merrick plantation in Louisiana not only ran the kitchen but determined who could have access to it. Caroline Merrick, at one time the plantation's Young Miss, remembered being driven out of the room by the cook's stern rebuke: "*Go inter de house*, Miss Carrie! Yer ain't no manner er use heah only ter git yer face red wid de heat."[50]

After years of toil in the fields, slaves sometimes began to feel that the harvest was their achievement rather than their master's. He may have owned the crop, but they had created it. There is no more eloquent expression of a slave's identification with the soil he worked than the claim made by a former South Carolina slave named Morris. Early in the twentieth century, when he was about to be thrown off the plantation where he had lived all his life, he went to the landlord to state his case.

I was born on dis place before Freedom. My Mammy and Daddy worked de rice fields. Dey's buried here. De fust ting I remember are dose rice banks. I growed up in dem from dat high. . . . De strength of dese arms and dese legs and of dis old back . . . is in your rice banks. It won't be long before de good Lord take de rest of pore old Morris away too. An' de rest of dis body want to be with de strength of de arms and de legs and de back dat is already buried in your rice banks. No . . . you ain't agoin' to run old Morris off dis place.[51]

The ironies of plantation slavery were many and profound, for although the plantation system was the very reason people of African descent were enslaved, it also provided them with an arena in which they could begin to piece back together their shattered lives. While ownership of a plantation clearly divided whites into distinct have and have-not classes, blacks generally found themselves drawn together in sufficient numbers to constitute coherent social groups. Comforted by the fellowship of the quarters, they were able to confront the injustice of their captivity in ways both subtle and obvious; among their various strategies of accommodation and resistance was the creation of their own version of the plantation. Recognizing that they could define a space for themselves, they took back the quarters, fields, gardens, barns, and outbuildings, claiming them as parts of a black landscape. Empowered by this territorial gesture, they were able to forge an even stronger sense of community, which few planters would ever recognize or acknowledge.

Even when slaves were most persistent in establishing their own landscapes, they attempted few bold gestures. Instead, they prudently relied on subtle adjustments to their dwellings, or they sought out spaces where their masters were unlikely to intrude. Their domains, consisting mainly of rough and ungainly dwellings together with their cluttered yards, reflected not a lack of ability but their material poverty. Denied the time and resources needed to design and build as they might have wanted, they simply appropriated, as marginalized peoples often do, the environments to which they were assigned.

The slaves' agenda is the hidden dimension of a southern plantation. Looking over these places, one sees most clearly the pattern of well-known, European-derived fashions. The ordered surfaces of building facades and well-tended grounds, however, were underpinned by a slave community whose labor provided the wealth with which planters created their impressive estates. The more than two-and-a-half-million slaves held on plantations in 1860 clearly dominated the southern countryside. It was, finally, their formidable demographic presence that transformed plantations into undeniably black places. This circumstance fostered such a self-reliant attitude among slaves that they were inspired to think about their captivity and its various physical contexts in ways that they found most reassuring. Just as slaves usually did not consider it a crime to take extra rations from the master's storehouse in order to satisfy their hunger, neither did they consider the buildings and spaces in which they were forced to work to be solely his property.[52] Thus the kitchen might be claimed by the slave cook, the dining room by the house servant, the loom house by the weaver, the barn by the field hand.

Acts of appropriation leave few physical marks, and therefore they must be consciously recalled in order to be factored into our interpretation of surviving slave buildings and spaces. Consequently, southern plantations can only be described accurately and analyzed fully if we remember the territorial prerogatives claimed and exercised repeatedly by slaves.

# TWO

# Big House Quarters

Only a small percentage of plantation slaves was employed as domestic servants; from a group of fifty slaves, only six or so would be assigned to work at the Big House.[1] Even if a plantation's labor force included hundreds of slaves, the domestic staff would usually not number much more than half a dozen. An 1854 inventory listing the occupations of slaves at the Laurel Hill plantation in Georgetown County, South Carolina, for example, indicates that of 171 slaves, only 7 were employed at the main house. At nearby Chicora Wood, planter Robert F. W. Allston kept ten slaves at his residence: a cook, a laundress, a housemaid, a seamstress, a butler, a second dining-room man, a coachman, a scullion, a gardener, and a yard boy. His wife Adele, however, complained: "There are too many servants; I do not know what to do with them. . . . I cannot find work for them! . . . Please send them away, half of them at least."[2]

Some planters, however, did not mind if house slaves sat idle; they enjoyed the display of numerous servants waiting at the ready to do their bidding. In 1857 Indiana native George Cary Eggleston reported, after visiting the home of his relatives in Locust Grove, Virginia: "In hardly anything else was the extravagance of the Virginians so manifest as in their wastefulness of labor. On nearly every plantation there were 10 or 12 able-bodied men and women employed about the house, doing the work which 2 or 3 ought to have done, and might have done; and in addition to this there were usually a dozen or a score of others with merely nominal duties or no duties at all. The master liked to have plenty of servants always within call."[3] Used to the plain living of a small midwestern town, Eggleston was clearly surprised when three or four slaves were called to take his horse or to fetch a pitcher of water. Because so much personal service was directed at him, it is easy to understand why his estimate of the number of house servants was double the usual average.

Although it is usually imagined that work in the Big House was considerably easier than toiling in the fields, domestic labor could be equally onerous. Elizabeth Fox-Genovese summarizes some of the tasks that were performed by the female servants:

> Slaves worked in the kitchens and smokehouses . . . to produce three meals a day, except perhaps on Sunday, and to hang and smoke innumerable pounds of pork. Slaves waited on table. Slaves washed and ironed; took up and put down carpets; carried the huge steaming pots for the preservation of fruits; lifted the barrels in which cucumbers soaked in brine; pried open the barrels of flour; swept floors and dusted furniture; hoed and weeded gardens; collected eggs from the poultry. Slaves suckled, washed, and minded infants. . . . Slaves spun and wove and sewed household linens and "negro clothes." Slaves quilted.[4]

Work in the Big House—unlike field labor, which would usually end at sunset—had a perpetual quality because house slaves were always on call. At any time of the day or night—even if they had completed their assigned tasks—they were still expected to anticipate and tend to their owners' personal needs. Field slaves were at least given the day off on Sundays and certain holidays.[5]

The childhood recollections of former slave Mingo White confirm the demanding nature of domestic service. Describing a plantation near Burleson, Alabama, where his mother struggled to complete all of her daily chores, he testified: "I helped her with her work. Her task was too hard for any one person. She had to serve as maid to Mr. White's daughter, cook for all of de hands, spin and card four cuts of thread a day, and den wash. Dere was one hundred and forty-four threads to de cut. If she didn't get all dis done she got fifty lashes that night. Many the night me and her would spin and card so she could get her task [done by] the next day. No matter what she had to do de next day she would save to get dem cuts of thread, even on wash day."[6]

A more considerate slaveholder might be inclined to reward his house slaves, particularly his personal servants, with certain favors: reduced work loads, better than usual food, nice clothing, superior living quarters.[7] Joseph Ball, master of Morattico plantation in Lancaster County, Virginia, saw that his favored slave Aron Jameson was provided with several sets of clothes, including a new pair of boots, three hats, and a dozen neckcloths. He also gave explicit directions to his plantation manager to "have one of the worst of my old Bedsteads cut short and fit for his Mattress" and requested further that a separate cabin be built for his exclusive use.[8]

Some masters kept their house slaves close at hand. Cheney Cross, a former slave who had once belonged to the Purifoy estate in Alabama, testified that she "was brung up right in de house with my white folks. I slept on the little trundler bed what pushed up under de big bed, during the day."[9] More often, however, the house slaves lived in a separate building adjacent to the planter's residence; occasionally there might be two or three small houses for domestic servants. Because these quarters were usually better constructed than the cabins built for the field hands, they conveyed the favored status granted to their occupants. Henry Clay, a former slave from near Rayville, North Carolina, apparently was well cared for in such a building: "Mammy and Pappy and me lived in a house close to the Big House back there [in North Carolina], and Pappy was the coach boy and horse boy. The Big House was two stories high with a big porch what run clean to the top, and more window blinds than I ever seen in a house since. Our little house was made of planks, heavy oak lumber, all whitewashed with lime, and we had good furniture Old Mistress give us what she was through with. The bed was high like you could hang a curtain on, and had springs like we got today."[10]

But serving at the Big House provided no guarantee of favors. At the Davenport plantation in Linden, Texas, former house slave John White found that his domestic role carried no privileges in the matters of either housing or work load:

I remembers the house. A heavy log cabin with a gallery clear across the front. The kitchen was back of the house. I work in there and live in there. It wasn't built so good as the master's house. The cold winds in the winter go through the cracks between the logs like the walls was somewheres else, and I shivers with the misery all the time. The cooking got to be my job. The washing too. Washday come around and I fills the tub with clothes. Puts the tub on my head and walks half a mile to the spring where I washes the clothes. Sometimes I run out of soap. Then I make ash soap right by the spring. I learns to be careful about streaks in the clothes. I learns by the bullwhip. One day the master finds a soapy streak in his shirt. Then he finds me.[11]

The plan of Magnolia Grove plantation near Greensboro, Alabama, shows that Isaac Croom placed the quarters for his house servants as far away from his house as was practical. They were pushed out toward the northwestern corner of the yard (fig. 2.1). Although most of their tasks were performed inside a fenced work yard—

an enclosure directly behind the main house containing the cookhouse, smokehouse, well, and bathhouse—the slaves' own quarters were placed roughly one hundred feet beyond this area. The distance suggests that Croom felt it imperative that he rigorously monitor the routines of his slaves and thus separate their work space from their residential space. The contrast between Croom's strategy and that used by James C. Johnston at Hayes Manor, located outside Edenton, North Carolina, is readily apparent (fig. 2.2). Johnston mixed the quarters for his house slaves in among the different service structures that were gathered together next to his mansion, treating them essentially as workplaces where the personal lives and the domestic chores of his servants merged into one seamless experience.

Big House slave quarters were generally set behind or to the side of the planter's residence, where they would not contend with it visually. Even if they were visible, they were obviously smaller, subordinate buildings. However, on some estates, such as Tuckahoe or Howard's Neck in Virginia, an ensemble of service structures, including several slave quarters, might flank the roadway leading to the mansion.[12] Although the usual commotion and goings-on in the slave yard may have distracted some visitors from giving their full attention to the prospect presented by the main house, it may in fact have been the planter's intention to impress them first with the number of slaves he owned before they took in the view of his residence. In these cases, the slave houses may have been placed in front of the big house deliberately in order to enhance the visitor's perception of the planter and his estate.

The placement of Big House quarters as an indicator of wealth can be seen clearly in the photograph of Boone Hall plantation in South Carolina (fig. 2.3). In 1843 the Horlbeck brothers built a long row of slave cabins that ran parallel to the oak-lined avenue leading up to the main house.[13] Passing by this so-called slave street allowed visitors to inventory at a glance a portion of the plantation's labor force. Moreover, the long row of small buildings made the main house seem more impressive. The long road approaching the Hermitage, the mansion built for Georgia rice planter Henry McAlpin in 1830, was lined with more than seventy diminutive brick slave houses (see fig. 11.10). At the end of the road sat a Regency-style house raised on a one-story basement that was graced by delicate Corinthian columns and curving stairways.[14] The contrast in scale and degree of finish between this building and the slave cabins served to underscore McAlpin's obvious authority.

Several building types were used as Big House quarters. The smallest consisted of only one room, usually square in plan. The quarters belonging to the Hurt house near Tuskegee, Alabama, provide an example (figs. 2.4, 2.5). Although this particular building was eventually expanded by the addition of a second room, close inspection of the structure reveals that it originally consisted of one square room plus a small porch. The most common type of Big House quarter during the late antebellum period was a two-room structure that usually had its fireplace and chimney centrally located between the two rooms (figs. 2.6, 2.7). This "saddlebag" configuration was common all across the South, although occasionally the fireplaces were placed at the gable ends (fig. 2.8). That two separate slave families were likely to be housed in these double-pen buildings is indicated by the presence of two front doors, one for each half of the house.[15] At the estate developed in 1818 by slave dealer Edward Stone outside of Millersburg, Kentucky, the house servants were quartered in a three-room brick structure, a building created by "adding" a single-pen unit to the end of a double-pen house (fig. 2.9). Another type of slave quarter was, in its plan, essentially a double-pen house built two stories high (fig. 2.10). Sometimes, as was the case at William-son Glover's Rosemount plantation in Greene County, Alabama, the lower level might serve as a kitchen, while bedrooms occupied the second floor (fig. 2.11). But if the cooking was done in another building, four different slave families could be quartered in such a building, one in each of the four rooms.[16]

Basic slave quarter plans were also modified to suit personal needs and to honor local building customs. The slave quarter at the Oakleigh mansion in Mobile, Alabama, for example, basically consists of three one-room cabins linked end to end (figs. 2.12, 2.13). The most distinctive feature of this structure is its overhanging front eave. The building has, in effect, the inset type of porch found on many houses in the Gulf Coast area. The quarter thus resembles, in its profile, a creole cottage, a commonplace local building type generally attributed to the influence of early French settlers. It also very similar in form to service buildings constructed at other nearby coastal sites.[17]

The Big House slave quarters were likely to be decorated in a manner that enhanced the planter's view of his estate. The quarters at Boone Hall, for instance, being constructed with brick masonry and covered with distinctive pantile roofs, had a pleasant, picturesque appearance. The plantation house built for Robert Gracey near Demopolis, Alabama, was a fashionable 1840s Gothic villa, its design apparently derived from the published writings of architect William H. Ranlett.[18] To preserve the fashion statement of his house, Gracey also decorated the quarters for his domestic slaves with Gothic embellishments, including board-and-batten siding, scalloped bargeboards along the eaves, and lancet windows in the gables near the peak of a steeply pitched roof (fig. 2.14). The quarters that James Watson built for his house servants at Westend, his plantation in Virginia's Louisa County, were decorated with modest classic cornices, faint echoes of the full-blown classic revival details found his own temple-form mansion (fig. 2.15). These quarters were fenestrated in a symmetrical door-window-window-door pattern on their fronts—the sides visible from the Big House—whereas the rear facades facing away from the mansion were simpler, having only doors or an asymmetrical pattern of one door and one window. Clearly these facades were contrived to present Watson with a pleasingly balanced and harmonious view. The blending of the servants' houses into an ensemble with the planter's residence is best seen at the Hurt house. Like the mansion it served, the Hurt slave quarter also had brick masonry walls covered with stucco. Both buildings featured the same low, hipped roof, plain cornice, and porch supported by a series of posts. The quarter was essentially the mansion in miniature.

At Keswick, the plantation in Powhatan County, Virginia, belonging to John Clarke, a mysterious round building thought to have once served as a slave quarter sits in the yard close to the main house (figs. 2.16, 2.17, 2.18). Built early in the nineteenth century, it is a brick structure, roughly thirty-six feet in diameter, topped with a conical roof. Although there is only a single entrance into the building, the structure's possible use as a communal shelter for several families is suggested by a round, centrally located fireplace containing three hearths. The twelve-foot-high ceiling was originally lathed and plastered, and a "gallery" or ledge was once affixed tó the walls all around the interior of the building, just above the windows and about three feet below the ceiling. Eyewitness accounts confirm the existence of this feature, but its function remains unclear. If it was built for storage, it was certainly a device without any local precedents. Indeed, the whole building is unusual, matching no other known slave quarters in the area.

Because the Keswick quarter bears a general resemblance to round, conical-roofed houses in Africa, its design has usually been explained as an instance of African influence on the design of slave housing.[19] However, the fact that most of the Africans brought into Virginia came from regions where square and rectangular buildings were most common makes this claim problematic.[20] Because Clarke was a noted industrialist and thus committed to progressive technologies and innovative designs— one example of his mechanical genius was his scheme to bring running water into the state capitol in Richmond—it is likely that he, more than his fellow planters, would have been inclined to experiment with new and unusual ways to provide adequate housing for his slaves.[21] The most plausible explanation is that the round slave house at Keswick resulted from Clarke's design rather than from a memory of Africa. Beyond the issue of design source, however, it is clear that the occupants of Clarke's round quarter saw themselves as a people apart. Their dwelling not only distinguished them from the residents of the Big House at Keswick, but from other slave communities throughout middle Virginia.

**2.1**

Site plan of Magnolia
Grove, Hale County,
Alabama. Drawn by
Kirby Stringer, 1936.

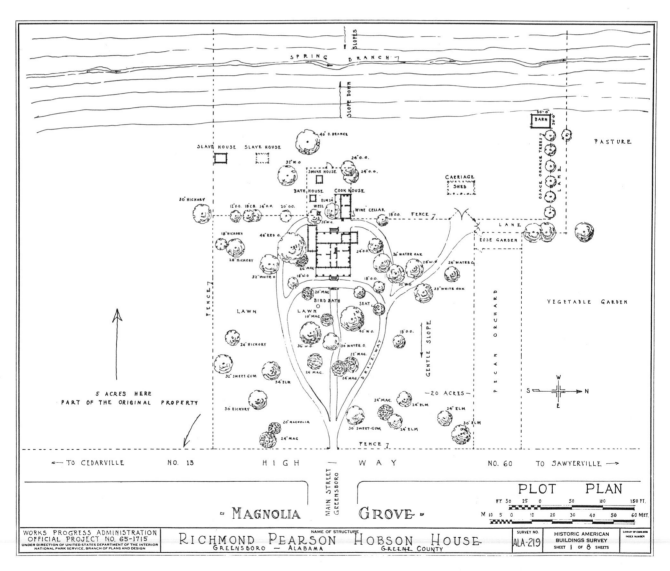

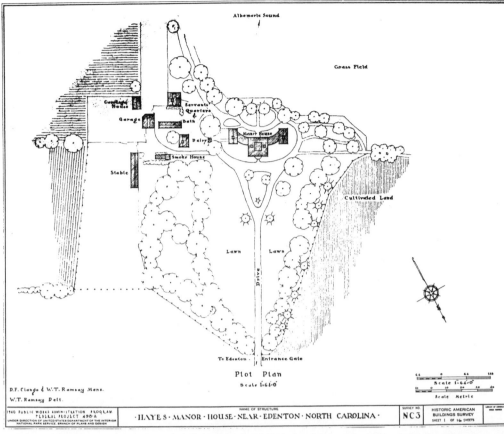

**2.2**

Site plan of Hayes Manor, Chowan County, North Carolina. Drawn by W. T. Ramsey, 1940.

**2.3**

The oak-lined approach to Boone Hall, Berkeley County, South Carolina. A row of brick slave houses is visible on the left. Photograph by C. O. Greene, 1940.

**2.4**

Slave quarter at the Hurt house, Macon County, Alabama. Photograph by W. N. Manning, 1935.

**2.5**

Front elevation and floor plan of the slave quarter at the Hurt house. Drawn by J. L. Irving, 1935.

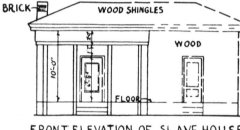

FRONT ELEVATION OF SLAVE HOUSE
SCALE "C"

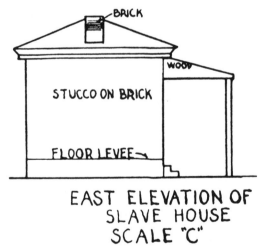

EAST ELEVATION OF SLAVE HOUSE
SCALE "C"

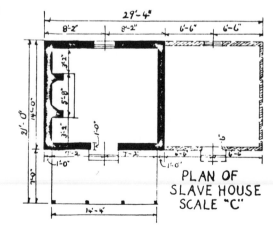

PLAN OF SLAVE HOUSE
SCALE "C"

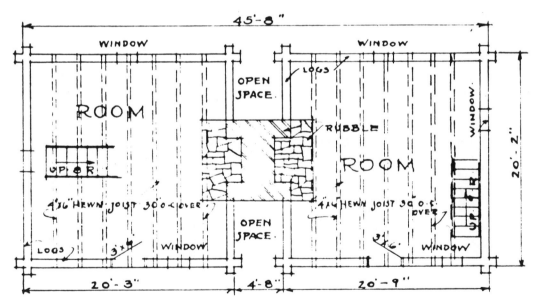

**2.6**

Slave quarter at
The Forks of Cypress,
Lauderdale County,
Alabama. Photograph
by Alex Bush, 1935.

**2.7**

Floor plan of the
slave quarter at The
Forks of Cypress.
Drawn by Harry J.
Frahn, 1935–36.

**2.8** [top l.]
Slave quarter at
Rocky Hill mansion,
Lawrence County,
Alabama. Photograph
by Alex Bush, 1935.

**2.9** [top r.]
Slave quarter at
The Grange, Bourbon
County, Kentucky.
Photograph by
Theodore Webb,
1934.

**2.10** [above]
Slave quarter at
Wickland, Nelson
County, Kentucky.
Photograph by
Theodore Webb,
1934.

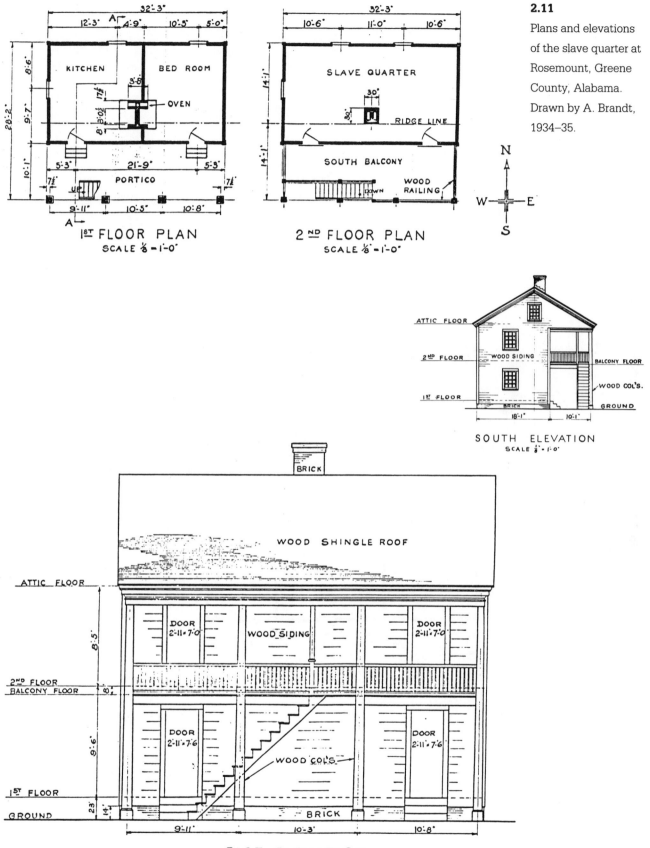

**2.11**

Plans and elevations of the slave quarter at Rosemount, Greene County, Alabama. Drawn by A. Brandt, 1934–35.

1ST FLOOR PLAN
SCALE ⅛ = 1'-0"

32'-3"
12'-3" 4'-9" 10'-5" 5'-0"
8'-6"
9'-7"
28'-2"
10'-1"
KITCHEN BED ROOM
3'-8"
17½"
OVEN
8'-3" 0½"
7½"
5'-3" 21'-9" 5'-3"
PORTICO
UP
9'-11" 10'-5" 10'-8"

2ND FLOOR PLAN
SCALE ⅛ = 1'-0"

32'-3"
10'-6" 11'-0" 10'-6"
14'-1"
SLAVE QUARTER
30"
30"
RIDGE LINE
14'-1"
SOUTH BALCONY
DOWN
WOOD RAILING

N
W E
S

SOUTH ELEVATION
SCALE ⅛ = 1'-0"

ATTIC FLOOR
2ND FLOOR
WOOD SIDING
1ST FLOOR
BRICK
18'-1"
BALCONY FLOOR
WOOD COL'S.
GROUND
10'-1"

EAST ELEVATION
SCALE ¼ = 1'-0"

BRICK
WOOD SHINGLE ROOF
ATTIC FLOOR
8'-5"
DOOR 2'-11" 7'-0"
WOOD SIDING
DOOR 2'-11" 7'-0"
2ND FLOOR
BALCONY FLOOR
8'
9'-6"
DOOR 2'-11" 7'-6"
WOOD COL'S
DOOR 2'-11" 7'-6"
1ST FLOOR
GROUND
23"
14"
9'-11" 10'-3" 10'-8"
BRICK

**2.12**

Slave quarter at
Oakleigh, Mobile
County, Alabama.
Photograph by
E. W. Russell, 1935.

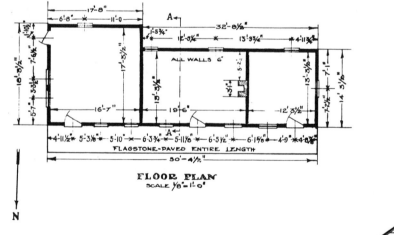

FLOOR PLAN
SCALE 1/8"=1'-0"

N

**2.13**

Floor plan and end
elevation of the slave
quarter at Oakleigh.
Drawn by P. DeV.
Chaudron, 1935.

EAST ELEVATION
SCALE 1/8"=1' 0"

**2.14**
One of the slave quarters at the Gracey house, Hale County, Alabama. Photograph by Alex Bush, 1935.

**2.15**
Slave quarters at Westend, Louisa County, Virginia. Photograph by Jack E. Boucher, 1983.

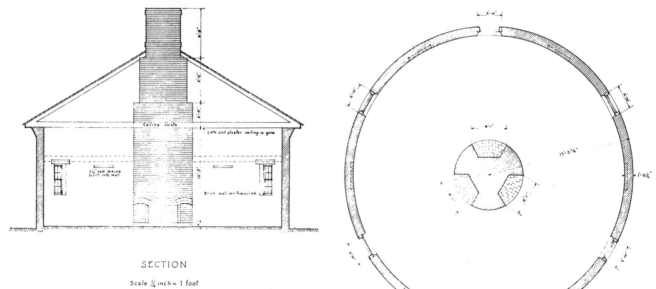

SECTION

Scale ¼ inch = 1 foot

**2.16** [top]
Slave quarters at
Keswick plantation,
Powhatan County,
Virginia. Photograph
by C. O. Greene, 1940.

**2.17** [above l.]
Sectional view of
the slave quarters at
Keswick. Drawn by
E. Bradbury, 1940.

**2.18** [above r.]
Floor plan of the
slave quarters at
Keswick. Drawn by
E. Bradbury, 1940.

# THREE

# The Yard

The buildings that sat close to a planter's residence defined the yard, a space where slaves performed many of their household chores. R. C. Smith, a former slave from Arkansas, remembered from his youth that his master's house was surrounded with large trees that "made a heavy shade. Old Mistress had lots of purty flowers and they had a row of cedars."[1] But there were no ornamental plants in the yard; the yard was work space. This arrangement is clearly visible in the site plan of Gunston Hall, George Mason's plantation in Fairfax County, Virginia (fig. 3.1). Mason entertained his guests in an elaborate formal garden located behind his house. Marked with tall hedges and marled pathways, the site was created by leveling the top of a low hill. The service yard at the side of the house was described by Mason's son John as "a high paled yard, adjoining the house, into which opened an outer door from the private front; within or connected with which yard, were the kitchen, well, poultry houses, and other domestic arrangements."[2]

It was here that one expected to find the slaves busy tending to their various chores. Behind their high, enclosing board fence, they were confined to a world of work, while just a few feet away Mason's guests promenaded in a pleasant garden. What Mason's slaves may have thought about their yard is unknown, but during the eighteenth century some Virginia slaves overturned their owners' intended hierarchies by exerting territorial claims over such work spaces. Philip Fithian, tutor at Nomini Hall, reported that on several occasions he had been assessed fines by the plantation's slaves because he had entered buildings and areas where they were working without first asking their permission. The plantation's baker, for example, charged Fithian seven-and-one-half pence for an uninvited intrusion into his kitchen.[3]

Because the structures surrounding the yard routinely included at least the kitchen, dairy, smokehouse, and well, it follows that cooking meals and cleaning up afterward were the most common chores performed there. Furthermore, given the scale of cooking and cleaning on the larger plantations, much of that work had to be done outdoors. The yard, then, served as an extension of the kitchen and the laundry. It was seen less as the space between outbuildings than as an area reserved for specific tasks. According to Silvia King, a former slave cook and housekeeper at a Texas plantation, "Dere always a big woodpile in de yard, and de big caboose kettle for renderin' hog fat and beef tallow candles and makin' soap."[4] The yard was the place where big jobs were done, those requiring the coordinated efforts of many hands.

Huge cast-iron kettles, like those photographed at various sites, were standard pieces of equipment in any plantation yard (fig. 3.2). At the Askins plantation near Steelville, Missouri, for example, the household slaves used them to make soap. In great detail, former slave Marie Askins Simpson recalled the process:

> The ash-hopper was made of boards, a sort of trough that was set slant-wise over a big iron kettle. The wood ashes from the fire place were dumped into this hopper. Hot water was poured over the ashes and they drained down into the kettle. It dripped slowly. When we thought the lye was strong enough, we got a turkey feather (a chicken feather won't do, 'cause it would eat up too quick), and if the lye from the hopper was strong enough it would eat up the turkey feather. Then the fire was started under the kettle.
>
> Into this big kettle of boiling ash-lye, we stirred in "cracklin'." This was the fried out fats left over from hog killin'. Old meat rinds, old meats that had turned strong, any kind of fat meat that was not used to eat, was thrown into this hot boiling lye. When the meat did not melt any more we know that there was enough fat in the lye to make soap.
>
> This was boiled down until it got "ropey." We tested it by dripping some of it in cold water. If it floated on top, it wasn't done. If it sunk to the bottom, we pulled the fire from under it and let it get cold. That was called hard soap. Next day, it was cut into chunks, placed on boards and put in the smoke house or attic to dry.[5]

Soap making required collective effort; a gang of slaves was needed to lift the kettles, to keep the fires burning, and to carry out the various stages of production.

The soap made on plantations was, of course, intended to be used for washing clothes or dirty dishes. Much of this washing would be done in the same iron kettles used to make the soap or in other large wooden tubs kept in the yard. The recollections of Sally Brown, a former slave from Georgia, add more details to our view of laundry day: "We took the clothes out'n the suds, soaped 'em good and put 'em on the block and beat 'em with a battlin' stick, which wuz made lak a paddle. On wash days you could hear them battlin' sticks poundin' every which way."[6] This description is confirmed by Georgina Gibbs, former slave from Virginia, who reported that "Dere wuz five women who done de washing an' ironing. Dey had to make de soap. . . . After de clothes had soaked in dis lye-soap and water, dey put de clothes on tables and beat 'em 'till dey wuz white."[7]

Slave women usually knelt on the ground and leaned over the tubs while doing the wash, but at Effingham, a plantation in Prince William County, Virginia, they apparently were spared some of the back strain. The yard at Effingham was equipped with a waist-high sink carved out of a rectangular block of sandstone so that some of the washing could be done standing up (fig. 3.3).

Most yard tasks were performed by groups of slaves. Glascow Norwood of Simpson County, Mississippi, who was only a small boy during the period of slavery, was excited by the work gangs he encountered in the yard:

I was a little chap running around in my long shirt and playin' in the sand, mud holes and ash heaps. I liked a big noise and to stir up a dust or splash in de water. I wuz alwas 'round when de slave women wuz a making soap with de fires a burnin 'round de pots. Hit wuz de same way at mollasses makin' time, I liked de muss and de stur. . . . I liked de bustle ob hog killing time where dey would hab big fires a burning 'round de pots to heat de water to scald de hogs. After dey wuz scraped dey wuz strung up to be dressed, dey would be long rows ob 'em. Den dey would be put on long tables under de trees and cut it up. De meat den wuz hung in smoke houses and smoked.[8]

Clearly a communal spirit could pervade the yard as the slaves labored to produce supplies of preserves, candles, syrup, soap, or sausage. During periods of intense activity, they probably felt that the yard was their domain.

The yard was definitely seen as slave territory by the slave children who were kept there while their parents were working in the fields. It served both as an open-air nursery where the children amused themselves with various games and as a mess hall where they were fed. According to Charity Jones of Amite County, Mississippi, those meals were served in a large wooden trough "made of a big log hallowed out an' had legs under it." Upon hearing the blast blown on a conch shell by the overseer, she and her playmates would all rush to the trough and try to scoop out their share of bread soaked with milk.[9] Robert Shepherd, a former slave from Lexington, Georgia, similarly recalled eating from a "great long trough what went plum across de yard."[10] The yard photographed at Pitts Folly near Uniontown, Alabama, could easily have accommodated the scenes described by Jones and Shepherd (fig. 3.4).

Wells were particularly prominent yard structures. In some instances, a well would be sheltered by a small house or at least by a roof supported on four cornerposts. The most elaborate of these structures had walls composed of ornamental latticework (fig. 3.5). The well house not only prevented debris from contaminating the water but also sheltered the ropes and pulleys used to draw the water buckets up from considerable depths, often more than seventy feet. When the water level was closer to the surface, the bucket was raised or lowered by means of a weighted pole called a well sweep. A good example of this type of well structure, actually a simple type of lifting machine, was recorded at the Smith house in Gates County, North Carolina (fig. 3.6).[11]

Throughout much of southern Louisiana, ground water proved to be so brackish that wells were useless as sources of drinking water. Suitable water was obtained by diverting the rain that fell on the roof of one's house into a large cistern, usually a large barrel constructed of cypress staves. The Fannie Richie mansion in Pointe Coupee Parish once had two such cisterns set on tall brick bases at the rear of the building (fig. 3.7). The immense size of the cypress barrels, ten feet by eight feet, was typical for such containers.[12]

Probably one of the most exceptional yard structures ever built on a plantation was the water tower at Milford in Sumter County, South Carolina (fig. 3.8). The mansion built there in 1850 by soon-to-be Governor John C. Manning was so large and so expensive that it was known at the time as Manning's Folly. Manning was an extravagant man; the granite that he used to build his house was shipped from a quarry in Rhode Island. Among the features of his home that were then regarded as particularly frivolous were two second-floor bathrooms equipped with running water. The lead pipes that carried the water were supplied from the tower in the yard. Standing thirty feet high with a base almost ten feet in diameter, the tower held a tank that was fed by a spring located several hundred feet away. The springhouse was equipped with a hydraulic ram that forced the water up into the tank. The force of gravity on the water in the tank in turn provided enough pressure to serve the second floor of the big house. Although this structure was at first of only marginal interest to the slaves at Milford, they all had their minds focused on it a few years later when it was transformed into a bell tower. The plantation's bell was housed in an elaborate hexagonal cupola set atop the water tank. In this way the tower, designed initially to provide the house with a convenient luxury, was cloaked in the guise of a practical device.

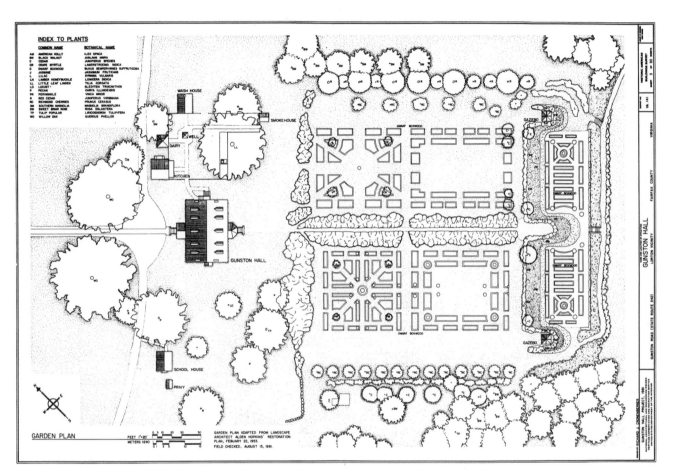

**3.1**

Site plan of Gunston Hall, Fairfax County, Virginia. Drawn by Richard J. Cronenberger, 1981, after a 1963 restoration plan.

**3.2**
Yard at the Seward home, Washington County, Texas. Photograph by Harry L. Starnes, 1936.

**3.3**
Stone sink in the yard of Effingham plantation, Prince William County, Virginia. Photograph by Russell Jones, 1959.

**3.4**
Yard at Pitts Folly,
Perry County,
Alabama. A structure
that once covered
a well stands in the
foreground, with the
old kitchen off to the
right. Photograph by
Alex Bush, 1936.

**3.5**
Well house at the
Vinson home, Colbert
County, Alabama.
Photograph by
Alex Bush, 1936.

View of the Smith
house, Gates County,
North Carolina,
showing both a
well sweep and a
dairy in the yard.
Photograph by
Thomas T. Waterman,
1940.

**3.7**

Elevation of the main house at the Fannie Richie plantation, Pointe Coupee Parish, Louisiana, showing the location of one of the house's two cypress cisterns. Drawn by George Fisher, 1936.

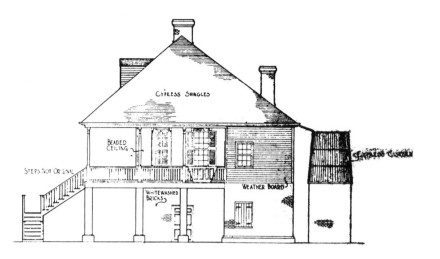

WEST ELEVATION
SCALE-⅛·1·0'

**3.8**

Water tower at Milford plantation, Sumter County, South Carolina. The cupola at the top holds the plantation's bell. Photograph by Jack E. Boucher, 1960.

# FOUR

# Kitchens

**B**y the first decades of the eighteenth century, it was already customary for the owners of large plantations to confine various cooking tasks to separate buildings located some distance from their residences. This move is usually interpreted solely as a response to practical considerations: the heat, noise, odors, and general commotion associated with the preparation of meals could be avoided altogether by simply moving the kitchen out of the house. In 1705 Virginia planter Robert Beverley praised this strategy for making one's house more comfortable, observing: "All . . . [the] Drudgeries of Cookery, washing, Dairies, &c. are perform'd in Offices detach from their Dwelling-Houses, which by this means are kept more cool and Sweet."[1]

There were, however, other important if less immediately evident reasons for planters to detach the kitchens from their residences. Moving such an essential homemaking function as cooking out of one's house established a clearer separation between those who served and those who were served. Until the last decades of the seventeenth century, slaves and their masters (at least in the Chesapeake region) lived and worked in close proximity, often in the same rooms, and sometimes shared a common identity as members of a plantation "family."[2] But this day-to-day intimacy was progressively replaced by a stricter regimen of racial segregation that was expressed by greater physical separation. The detached kitchen was an important emblem of hardening social boundaries and the evolving society created by slaveholders that increasingly demanded clearer definitions of status, position, and authority.

Separating the kitchen from the main plantation house was one of several related architectural gestures that signaled the onset of a more rigid form of chattel slavery that would persist until the middle of the nineteenth century.[3] Robert Q. Mallard emphasized the slaveholder's need to maintain absolute control when he observed that the buildings on a large plantation in Liberty County, Georgia, were arranged according to "the principle of placing everything under the master's eye." In fact, this particular slaveholder seemed even to watch over the preparation of meals, at least symbolically, by situating those buildings directly associated with food in his front yard—the smokehouse to the right side and the kitchen to the left.[4]

The talents of slave cooks were fondly remembered by both black and white plantation residents. Minnie Davis, a former slave from Greene County, Georgia, testified about her mother, who had served as the plantation's cook and housekeeper: "Oh, yes indeed, we had good food to eat. . . . I have seen my mother bake beautiful biscuits and cakes. . . . Mother's batter cakes would just melt in your mouth and she could bake and fry the most delicious fish."[5] This enthusiasm is matched by Mallard's when he claimed that kitchen slaves possessed so much "natural genius" that they "completely distanced" French cooks "in the production of wholesome, dainty and appetizing food."[6] One wonders if planters sensed the irony of their actions: At the very moment that they were taking so much pleasure from their slaves' culinary talents, they were confining their prized cooks to peripheral buildings beyond the Big House.

Photographs of plantation kitchens illustrate the use of two major building types. The first of these consisted of only a single room with a fireplace and chimney at one end. These small, elemental structures, constructed mainly in frame or with hewn logs, were in use from Virginia to Texas. An example from Road View Farm in New Kent County, Virginia, apparently built in the nineteenth century, surprisingly retained a number of archaic features traceable back to seventeenth-century Chesapeake custom: the posts that supported the walls and roof were sunk directly into the ground, and the chimney was actually a smoke bay, an open space between the gable wall and a slanting attic partition (figs. 4.1, 4.2).[7] External masonry fireplaces and chimneys represent the more common southern practice (figs. 4.3, 4.4).[8]

The second major building type used as a kitchen was a two-room structure with its fireplaces located either centrally or at the gable ends (figs. 4.5, 4.6, 4.7). Both rooms could be used for food preparation, but frequently, as was the case at the Cunningham plantation in Colbert County, Alabama, one of the rooms was used as a slave quarter, usually for the cook and her family (fig. 4.8). Some of the larger cooking structures developed from this two-room plan, such as the kitchen at the Marmion plantation in King George County, Virginia, had lofts large enough to be used either for storage or as extra living space (fig. 4.9). At Magnolia Grove, a plantation located just at the edge of Greensboro, Alabama, a two-unit building was set above a three-room basement (figs. 4.10, 4.11). The cooking was done in the two rooms on the upper level, with the largest room in the basement serving as a slave quarter. The two smaller basement rooms, which were closer to the main house, were used for storage; one of them was set up as a wine cellar.

The kitchen at Pond Spring, the plantation in Lawrence County, Alabama, belonging originally to John P. Hickman, was nothing more than a single-pen log cabin in 1818 (figs. 4.12, 4.13). However, when a second room was added as a bedroom (probably for the cook and her family), the building was transformed into a "dogtrot" house, a building type more often used as a quarter for field hands. The wide passage left between the two rooms not only helped to draw cooling breezes through the structure but also made the bedroom somewhat more private.[9] As the kitchen segment retained its front door, whereas the bedroom was entered only from the passageway, it was easy to tell which was the working end of the building. Work space was further distinguished from residential space by the fact that the rooflines of the two halves of the structure did not quite match; the older kitchen section was slightly taller.

A detached kitchen was a distinctive feature of the plantation ensemble, second in prominence only to the Big House. Occasionally the kitchen's separation from the main house might be further emphasized by a covered arcade that literally reattached the kitchen to the planter's residence. Former slave Charity Jones recalled that, on her Mississippi plantation: "De kitchen was a log house set 'way back in de yard, an' de cook had ter tote de grub frum de kitchen ter de Big House. Dere was a shed dat re'ched frum de Big House ter de kitchen ter keep de rain off'n us an' de grub."[10] A covered walkway photographed at the Reynolds home near Sylacauga, Alabama, nicely illustrates the sort of kitchen environment that Jones described (fig. 4.14).[11]

Arlington House, the mansion sited on the Virginia side of the Potomac River overlooking the nation's capital, was formerly the centerpiece of an 1,100-acre estate belonging first to George Washington Parke Custis and later to Robert E. Lee. The main kitchen for Arlington was located in the basement of its northern service wing, but just a few steps behind the mansion was a large, stucco-covered brick structure, built around 1818, which contained a summer kitchen (fig. 4.15). However, because four of the building's five rooms served as quarters for the slave cooks and other house servants, it was finally more slave quarter than kitchen (figs. 4.16, 4.17). Decorated with features intended to match the classical motifs employed by architect George Hadfield on the facade of the mansion, it was a very imposing outbuilding. The side opening onto the work yard was extremely plain, but the outward-facing northern facade was pierced by nine windows and graced by four Doric columns set under a sweeping arch that was created by recessing a section of the wall about a foot. The building's size, superior construction materials, and degree of finish all combined to mark its occupants as members of Arlington's slave "aristocracy." Their housing, at least, was decidedly better than the wooden cabins provided for the fifty or so field hands.[12]

Because the same range of domestic chores performed out in the house yard might also be performed inside the kitchen, it was not uncommon for plantation kitchens to be designed to serve more than one function. At the Foster house near Union Springs, Alabama, for example, one half of a two-room kitchen served as a laundry (fig. 4.18). The summer kitchen at Poplar Forest, the retreat built by Thomas Jefferson in Bedford County, Virginia, was combined, appropriately enough, with a dairy (fig. 4.19). Four components were configured into a single structure at Greenwood plantation in West Feliciana Parish, Louisiana (figs. 4.20, 4.21). Contained within a squarish brick building measuring approximately thirty by twenty-seven feet were a kitchen, a well, a dairy, and a smokehouse. It is evident that this building's designer was trying to cluster related tasks in the hope that the work might be done more efficiently (compare fig. 12.54). Many steps were undoubtedly saved by this unique structure.

The fireplace was the central element of a kitchen's interior. Of one such plantation kitchen, former slave Cicely Cawthon recalled: "The kitchen was bigger than this house [here]; and that fireplace! I never saw such a big one. The stick of wood for this fireplace was twelve foot long. There was hooks, two big hooks up in the chimney. I've seen em hang lambs' and calves' hind quarters up in that chimney to smoke."[13] Some sense of this huge fireplace can be gained by considering the generous proportions of the fireplace in the slave kitchen at the Borders-Blackman home near Oxford, Alabama (fig. 4.22).

Other slave testimony focused on the equipment used in the fireplace. Minnie Davis described a fireplace with a long iron bar extending across it: "The great cooking pots were suspended over the coals from this bar by means of pot hooks. Heavy iron skillets with thick lids were much used for baking, and they had ovens of various sizes."[14] Robert Shepard of Athens, Georgia, reported that his fellow slaves "cooked some of de victuals in big old washpots and dere was sure a plenty for all. All the cookin' was done in big fireplaces what had racks made inside to hang pots on and dey had big old ovens for bakin' and thick iron skillets, and long-handled fryin' pans. You just can't imagine how good things was cooked dat way on de open fire."[15] Although the exact taste of slave-cooked food might be hard to re-create, the processes involved in its preparation can be visualized. For example, the photographs made at Effingham plantation in Virginia and at the Refuge plantation in Camden County, Georgia, depict in rich detail the cooking equipment recalled in the testimonies of former slaves (figs. 4.23, 4.24).

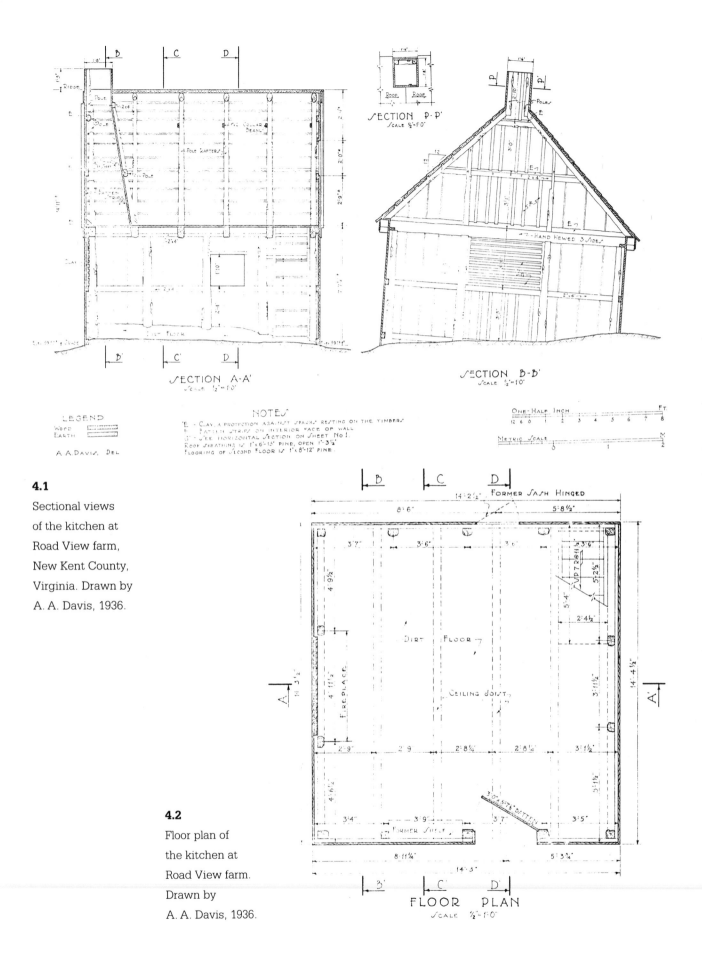

**4.1**

Sectional views
of the kitchen at
Road View farm,
New Kent County,
Virginia. Drawn by
A. A. Davis, 1936.

**4.2**

Floor plan of
the kitchen at
Road View farm.
Drawn by
A. A. Davis, 1936.

**4.3**
Kitchen at
the Kilpatrick
place, Wilcox
County, Alabama.
Photograph by
Alex Bush, 1937.

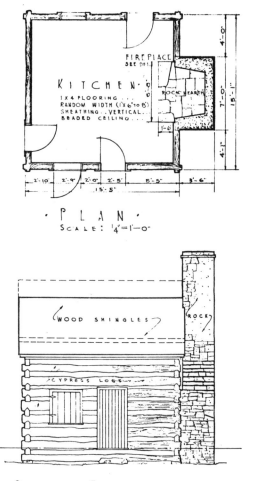

**4.5**

Kitchen at
Kensington plantation,
Richland County,
South Carolina.
Photograph by Harlan
Hambright, 1982.

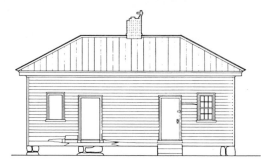

EAST ELEVATION
1/4" = 1'-0"

**4.4**

Floor plan and
front elevation of
the kitchen at the
Polley plantation,
Wilson County,
Texas. Drawn by
W. Cook, 1936.

**4.6**

Front elevation
of the kitchen
at Kensington.
Drawn by Valerie
Sivinski, 1982.

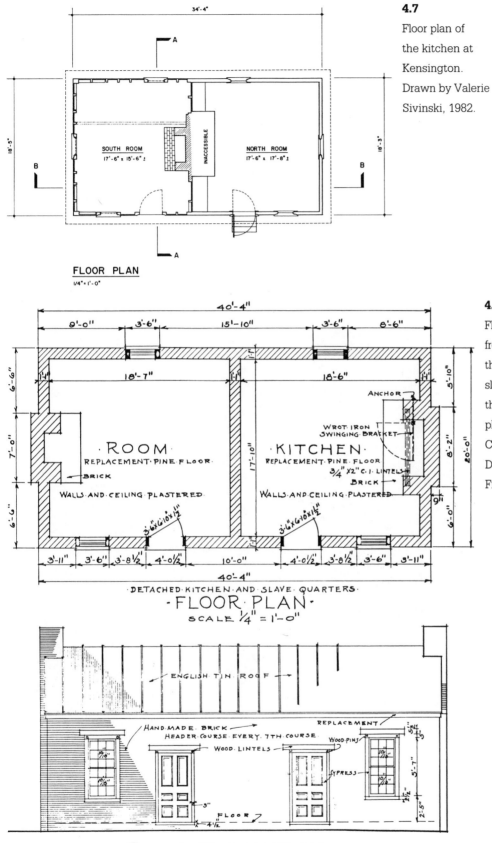

**4.7**

Floor plan of
the kitchen at
Kensington.
Drawn by Valerie
Sivinski, 1982.

FLOOR PLAN
1/4"=1'-0"

**4.8**

Floor plan and
front elevation of
the kitchen and
slave quarter at
the Cunningham
plantation, Colbert
County, Alabama.
Drawn by Harry J.
Frahn, 1937.

·DETACHED·KITCHEN·AND·SLAVE·QUARTERS·
·FLOOR·PLAN·
SCALE 1/4" = 1'-0"

·EAST·ELEVATION·
SCALE 1/4" = 1'-0"

**4.9**

Kitchen and slave
quarter at Marmion
plantation, King
George County,
Virginia. Photograph
by Frederick D.
Nichols, 1936.

**4.10**

Kitchen and slave quarter at Magnolia Grove, Hale County, Alabama. Photograph by Alex Bush, 1934.

**4.11**

Floor plans and front elevation of the kitchen and slave quarter at Magnolia Grove. Drawn by Kirby Stringer, 1936.

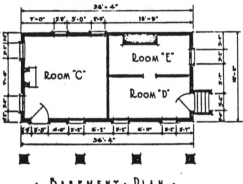

· BASEMENT · PLAN ·
SCALE ¼" = 1'-0"

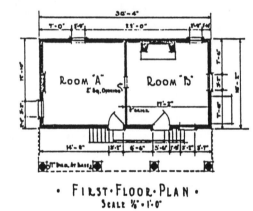

· FIRST · FLOOR · PLAN ·
SCALE ¼" = 1'-0"

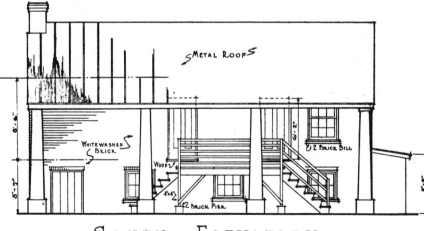

· SOUTH · ELEVATION ·
SCALE ¼" = 1'-0"

**4.12**

Kitchen and slave
quarter at Pond
Spring plantation,
Lawrence County,
Alabama. Photograph
by Alex Bush, 1935.

**4.13**

Floor plan and
front elevation
of the kitchen
and slave quarter
at Pond Spring.
Drawn by W. A.
Hotchkiss, 1935.

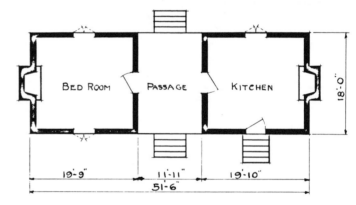

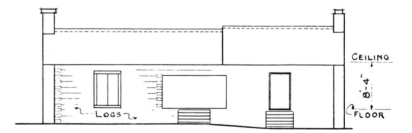

**4.14**

Detached kitchen and covered walkway at the Reynolds home, Talladega County, Alabama. Photograph by Alex Bush, 1935.

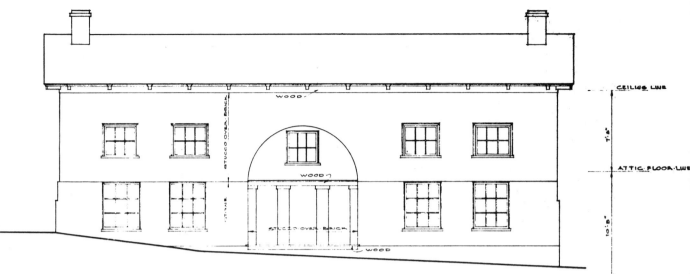

**4.15**

Southern facade
of the combined
summer kitchen
and slave quarter
at Arlington House,
Arlington County,
Virginia. Drawn by
D. F. Ciango, 1940.

**4.16**

Floor plan of the
lower level of the
summer kitchen
and slave quarter
at Arlington House,
along with a site
plan of the property.
Drawn by C. F.
Ciango, 1940.

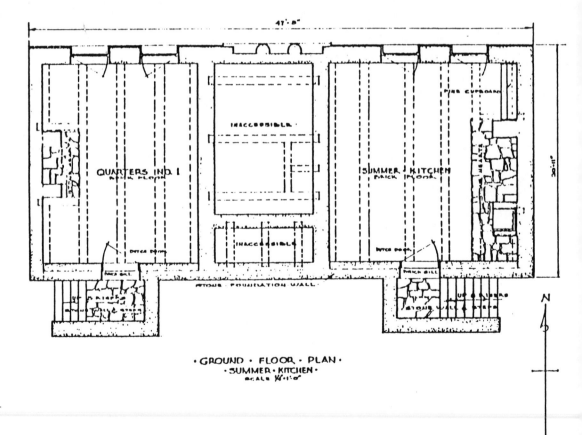

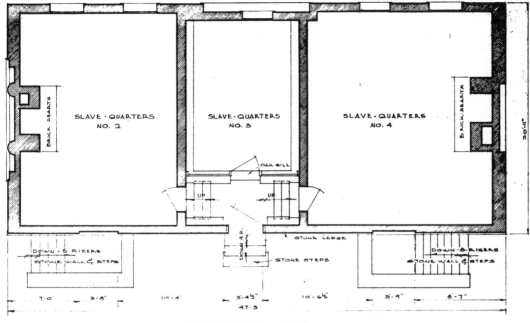

**4.17**
Floor plan of the
upper level of the
summer kitchen
and slave quarter
at Arlington House.
Drawn by C. F.
Ciango, 1940.

**4.18**
Combination kitchen
and laundry at the
Foster house, Bullock
County, Alabama.
Photograph by
W. N. Manning, 1935.

**4.19**

Elevation and floor plan of the combination kitchen and dairy at Poplar Forest, Bedford County, Virginia. Drawn by Eric Zehrung, Timothy Buehner, Elizabeth White, and Stephen Jackman, 1985.

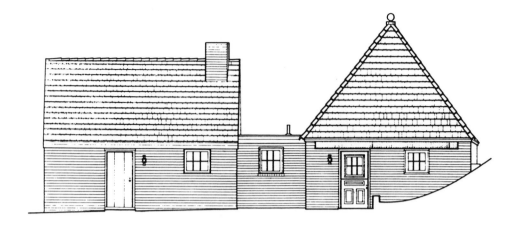

SOUTH ELEVATION

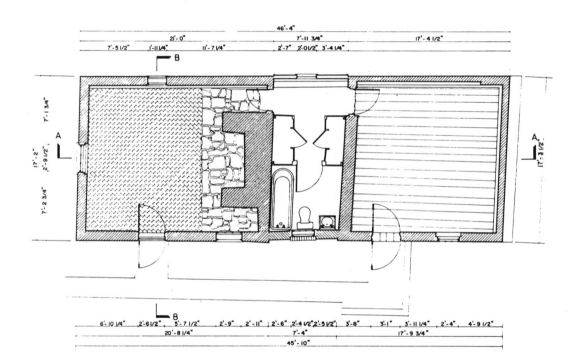

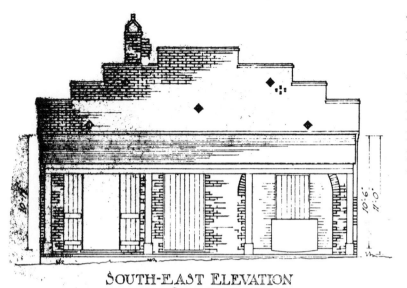

SOUTH-EAST ELEVATION
SCALE - ¼" = 1'-0"

**4.20**

Front elevation of the kitchen building at Greenwood plantation, West Feliciana Parish, Louisiana. Drawn by Chester H. Wicker, 1936.

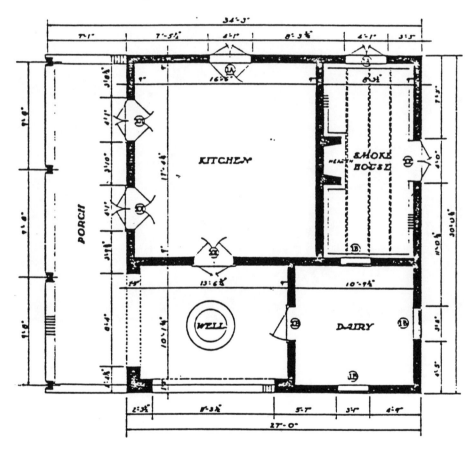

PLAN

Scale ¼" = 1'-0"

**4.21**

Floor plan of the kitchen building at Greenwood showing the locations of the food preparation area, the smokehouse, the dairy, and the well. Drawn by Samuel Wilson, Jr., 1938.

**4.22**
Fireplace in the
detached kitchen of
the Borders-Blackman
home, Calhoun County,
Alabama. Photograph by
W. N. Manning, 1935.

**4.23**
Fireplace in
the kitchen at
Effingham plantation,
Prince William
County, Virginia.
Photograph by
John O. Brostrup,
1936.

**4.24**

Fireplace in the kitchen at Refuge plantation, Camden County, Georgia. Photograph by L. D. Andrew, 1936, from an older picture taken ca. 1880.

# FIVE

# Smokehouses

A plantation's smokehouse was more than just a building where meat was preserved and stored. It also served as an index of regional diet and thus was perceived as an important symbol of southern identity by local people and outsiders alike. Certainly Emily Burke, a northern visitor to a Georgia plantation, recognized this when she wrote: "Pork at the South is never to my knowledge, salted and barreled as it is with us, but flitches as well as hams are hung up without being divided, in the house built for that purpose, and preserved in a smoke that is kept up day and night."[1] Although various kinds of meat might be smoked, a plantation's smokehouse was mainly filled with "hog meat." The popularity of pork in the southern diet inspired Dr. John S. Wilson of Columbus, Georgia, to refer to the South as "the great Hog-eating Confederacy" and to suggest that the region be dubbed the "Republic of Porkdom." Observing in 1860 that pork was consumed in some form "continually morning, noon, and night" by "all classes, sexes, ages, and conditions," he claimed that "hog's lard is the very oil that moves the machinery of life."[2] According to geographer Sam Bowers Hilliard, as cotton was understood to be the "king" of the antebellum southern economy, the title of "queen" should go to the pig.[3]

These opinions of southern foodways are confirmed by census figures. Between 1840 and 1860, there were 2.2 hogs for each man, woman, and child living in the South. This ratio meant that every southerner potentially had access to approximately three hundred pounds of pork per year. Even the slave diet featured relatively large portions of hog meat; full field hands were commonly allotted three pounds per week, or slightly more than one hundred and fifty pounds per year.[4] Because there was no established meat-packing industry in the South during this period, planters were faced with a tremendous task if they were to satisfy their desire for pork.

Even the smallest plantation, run with only twenty slaves, had to process and store over two tons of meat each year. One can easily appreciate, then, the importance of a smokehouse to the plantation routine. Former slave Eliza Overton reported that her master, John Coffman, who resided near Sikestown, Missouri, "used to kill about one hundred hogs at one time and then put them in the smokehouse."[5] If her calculation is correct, seven tons of pork were processed yearly at the Coffman plantation. When hogs were slaughtered on such a scale, the smokehouse had to be large and strongly constructed in order to protect its valuable contents. Overton's testimony brings to mind a substantial smokehouse like the one at the Stone-Young plantation in Lowndes County, Alabama (fig. 5.1). Larger than many of the dwelling houses in the county, this building stood more than thirty-five feet high and had a storage volume of almost 22,000 cubic feet. Constructed with brick masonry and decorated with diamond-shaped ventilators, it no doubt symbolized plantation owner Barton Stone's pride of place.

A smokehouse was first a machine for preserving meat. Hogs slaughtered late in the fall would keep until the next year's butchering if their quartered carcasses were salted and then dried over a smoldering fire. But once it was full of hams and sides of bacon, the smokehouse also became a vault. A meat-filled smokehouse symbolized the self-sufficiency of a plantation. It demonstrated a planter's ability to manage his affairs and adequately provide for his family and his slaves. The smokehouse also symbolized a planter's mastery over his work force. Because the slaves' survival and well-being was directly linked to the contents of the smokehouse, food allotments were often used as means of social control; productive workers were given extra or better cuts of meat as a way to inspire the others to work harder.[6] Once a week James Henry Hammond, master of Silver Bluff plantation in Edgefield County, South Carolina, made all of his servants put on clean clothes and stand before him to receive their weekly provisions. This ritual was clearly intended not only to convince the slaves that Hammond was a generous master but also to emphasize their dependence on him.[7]

Although the planter could use food to enhance his social power, slaves could just as easily strike back by manipulating the same symbolic means. A plantation's smokehouse was one of the chief targets for pilferage. Planters' letters and daybooks frequently mention thefts of small amounts of food—usually enough for a single meal—and the testimonies of former slaves contain numerous admissions that their diets were supplemented by nocturnal visits to their masters' storehouses.[8] Sarah Fitzpatrick from Tuskegee, Alabama, recalled that slave thefts of extra rations were very common. "Fak' is," she testified, "dey didn't call it stealin', dey called it takin'."[9] The smokehouse was thus a site of conflict where a planter's authority was sure to be challenged.

The connection between the smokehouse and the planter's power was made very clear to Missouri slave William Wells Brown. After a failed escape attempt, he was taken to the smokehouse, where he was hung by the wrists from a collar beam and severely whipped. Then his master, Major Freeland, "sent out his son Robert, a young man eighteen or twenty years of age, to see that I was well smoked. He made a fire of tobacco stems, which soon set me to coughing and sneezing. This, Robert told me, was the way his father used to do to his slaves in Virginia. After giving me what they conceived to be a decent smoking, I was untied and again set to work."[10] Clearly Freeland meant to show Brown that he was literally no more than a piece of meat. It was also equally clear that he thought the smokehouse was the best place to convey that message. That smokehouse punishments were not merely Freeland's unique form of discipline is indicated by the testimony of former slave B. E. Rogers from Raleigh, North Carolina: "Once on a neighboring plantation I saw two Negro boys hanged up in a smokehouse by the thumbs and beat for leaving the plantation without permission. Their shirts were so bloody they had to be greased before they would come off."[11] Samuel Burges, a planter from Cheraw, South Carolina, once used the smokehouse as a temporary jail for a runaway slave whom he had tracked down for friend.[12]

So many slaves understood the smokehouse to be the plantation's punishment site that, upon learning of their emancipation, their songs of celebration used the place to lampoon their former owners:

> De oberseer he make us trouble,
> An' he dribe us round a spell;
> We lock him up in de smoke-house cellar,
> Wid de key trown in de well.[13]

If we assume that the song celebrates an actual event, then certainly the punitive function of the smokehouse had been completely, and deliberately, overturned.

In Virginia smokehouses commonly were square in plan and topped with pyramidal roofs. The photograph of Saratoga plantation near Millwood, Virginia, shows that a smokehouse was easily recognizable as a storage building when seen within its architectural setting (fig. 5.2). Its scale, shape, and roofline distinguish it from the nearby kitchen. The square, pyramidal-roofed smokehouse was used on plantations all across the South; its presence in West Virginia, Kentucky, Alabama, and other states can be taken as evidence of the influence of Virginia families on the westward-moving plantation frontier throughout the first half of nineteenth century (figs. 5.3, 5.4, 5.5, 5.6).[14] The Virginia origins of these smokehouses are indicated not only by their form but occasionally in the details of their construction as well. The walls of the smokehouse built during the early 1820s at the Forks of Cypress, a plantation outside Florence, Alabama, for example, were framed basically in the Virginia Tidewater mode; the small framing members, the down braces at the corners, and the overhanging ceiling joists are a collective signature of Virginia-derived technique (figs. 5.7, 5.8).[15]

The square-plan smokehouse was also built with the more commonplace saddle-gable roof. Buildings roofed this way had a definite front and back as well as two side walls (fig. 5.9). Their entrances were located either in the front wall or in one of the ends. If the first option were followed, the building resembled a diminutive cabin. When the doorway was placed in a gable end, the smokehouse could look more like a small barn, especially if the building was constructed with logs (figs. 5.10, 5.11).

A smokehouse with a rectangular floor plan generally had its entrance in one of its narrower end walls, and frequently its roof projected several feet over the doorway (fig. 5.12). During the slaughtering season, animal carcasses were suspended from this overhanging gable while the meat was butchered and prepared for further processing. This type of smokehouse, thought to derive ultimately from a Pennsylvanian prototype, reflected mainly an upland South regional identity.[16] However, square and rectangular smokehouses could be found on neighboring plantations throughout the Deep South.

The meat hung in a smokehouse was already preserved by a "dry salting" process. Pieces of the freshly butchered meat were rubbed with raw salt and placed in wooden box or trough for up to six weeks (fig. 5.13). Meat was only smoked for about a week, mainly to give it a particular flavor. Any sort of green wood or slow-burning fuel could be used for the smoking process—even corncobs. The choice of fuel was determined largely by one's taste buds.[17] Blanche Wilson, who grew up on a black farmstead in Calvert County, Maryland, noted that her family had developed a preference for using apple wood when smoking their pork and observed further that fallen apple tree branches were collected throughout the year and saved especially for that purpose.[18]

The interior of a smokehouse was very dark. Its walls were blackened with soot, and the only light that entered the building came in through the single door when it was opened or through small vent holes. The floor was invariably bare earth with a shallow pit in the center to hold the fire. Pieces of meat were either set on low shelves built around the edges of the building or hung from horizontal poles set at about head height. If a smokehouse was particularly tall, additional rows of poles would be placed at regular intervals all the way to the top of the walls (fig. 5.14). Meat might also be hung from the building's rafters and collar beams if a large number of hogs had been butchered.

The interior of the smokehouse at Sherwood Forest plantation in Charles City County, Virginia, suggests some of the more onerous aspects of working in a smokehouse (see fig. 5.14). It provides a visual analog for the observation of an unnamed planter who in 1851 wrote: "A filthy smokehouse is a disgusting subject to write about, but as they are so numerous, I hope to be pardoned. It is enough to restrain the most inordinate appetite to be shown into the smokehouse and be regaled with the scent from its ground floor, spread with fragments of meat and bones and its walls decorated with fat cans and soap gourds."[19]

**5.1**

Smokehouse at
the Stone-Young
plantation, Lowndes
County, Alabama.
Photograph by W. N.
Manning, 1935.

**5.2**

View of Saratoga plantation, Clarke County, Virginia, showing the relationship of the smokehouse to the kitchen and mansion house. Photographer unknown, 1936, from an older photograph of unknown date.

**5.3**

Smokehouse at
Marmion plantation,
King George County,
Virginia. Photograph
by Frederick D.
Nichols, 1936.

**5.4**

Smokehouse at
Wheatland plantation,
Jefferson County,
West Virginia.
Photograph by Ian
MacLaughlin, 1937.

**5.5**
Smokehouse at
Mt. Lebanon
plantation, Bourbon
County, Kentucky.
Photograph by
Theodore Webb,
1934.

**5.6**
Smokehouse at
the Kilpatrick place,
Wilcox County,
Alabama. Photograph
by Alex Bush, 1937.

**5.7**

Framing diagram
for the smokehouse at
Marmion plantation.
Drawn by
Frederick D. Nichols
and A. Biggs, 1936.

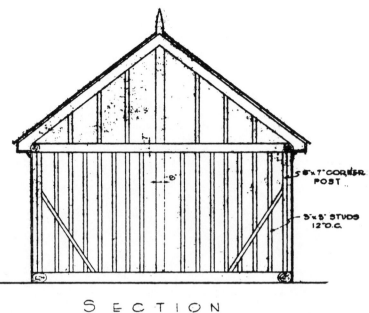

SECTION

**5.8**

Framing diagram
for the smokehouse at
The Forks of Cypress,
Lauderdale County,
Alabama. Drawn by
C. K. Rand, 1935–36.

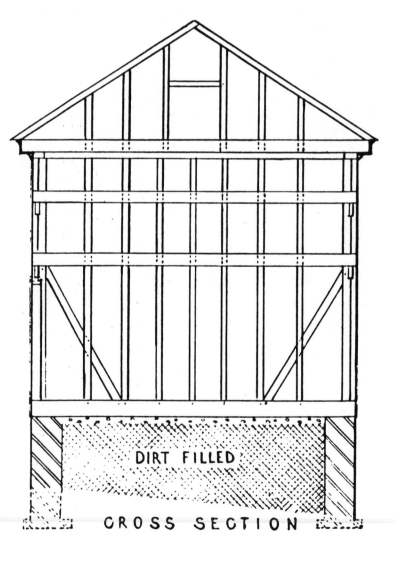

DIRT FILLED

CROSS SECTION

**5.9**
Smokehouse at
Berry Hill plantation,
Halifax County,
Virginia. Photograph
by C. O. Greene, 1940.

**5.10**
Smokehouse at the
Whitehall house, Hale
County, Alabama.
Photograph by W. N.
Manning, 1935.

**5.11**
Smokehouse at The
Oaks plantation,
Colbert County,
Alabama. Photograph
by Alex Bush, 1935.

**5.12**
Smokehouse at
the Grant house,
Marengo County,
Alabama. Photograph
by Alex Bush, 1935.

**5.13**
Salting trough at
Woodlands planta-
tion, Northampton
County, Virginia.
Photograph by
Jack E. Boucher,
1960.

**5.14**
Interior of
smokehouse at
Sherwood Forest
plantation, Charles
City County, Virginia.
Photograph by
William Barrett, 1975.

# SIX

# Outbuildings

The Big House setting was characterized by a distinctive array of outbuildings. Besides the freestanding kitchens and smokehouses already considered, there were more buildings that sheltered tasks related to food production, preservation, and storage. These buildings might include a dairy, an icehouse, and a chicken coop as well as other small sheds. In fact, by the middle of the nineteenth century, a large gathering of outbuildings commonly identified a place as southern. Union officer Theodore Lyman, while stationed in northern Virginia, was quick to note the distinctive pattern of rural estates. He wrote of southern planters, "They have a queer way of building on one thing after another, the great point being to have a separate shed or out-house for every purpose. . . . You will find a carpenter's shop, tool room, coachshed, pig-house, stable, kitchen, two or three barns, and half a dozen negro huts, besides the main house."[1] Emily Burke joked that on a southern plantation "there were nearly as many roofs as rooms."[2] A similar comic observation was made half a century earlier by architect Benjamin H. Latrobe when he wrote that outbuildings seemed to cluster around southern houses "as a litter of pigs their mother."[3] Although the number and purposes of the structures on any given plantation could vary with the size of the holding and its degree of self-sufficiency, no estate—however modest—lacked a set of small service buildings.

Regarded as an ensemble, a set of outbuildings could be used to define the boundaries of a planter's yard in much the same way that they were used to outline the slaves' work space. A photograph of Kendall Lee's Ditchley plantation, located in Northumberland County, Virginia, for example, shows that Lee placed his dairy and icehouse behind the mansion, where they stood like sentinels at the ends of an imaginary fence (fig. 6.1). A similar pattern is visible in the site plan of Marmion in King George County, Virginia, the plantation developed in the eighteenth century for John Fitzhugh (fig. 6.2). In this case, however, the yard was enclosed by an actual wall. Fitzhugh placed his dairy, smokehouse, kitchen, and office at the corners of his yard in an apparent attempt to underscore its geometrical layout and to emphasize the separation between his residential space and the adjacent fields.

During the nineteenth century, plantation outbuildings were more frequently strung out in rows running either parallel or perpendicular to the alignment of the Big House.[4] Photographs from two Virginia plantations, Dan's Hill in Pittsylvania County and Upper Bremo in Fluvanna County, illustrate strings of small service outbuildings (figs. 6.3, 6.4; also see fig. 10.3). At both properties, various food preparation and storage functions, although housed in discrete buildings, were nonetheless perceived as a related set of activities. The linear arrangement of these outbuildings was, however, not entirely novel. Eighteenth-century precedents can found in the layout of at least two Virginia plantations, Tuckahoe in Goochland County and Nomini Hall in Lancaster County.[5]

## Dairies and Springhouses

Throughout the greater Chesapeake region, a dairy, like the smokehouse with which it was frequently paired, was a small building, roughly fourteen feet square, that was topped with either a pyramidal or gable roof (figs. 6.5, 6.6; also see fig. 3.6).[6] These structures were distinguished particularly by their extended overhanging eaves and louvered ventilators, two features designed to keep the interior of the building— and hence its contents—cool. According to agricultural historian John Martin Robinson: "A cool even temperature was very important in a dairy; about 50°F was considered the ideal. If conditions were too hot the cream would turn sour; if too cold it would not coagulate properly, and so could not be churned."[7] A dairy was basically a clean room where milk sat undisturbed in shallow dishes or "pans" for about ten hours, until the cream rose to the surface. After the cream was collected, it was usually taken by the slave cook or her assistant to the kitchen to be churned into butter. However, in some places the dairy functioned as a specialized workroom. Mary Fowler, a former slave from Lowndes County, Alabama, recalled that, at the dairy on the Shepard plantation, "there was a stove there too, to heat plenty of water for the milk things—

vessels and strainers an' cloths. . . . The dairy was big an' cool an' we strained up the milk an' churned an' worked up the butter here."[8]

Maintaining a suitable temperature inside a dairy could prove quite difficult, particularly during the long, hot southern summers. Some planters attempted to maintain the required temperature by thoroughly insulating the walls and ceiling of the structure. Another widely used strategy, the one employed by John Fitzhugh at Marmion, was to sink the floor of the dairy several feet below ground level (fig. 6.7). At Perry Hall plantation in Talbot County, Maryland, water was carried in from a nearby well and poured into a trough that ran around the perimeter of the dairy floor. The crocks of milk placed in this trough were kept cool by changing the water two or three times a day.[9]

Sam Bowers Hilliard has found that the South as a whole never developed a significant dairying capacity during the antebellum period. In both 1850 and 1860, the annual output for butter, the only recorded index of milk production, showed that southerners consumed less than seven pounds per person, a level only one-third of the rate for northern states.[10] This low figure suggests not only that there were relatively few milk cows in the region, but also that dairy buildings were exceptional elements in the built landscape. A dairy was thus an architectural emblem signaling the wealth of the planter class. The mere presence of a dairy among a planter's buildings immediately suggested the variety and richness of his table. The luxury of sweet cream, butter, and fresh milk was emphatically underscored at Folly plantation in Augusta County, Virginia, where the dairy was not only built in brick masonry but had a decorative cupola on its roof and a projecting gable porch supported by classical columns (fig. 6.8).

On plantations located in the trans-Appalachian South, when there were dairy products to be stored, they were usually placed in a springhouse, a rectangular masonry building with a gable entrance (fig. 6.9). Frequently built into the slope of a hill, a springhouse often had two levels that were entered from different sides of the building.[11] At the base of the structure was a pool of cool water, usually about two feet deep, supplied by a natural spring. Any overflow that built up was carried out of the building by a runoff spout. From the description provided by former slave Mary Fowler, the springhouse on the Shepard plantation in Lowndes County, Alabama, was apparently built in this way: "There was a spring at the foot of a little hill, with a wide, spreadin' tree shadin' it, an' Massa had a trench dug from the spring, an' walled with rock, an' lined along the bottom with rock, an' pieces of plank was put across, a little ways apart, to hold the vessels steady, an' that was where we kep' the milk an' butter cool an' sweet, as with ice." [12] Rachel Cruze, kept as a slave at the Strawberry Fields plantation in Knox County, Tennessee, had similar memories: "The spring house stood close to the big house, and here was kept the butter, cream, and milk and such like that had to be kept cool. There were shelves built in it to accommodate the food in case of heavy rains. Apples and other fruits were often kept in the upper part." [13] The placement of a springhouse was contingent on the location of the spring and thus might not always be near to hand. Such was the case with the two springhouses at Spring Station, an estate just outside Louisville, Kentucky. These structures were located several hundred yards away from the Big House belonging to Samuel Beall.

## Icehouses

The use of ice for preserving food became a part of the plantation routine as early as 1665, when Sir William Berkeley, governor of Virginia, was granted a patent "to gather, make and take snow and ice . . . and to preserve and keep the same in such pits, caves and cool places as he should think fit." [14] But even with such a long history of icehouses, effective ice preservation techniques remained elusive to Virginians for more than a century. In the late spring of 1784, George Washington wrote to Robert Morris of Pennsylvania: "The House I filled with ice does not answer, it [the ice] is gone already." Morris responded with a detailed description of a subterranean ice vault, which Washington studied carefully. But even with this new information, he still could not maintain a supply of ice past late spring. On June 5, 1785, Washington wrote in his diary: "Opened the Well in my Cellar in which I had laid up a store of Ice, but there was not the smallest particle remaining." [15]

Washington and his fellow southerners eventually came to understand how to pack their ice in grass or sawdust and how to drain off the water that built up from the inevitable melting that took place over the course of a summer. They also learned that an underground vault provided the greatest degree of thermal insulation. Thomas Jefferson, to cite just one example, built two icehouses at Monticello; one of them was a sixteen-foot-deep pit that held sixty wagonloads of ice. [16]

Plantation icehouses varied considerably in form and appearance. At Marmion the icehouse looked like nothing more than a gabled roof resting close to the ground, whereas at Folly plantation, the icehouse was a small, square building with brick walls that stood around five feet high on the front (figs. 6.10, 6.11). The icehouse at Toddsbury in Gloucester County, Virginia, was an exotic-looking cylindrical structure topped with a conical roof (fig. 6.12), whereas all that was visible of Charles Ridgely's icehouse at Hampton, just north of Baltimore, Maryland, was a mound of earth. As scaled drawings make very clear, the greater part of an icehouse was located underground. Beneath the large grassy dome on the north lawn at Hampton was a brick- and stone-lined vault measuring twelve feet in diameter and almost thirty-four feet deep, which was reached by a stairway and subterranean passage (fig. 6.13; see also fig. 12.2). The pits under the Marmion and Folly icehouses also extended nearly thirty feet below ground level. Although these icehouses differed on the surface, they were all still the same type of structure.[17]

The icehouses from the Chesapeake region seem to correspond closely to out-buildings reported by former slave Mary Anderson, who lived in the Piedmont region of North Carolina. In describing the Bodie plantation near Franklinton, she remembered:

> A pond was located on the place and in winter ice was gathered there for summer use and stored in an icehouse which was built in the grove where the other build-ings were. A large hole about ten feet deep was dug in the ground; the ice was put in that hole and covered. A large frame building was built over it. At the top of the earth there was an entrance door and steps leading down to the bottom of the hole. Other things besides ice were stored there. There was a still on the plan-tation and barrels of brandy were stored in the icehouse, also pickles, preserves, and cider.[18]

In the parts of the South where ponds and streams froze over during the winter months, procuring ice was relatively easy. In the warmer areas of the Deep South, particularly in South Carolina and Georgia and along the Gulf Coast, a large-scale interstate ice trade developed. Beginning in 1799, shiploads of ice were brought in regularly from New England. Later another route was established down the Missis-sippi River from ice ponds in Illinois and Wisconsin.[19] Consequently, icehouses were found all across the South, even on the estates of planters living along the semitropical Rice Coast of South Carolina.[20]

## Chicken Houses and Dovecotes

Southern planters raised a variety of fowls: turkeys, ducks, geese, pigeons, and chickens. Although there are no records to provide an accurate estimate of the number of birds raised in the South during any decade of the antebellum period, it is clear that domesticated fowl, particularly chickens, were a mainstay of the region's foodways.[21]

There were several important advantages to raising chickens: they provided both meat and eggs; they could be maintained on very small amounts of feed; and they could be killed on short notice, thus reducing the risk of spoilage. Because it was common practice to let chickens nest wherever they felt secure, coops or poultry houses were rarely seen in a southern farmyard. A nineteenth-century visitor to Mississippi reported that in the "evenings all the trees of the plantations are covered with chickens and turkeys."[22]

Indeed, on most plantations, raising chickens was seen as a slave activity. Landon Carter, master of Sabine Hall in Richmond County, Virginia, to cite an eighteenth-century example, ordered his slaves to swap the chickens they raised at their quarters for the cloth they needed to make their clothes.[23] Frances Kemble, in her description of life on Butler Island, a Georgia rice plantation, complained that the estate was nearly overrun by slave-owned poultry: "[They] cluck, scream, gabble, gobble, crow, cackle, fight, fly, and flutter in all directions, and to their immense concourse, and the perfect freedom with which they intrude themselves even into the piazza of the house, the pantry, and kitchen, I partly attribute the swarms of fleas, and other still less agreeable vermin, with which we are most horribly pestered."[24]

According to former slave Rachel Cruze, even when planters supervised the raising of chickens, slaves still maintained their own flocks: "Miss Nancy [the plantation mistress] had a hen house up near the big house where she kept the chickens for the family, and then there was another group around the barn, for the hands. Sometimes Miss Nancy's chickens wouldn't get as nice and fat as the ones down at the barn; then she would go down and get some of them."[25] The different chicken houses described by Rachel Cruze can be visualized, perhaps, by comparing the outbuildings located on the Blakely plantation near Vicksburg, Mississippi, and on the Dry Forks plantation just outside of Camden, Alabama (figs. 6.14, 6.15). At Blakely the chicken coop was a stylish frame structure with a pyramidal roof, whereas the hen house at Dry Forks was only a roughly framed pen. Clearly the Blakely coop, a building with an aristocratic flair reminiscent of an old Virginia estate, was meant to serve both practical and ornamental functions.

The dovecote, or pigeon roost, was another plantation outbuilding used to shelter domestic fowl. Although Hilliard reports that pigeons were only a minor ingredient in the southern diet, on some plantations these birds were clearly significant. An 1835 plan of the Harris-Rives plantation near Sparta, Georgia, indicates ten "dove houses" of varying sizes.[26] As sketched by an amateur draftsman, these structures appear to have been square boxes with pyramidal roofs raised off the ground on posts, very much like the dovecote at Bowman's Folly in Accomac County, Virginia (fig. 6.16). The dovecote at the Cox-Steward farm near Lexington, Georgia, was a different type of structure, basically a two-story tower with pigeon roosts above and storage space below (fig. 6.17). Similar structures have been noted at a several sites in Louisiana as well. In fact, the dovecote was once so commonplace in Louisiana that Frederick Law Olmsted referred to it in 1857 as the "universal appendage of a sugar planter's house."[27] Indeed, Louisiana dovecotes could be quite elaborate. The two at Uncle Sam plantation in St. James Parish, Louisiana, were hexagonal towers that stood slightly more than thirty-five feet tall (see fig. 12.48). The dovecote at Parlange plantation in Pointe Coupee Parish, Louisiana, was just slightly taller and octagonal in plan (fig. 6.18).

## Craft Shops

If a planter owned a significant number of gifted slave artisans, he would construct workshops or service buildings where they would practice their special skills. George Mason, who owned numerous slave artisans, including carpenters, coopers, blacksmiths, tanners, shoemakers, spinners, and even a distiller, must have had several craft shops at Gunston Hall. At Montpelier James Madison reportedly had shops for a blacksmith, a wood turner, a carpenter, and a wheelwright.[28] In a rendering of the Tower Hill plantation in Sussex County, Virginia, Major William N. Blow, the former owner of the estate, indicated that there had once been three sizable cabins reserved for craft activities.[29] The Bodie plantation in North Carolina was apparently quite self-sufficient. According to Mary Anderson, one of the plantation's former slaves: "Many of the things we used were made on the place. There was a grist mill, tannery, shoe shop, blacksmith shop, and looms for weaving cloth."[30] Very few buildings of this sort survived into the twentieth century, but there are photographs of the blacksmith shops at Effingham plantation in Prince William County, Virginia, and Rosemount plantation in Greene County, Alabama (figs. 6.19, 6.20; also see fig. 12.14). At these shops, many different tasks were performed in addition to metalwork. In plantation lingo, such a building was usually called a "workshop." Martha Colquitt, a former slave from Olgethorpe County, Georgia, recalled, "De workshop was a big lone shed off to itself, where dey had de blacksmith place, and where harness was mended and all sorts of fixin' done to de tools and things."[31]

If a plantation required a large amount of cloth on an annual basis, a special building was erected to house the necessary equipment. At Sabine Hall in Richmond County, Virginia, Landon Carter constructed a "weaving manufactory" where he kept two looms, one cotton gin, four flax spinning wheels, five "great wheels," five pairs of wool cards, and one hackle for processing linen fiber.[32] A similar structure was recalled by John Sneed, a former slave from Travis County, Texas: "Dere's one long, log house where dey spinned and weaved de cloth. Dere sixteen spinnin' wheels and eight looms in dat house. . . . Mos' all de clothes what de slaves and de white folks have was made in dat house."[33] The recollections of former slave Nelson Dickerson from Pike County, Mississippi, provide a similar description: "Old Mistiss had a big loom room an' when it rained she had de wimen to come in an' sum wud card de bats, sum wud spin de thread and sum wud make de cloth. Dey had great stacks uf cloth piled up on a table in dat room. She wud give sum uf dat cloth to her wimen folk to make deir clothes uf. None of her folks eber went naked."[34]

Textile production on plantations was housed in several different types of buildings. At the James Ridley place in Davidson County, Tennessee, the loom house was a modest, two-story log structure with gable entrances that looked very much like a small barn (fig. 6.21). This building contrasts markedly with the two-room dependency used for weaving at the Borough house near Stateburg, South Carolina, which was clearly meant to present an attractive front to the Big House (fig. 6.22). The two-story brick spinning house at the Reynolds home near Sylacauga, Alabama, illustrates yet another building form used for textile production (fig. 6.23).

### Storehouses

If slave artisans produced more goods than could be used immediately, the surplus was kept in a storehouse. Landon Carter used his to stockpile the bolts of cotton and wool cloth woven by his female slaves.[35] Olmsted reported that the plantation store at a large estate in coastal Georgia held provisions, tools, and materials as well as housing the plantation's produce before it was shipped to market.[36] Robert "King"

Carter maintained a building at Corotoman, his plantation in Lancaster County, Virginia, called the "Brick House Store" where he kept imported goods, which he sold or bartered to local farmers. Listed in a 1730 inventory of this building were not only essential supplies and goods such as cloth, tools, gunpowder, and home furnishings but also many luxury items including spices, ivory combs, and brass candlesticks.[37] Because it held so many things of value, a store had to be solidly constructed, and it had to provide adequate storage space. The storehouse at Hillsborough plantation in King and Queen County, Virginia, built during the first quarter of the eighteenth century by tobacco planter and merchant Humphrey Hill, is a good example (figs. 6.24, 6.25). The building had brick walls more than a foot thick and three floors where goods could be stowed away.

The so-called shipping house at Chicora Wood, the plantation in Georgetown County, South Carolina, that served as the residence of Robert F. W. Allston, was a two-story frame structure (fig. 6.26). The plantation's rice crop was stored in this building, which was located at the edge of the Pee Dee River, until it could be sent to market. Because Allston owned five plantations with a collective work force of 630 slaves in 1860, he doubtless had several shipping houses. In 1858 the year's harvest at Chicora Wood alone totaled 27,078 bushels.[38] The storehouse at Middleburg, a South Carolina rice estate in Berkeley County, was a frame building raised up on a one-story brick masonry foundation. The upper storage level, containing a large open room plus a loft space, was reached by exterior stairways (fig. 6.27).

The storage building at Melrose plantation near Natchitoches, Louisiana, constructed sometime between 1800 and 1833, also has a masonry base with a wooden second story (figs. 6.28, 6.29, 6.30).[39] The building, which was used as the plantation's jail as well as for storage, has a spectacular hipped roof extending slightly more than nine feet beyond the walls on all four sides. Its steeply sloping sides almost completely obscure the upper story of the building, which is constructed with corner-notched logs. Because of the building's exotic form, it has been called the African House. However, all over southern Louisiana there are many plantation buildings—large mansions, smaller dwelling houses, outbuildings, and some barns—constructed with similar hipped roofs that extend well past their walls.[40] In fact, two of the dwelling houses at Melrose, the mansion commissioned in 1833 by Jean Baptiste Louis Metoyer and an earlier house called Yucca, also have this sort of roof. The claim for African origins is sometimes tied to the fact that the plantation's first owner, Marie Thereze Coincoin Metoyer, was the child of African slaves. In fact, the name Coincoin (just one of several spellings) appears to be derived from a name used among the Ewe people of West Africa; it is given to second-born daughters like Marie Thereze.[41] Unfortunately, this linguistic evidence provides a false architectural trail, for there is little resemblance between this building and the houses of the Ewe in either form or mode of construction. African House needs to be understood as a building based on local practices rather than on exotic custom. More than anything else, it resembles a French barn shorn of its usual encompassing sheds.

## Miscellaneous Structures

The firewood used on plantations was usually stacked in the yard near the kitchen, where it was needed most. However, a planter who was particularly concerned with the order and neatness of his property might build a woodshed. This was a minimal structure that provided little more than a roof to cover the woodpile. The open-sided example from Fort Mitchell, Alabama, provides a good example of the building type (fig. 6.31).

Tools and gear might end up anywhere on a plantation: in the barn, in the quarters, on the porch, in the yard. Joseph H. Ingram, upon visiting a Mississippi plantation in the 1830s, found its porch "strewed [with] saddles, whips, horse blankets, and the motley paraphernalia with which planters love to lumber their galleries."[42] But if a planter wanted to ensure the orderly appearance of his estate, he could build specialized sheds in which to store these items. Often these were small frame or log structures resembling smokehouses or small barns. The brick toolshed standing at the edge of the formal gardens at Westover plantation in Virginia represents probably the most refined version of this building type (fig. 6.32).

**6.1**

View of the yard at
Ditchley plantation,
Northumberland
County, Virginia.
Photograph by
C. O. Greene, 1940.

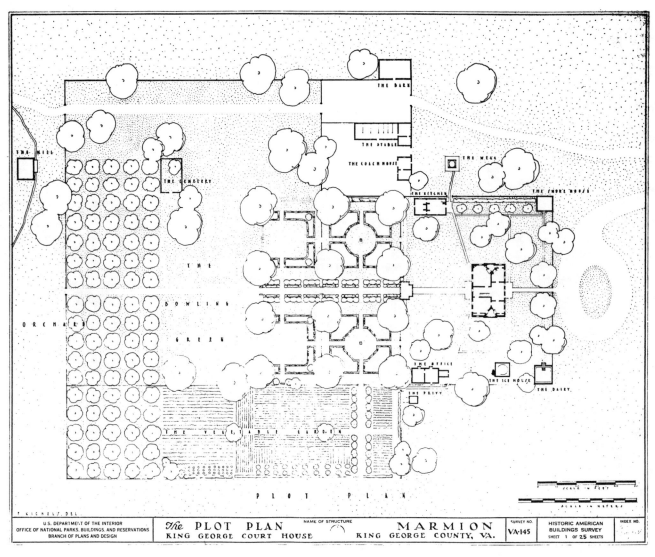

**6.2**

Site plan of
Marmion plantation,
King George County,
Virginia. Drawn
by Frederick D.
Nichols, 1936.

**6.3**
Outbuildings
at Dan's Hill,
Pittsylvania County,
Virginia. Photograph
by W. R. Crowe, 1934.

**6.4**
Outbuildings at
Bremo plantation,
Fluvanna County,
Virginia. Included
in this set, from
left to right, are a
smokehouse, wood
shed, and dairy.
Photograph by C. O.
Greene, 1940.

**6.5**
Dairy at Hayes
Manor, Chowan
County, North
Carolina. Photograph
by C. O. Greene, 1940.

**6.6**
Dairy at Wood-
lands plantation,
Northampton
County, Virginia.
Photograph by
Jack E. Boucher,
1960.

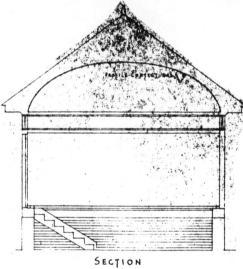

SECTION

**6.7**
Section of the dairy
at Marmion plantation.
Drawn by A. Biggs
and Frederick D.
Nichols, 1936.

**6.8**

Dairy at Folly
plantation, Augusta
County, Virginia.
Photograph by
S. J. Collins, 1934.

**6.9**

Springhouses at
Spring Station,
Jefferson County,
Kentucky.
Photograph by
Theodore Webb, 1934.

**6.10**
Icehouse at
Marmion plantation.
Photograph by W. M.
Haussman, in 1935.

**6.11**
Icehouse at
Folly plantation.
Photograph by
S. J. Collins, 1934.

**6.12**
Icehouse at
Toddsbury plantation,
Gloucester County,
Virginia. Photograph
by Charles E.
Peterson, 1933.

**6.13**

Cross section of the
icehouse at Hampton
plantation, Baltimore
County, Maryland.
Drawn by C. C.
Boldrick, 1959.

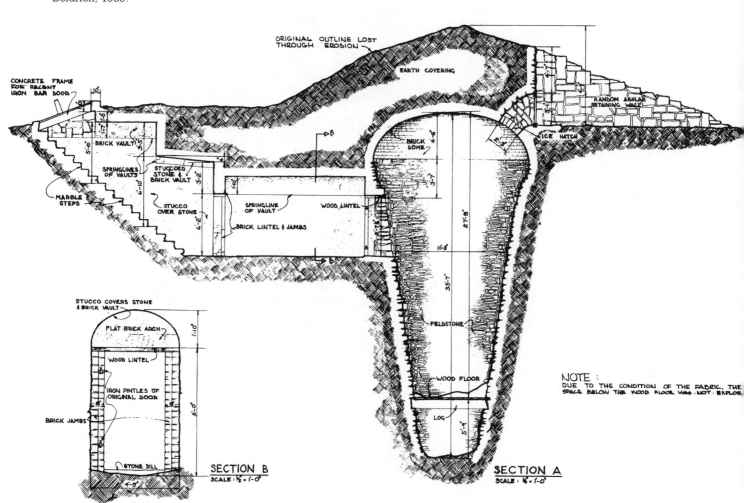

**6.14**
Chicken house at
Blakely plantation,
Warren County,
Mississippi.
Photograph by
Lester Jones, 1940.

**6.15**

Chicken house at
Dry Forks plantation,
Wilcox County,
Alabama. Photograph
by Alex Bush, 1936.

**6.16**

Dovecote at
Bowman's Folly,
Accomac County,
Virginia. Photograph
by Jack E. Boucher,
1960.

**6.17**
Dovecote at the
Cox-Steward
farm, Oglethorpe
County, Georgia.
Photograph by L. D.
Andrews, 1936.

**6.18**

Plan and elevation
of the dovecote at
Parlange plantation,
Pointe Coupee Parish,
Louisiana. Drawn by
A. E. Hoover and O. C.
Kottemann, 1936.

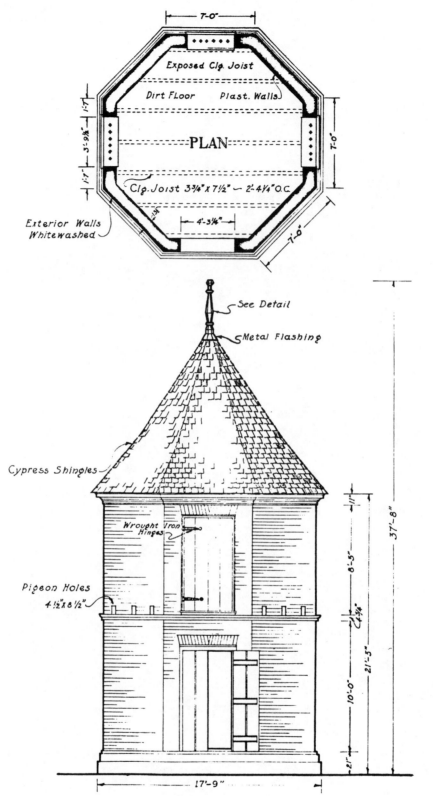

**6.19**
Blacksmith shop
at Effingham
plantation, Prince
William County,
Virginia. Photograph
by John O.
Brostrup, 1936.

**6.20**
Blacksmith shop at
Rosemount, Greene
County, Alabama.
A single-crib log
barn stands in the
distance. Photograph
by Alex Bush, 1934.

**6.21**
Loom house at
the Ridley house,
Davidson County,
Tennessee.
Photograph by
Lester Jones, 1940.

**6.22**
Weaving house at
the Borough house,
Sumter County,
South Carolina.
Photograph by
Jack E. Boucher,
1960.

**6.23**

Spinning house at
the Reynolds home,
Talladega County,
Alabama. Photograph
by Alex Bush, 1935.

**6.24**

Storehouse at
Hillsborough
plantation, King
and Queen County,
Virginia. Photograph
by H. Bagby, 1936.

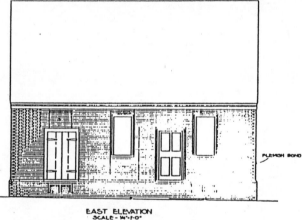

EAST ELEVATION
SCALE · ¼"·1'·0"

**6.25**

Front elevation
and first-floor plan
of the storehouse
at Hillsborough.
Drawn by G. C.
Pyne, Jr., 1936.

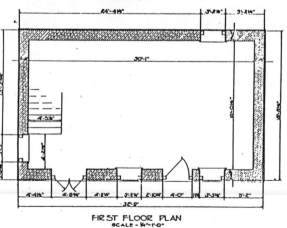

FIRST FLOOR PLAN
SCALE · ¼"·1'·0"

**6.26**
Shipping house
at Chicora Wood
plantation,
Georgetown
County, South
Carolina. Photograph
by Charles N.
Bayless, 1977.

**6.27** [top]

Storehouse at
Middleburg
plantation, Berkeley
County, South
Carolina. Photograph
by C. O. Greene, 1940.

**6.28** [above]

Storehouse at
Melrose plantation,
Natchitoches
Parish, Louisiana.
Photograph by Lester
Jones, 1940.

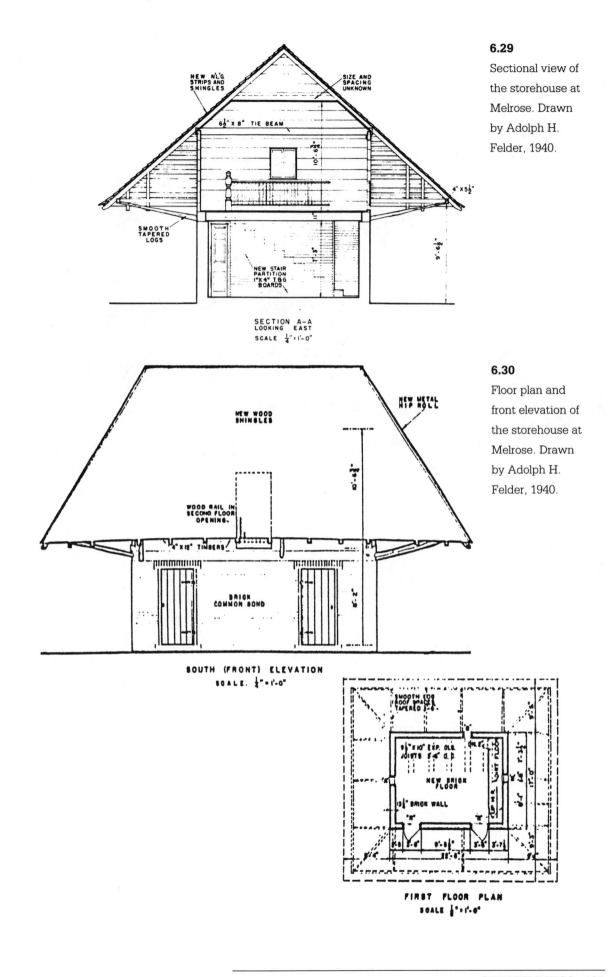

NEW N'L'G
STRIPS AND
SHINGLES

SIZE AND
SPACING
UNKNOWN

6½" X 8" TIE BEAM

10'-6"

4" X 5½"

SMOOTH
TAPERED
LOGS

7'-3"

9'-6"

NEW STAIR
PARTITION
1"X 4" T&G
BOARDS

SECTION A-A
LOOKING EAST
SCALE ¼"=1'-0"

**6.29**

Sectional view of the storehouse at Melrose. Drawn by Adolph H. Felder, 1940.

NEW METAL
HIP ROLL

NEW WOOD
SHINGLES

16'-0"

WOOD RAIL IN
SECOND FLOOR
OPENING.

4" X 12" TIMBERS

BRICK
COMMON BOND

8'-2"

SOUTH (FRONT) ELEVATION
SCALE ¼"=1'-0"

**6.30**

Floor plan and front elevation of the storehouse at Melrose. Drawn by Adolph H. Felder, 1940.

SMOOTH LOG
ROOF BRACE
TAPERED 3'-6"

9¼" X 10" EXP. OLD
JOISTS 1'-4" O.C.

NEW BRICK
FLOOR

13¼" BRICK WALL

"A"

11'-0"

16'-0"

FIRST FLOOR PLAN
SCALE ¼"=1'-0"

**6.31**
Wood shed at
the Alexander
house, Russell
County, Alabama.
Photograph by W. N.
Manning, 1936.

**6.32**
Elevations and floor
plan of the toolshed at
Westover plantation,
Charles City County,
Virginia. Drawn by
Susan Dornbusch,
1978–79.

SOUTH ELEVATION        WEST ELEVATION        PLAN

TOOL SHED        SCALE 1/4"=1'-0"

# SEVEN

# Barns and Stables

## Barns

The barns built on some plantations were enormous structures. Samuel Washington of Stafford County, Virginia, for example, reported in the *Virginia Gazette* in 1767 "a Barn finished this year, 72 by 48, framed work."[1] The tobacco barn at Green Hill plantation in Campbell County, Virginia, built early in the nineteenth century, measured seventy-five by sixty feet including its shed additions (see fig. 12.27). Although not specific about the size, William Henry Townes, a former slave from Tuscumbia, Alabama, testified that there was on his master's plantation a "great, big barn where all de stock an' stuff dat was raised [was] kep'."[2] But perhaps the most impressive barn, at least in Virginia, was the great barn begun in 1815 at Bremo plantation in Fluvanna County (fig. 7.1). Completed in 1817, it was constructed mainly with sandstone and stood two stories high; the largest segment of the T-plan building measured eighty-five by thirty-three feet.[3] The barn was covered by a hipped roof and topped by a cupola containing a large clock. Its main entrance was protected by a pedimented portico supported by four Tuscan columns. Soon after this barn was completed, John Hartwell Cocke, the master of Bremo, began an aggressive campaign of agricultural reforms, hoping to convince his fellow planters to abandon what he deemed to be their unhealthy dependence on tobacco as their single cash crop. Perhaps he considered his templelike barn to be an effective advertisement for the virtues of his new gospel of diversified agriculture and soil replenishment.[4]

Large barns were, according to historian of agriculture Lewis Cecil Gray, exceptional in the Deep South.[5] Virginia planters might refer to almost any storage structure, from a twelve-foot-square corncrib to a sizable stable, as a "barn," suggesting that they had only an approximate definition for this building type.[6] Such a lack of specificity probably stemmed from the widespread southern practice of sheltering various activities in several small buildings rather than gathering them under the roof of a single large structure.[7] An 1825 notice from a South Carolina newspaper confirms that this custom was observed at the Point plantation near Charleston; listed among the plantation's buildings were a cotton house, a corn house, a fodder house, a carriage house and stable, a mule stable, and an ox house.[8] Given the specialized purposes of each of these buildings, it is unlikely that any of them would have been as big as the average Pennsylvania barn.

Because the southern climate was relatively mild, planters generally believed that their livestock and produce did not need to be sheltered. One respondent to the *Southern Cultivator* wrote in 1849 that more than half of the farmers in his county never housed their oats and fodder at all, and that fewer than one-tenth of them provided any shelter for their cows.[9] Isaac Adams, a former slave belonging to Sack P. Gee in Louisiana, confirmed that the livestock was generally left out in the open: "Some of his [Mr. Gee's] land was in pasture but most of it was in open fields, with just miles and miles of cotton rows. There was a pretty good strip along one side he called the 'old' fields. That's what they called the land that was wore out and turned back. It was all growed up in young trees, and that's where he kept his horses most of the time."[10] Former slave Manus Robinson reported a variant of this custom in North Carolina. The livestock, he said, was left out year round to forage in open pasture, but should the weather turn cold, "Us had ter build 'em big fires of long logs ter keep 'em warm. Dese fires would burn fer days, wid a little stirrin' 'bout."[11] According to former slave Katie Darling, the cows at the McCarty plantation near Marshall, Texas, were not milked in a barn. They were, instead, gathered each morning into a fenced corral, milked, and then released back to their pasture.[12] The absence of substantial farm buildings was noted as well in central Georgia by a local newspaper editor who, after a trip through the Piedmont region—the core of the state's inland plantation zone—found only a half-dozen "respectable barns."[13]

Southern planters generally followed the example of their yeomen neighbors and opted for small, single-crib log barns when they thought it prudent to shelter their beasts or their feed. This certainly was the case at the Nassau plantation in central Texas, where Ferdinand Roemer found during the 1840s that "the farm buildings belonging to the plantation lie about a gunshot distance from the manor house at the foot of the hill. There are barns, storage houses, negro cabins and a house for the overseer. All are rough log houses made of roughly hewn logs, covered with shingles, which like most buildings of this kind on an American plantation have no particular pleasing appearance."[14] Hugh Davis, master of the Beaver Bend plantation in Perry County, Alabama, also had a preference for log buildings. Summarizing a very busy season, he noted in his plantation ledger on February 29, 1856, that during the previous month his slaves had cleared 180 acres of new land, providing him with 50,000 rails and the material to build thirty "houses of all kinds." Presumably his use of the term *house* covered all manner of log structures from slave cabins to barns to chicken coops.[15] In fact, small log cribs were so frequently used in Alabama as outbuildings that it seemed to one nineteenth-century traveler that a shower of rails must have fallen across the countryside.[16] The 1935 photograph of the log cribs scattered across the pasture of the Walter Henry Crenshaw plantation in Butler County, Alabama, records a scene that might have inspired such a view of the landscape (fig. 7.2).

The most basic southern barns were constructed of logs. The smallest consisted of nothing more than a pen of logs covered by a roof. The corncrib located at the Bracketts farm in Louisa County, Virginia, a squarish pen of slightly hewn poles with a doorway in the gable end, provides a good example (fig. 7.3; also see figs. 12.28, 6.20). Slightly more elaborate versions of the basic single-crib type could be created by adding sheds to the sides for additional storage (fig. 7.4). Another variant of the single-crib barn, built at the Hill of Howth plantation near Boligee, Alabama, was encircled by an arcade of posts that held up the ends of a broad, overhanging roof (fig. 7.5). Tools and other equipment were stored under the protected areas surrounding the barn. The granary at Northampton plantation in Prince Georges County, Maryland, built probably in the early nineteenth century, was a single-crib barn constructed in frame and flanked with shed additions to each side (fig. 7.6). To protect its contents against damage from moisture and rodents, the building was not only tightly sealed with a clapboard covering but also was raised a couple of feet off the ground on a foundation of brick masonry.[17]

Geographer Fred B. Kniffen identifies log barns as features of mid-Atlantic regional culture that were carried into the South beginning in the eighteenth century. Along the path of their southward diffusion, he explains, "The cribs grew smaller and smaller. From serving as stables they became more and more cribs for the storage of corn."[18] His assessment is supported by an 1854 description of standard plantation practice, which explained: "The common arrangement is a rail pen for corn, a rail pen for shucks, [with] fodder and oats in stacks."[19] One of the more typical barns, then, was a two-pen structure like the log barn at Belmont, the plantation in Colbert

County, Alabama, built in 1828 for Alexander Mitchell (fig. 7.7). If a larger building was needed, the plan of the double-crib barn was doubled again, producing a four-crib structure similar to the barn at Pond Spring plantation in Lawrence County, Alabama (fig. 7.8).[20] In this case, not only was the amount of storage space increased by two additional cribs, but a stabling area was provided by the lean-to shed added to one side of the barn.

Barn types varied across the South, not only with the commodity produced but with a master's ethnic and subregional allegiances. Nicholas Merryman Bosley, the owner of Hayfields, a sizable stock farm in Baltimore County, Maryland, run with slave labor, was evidently influenced in his choice of barn design by examples from southeastern Pennsylvania.[21] His farm buildings, all of them substantial stone or brick structures, included one set known as the "big barn group." The central building in this group was a large stone barn that stood two stories high and measured approximately eighty by forty feet (figs. 7.9, 7.10). A central runway on the ground floor separated two stabling areas, while hay was stored above in the vast loft area. The entrances to the stables were protected by a large, distinctive pent roof supported by projecting floor joists that extended ten feet beyond the building's southern wall (fig. 7.11). Even the manner in which Bosley defined his barnyard, that is, by flanking it with smaller buildings, suggested that he was following mid-Atlantic, if not Pennsylvanian, custom.[22] In fact, the overall plan of Hayfields followed the standard arrangement for mid-Atlantic farmsteads. All of the buildings were bracketed between the house and the barn and strung out in a row along the top of a low ridge.[23] Although Nicholas Bosley clearly looked southward to slaveholding plantations for his managerial model, he had looked north of the Mason-Dixon line for the architectural models upon which to base his farm.

Along the Mississippi River in southern Louisiana, barns, like many of the other domestic buildings, have French antecedents. One example at the Homeplace plantation in St. Charles Parish provides evidence of this connection (figs. 7.12, 7.13). The rectangular core of this frame structure measured about fifty by twenty-five feet and was covered by a thirty-foot-tall *pavilion* or hipped roof. The eaves of the roof extended slightly more than ten feet beyond the walls of the barn on all sides, shading the front wall and providing a roof for the stables that wrapped around the sides and back of the building. Although the hipped roof and extended eaves of this structure recall the designs of other local plantation houses, its plan and its framing system derive from barns in northern France.[24]

The barn or cotton house at the Hamilton plantation on St. Simons Island, Georgia, illustrates the preference among coastal planters for a local Sea Island building material (fig. 7.14). This structure, as well as the main residence and a number of slave dwellings on the estate, were all constructed with tabby, a coarse type of concrete made primarily from oyster shells.[25] Thomas Spalding is generally credited with the early nineteenth-century experiments that repopularized the use of tabby in the area. He proved that the material was not just inexpensive but durable. The tabby buildings on his Ashantilly plantation near Darien, Georgia, easily withstood the hurricanes that seasonally buffeted the area.[26] It is not difficult to understand why his "scientific" neighbor James Couper, manager of Hamilton plantation, decided to use tabby in the construction of the building in which he stored the estate's precious crop of Sea Island cotton before it was ginned and packed into bales for shipping.[27] The valuable fiber was protected from fire and storm alike in a large barn that was essentially a two-story concrete shell.

These barns from Maryland, Louisiana, and Georgia, when compared with the more commonplace log barns, reflect more than just the variety in southern plantation architecture; they also demonstrate the absence of a unified plantation ideal, at least for agricultural structures. Because planters tended to accept the prevailing local wisdom as to the best types of farm buildings, the overall southern plantation landscape shows a noteworthy diversity. Designs for barns and other buildings too might be borrowed from outside the region or adapted from Old World precedents. Local innovations in construction might be added to a repertoire of traditional practices. Barns are one of the clearest markers of subregional identities within the plantation South.

## Stables

The importance of horses among the planter elite cannot be overestimated; it was a commonly accepted dictum that "a man was only as good as his horse."[28] In 1862 Edmund Kirke found that the stables at a particular South Carolina plantation were exceptionally well constructed: "better built, warmer, more commodious, and in every way more comfortable than the shanties occupied by the human cattle of the plantation." When he asked the plantation's owner if this architectural gesture meant that he valued his horses more than his slaves, the man replied: "That may be true. . . . Two of my horses are worth more than any eight of my slaves."[29] In a similar vein, it was reported of Wade Hampton II of South Carolina that "no pilgrim ever knelt at the shrine of My Lady of Loretto . . . with more devotion than does Col. Hampton when he visits his stables in the morning."[30] Plantation stables are best understood in the light of this representative attitude.

Slaves learned quickly that horses were highly regarded. Born on a plantation in Spartanburg, South Carolina, John Petty was assigned, while still a young boy, to watch after the livestock, but he was specifically charged with caring for a prized stud horse named Max. The stable in which Max was kept, according to Petty, was "big enough for a dozen or more horses, 'cause it hardly ever been that Max get out, and his stable had to be so big so as he could exercise in it."[31]

The stable at Chachan plantation in Berkeley County, South Carolina, was not only large, but it also had a stylish baroque exterior featuring curved Jacobean gables (fig. 7.15). One of a pair of buildings forming the forecourt of the mansion house (the other being a carriage house), its decorative form and substantial masonry construction signaled the importance both of planter Antoine Cordes and the riding and carriage horses he owned.[32] Equally impressive but built in a different mode was the brick horse barn at Hayfields (fig. 7.16). It stood almost three stories high and had diamond-shaped ventilators in all four walls. Prize Black Hawk horses were stabled on the first floor, while their feed was stored overhead. Sheltering the entrances to the stalls on each side of the barn were ten-foot-wide pent roofs similar to the one on the farm's large stone barn.

Even when a stable lacked any ornamentation, just its mode of construction might suggest the building's importance. At Hikes Place in Kentucky, for example, the horse barn was built of stone, whereas the other buildings were either log or frame, indicating that horses were deemed the most valuable property on the plantation (fig. 7.17).[33] Substantially built plantation stables confirm the importance of horseflesh in the South. The extra care taken in their construction and the use of ornamentation may suggest that many planters considered horses a particularly powerful symbol of authority. Seated on the back of a horse, a man had unquestioned stature and mobility, two social attributes deliberately denied to slaves.

Although planters derived high prestige from their favored mounts, they earned their profits with mules. These homely draft animals were first bred in the South at George Washington's Mount Vernon plantation during the late eighteenth century and quickly were judged particularly well suited for plantation agriculture. By 1860 approximately 529,000 mules were reported in the lower South, a total equal to 47 percent of all the mules in the United States.[34] The popularity of these animals was based on the belief that they would work harder on less feed than a horse. Certainly this was the feeling of Henry S. Turner, a Shenandoah Valley planter who wrote in 1834: "Of all the animals subservient to agriculture the mule stands pre-eminent. I have no terms adequate to bespeak his merit—none that could be employed would exaggerate it; he is a long liver, a small consumer, a powerful, faithful and enduring laborer."[35] In his often-reprinted treatise on efficient cotton cultivation, D. A. Tompkins estimated that an average plantation of about three thousand acres, operated with the labor of one hundred slaves, would require twenty-five mules and only four horses.[36] According to former slave Sam Kilgore, the Peacock plantation near Memphis, Tennessee, had a large complement of work stock, including eighty mules, fifty horses, and fifteen yoke of oxen.[37] If we accept Kilgore's description as typical, then it follows that on many plantations the stables would actually have been mule barns, although it was widely believed that mules were such hardy beasts that they could stay out in the open without any ill effects. The mule barn at Hampton plantation in Maryland, however, suggests that mules could be sheltered almost as well as horses (see fig. 12.13).

**7.1**

Barn at Bremo
plantation, Fluvanna
County, Virginia.
Photograph by
C. O. Greene, 1940.

**7.2**
View of the Walter Henry Crenshaw plantation, Butler County, Alabama, showing the random location of three single-crib log barns. Photograph by W. N. Manning, 1935.

**7.3**
Single log crib at the Bracketts farm, Louisa County, Virginia. Photograph by Jack E. Boucher, 1983.

**7.4**
Barn at Magnolia Grove plantation, Hale County, Alabama. Photograph by Alex Bush, 1936.

**7.5**

Barn at the Hill of Howth plantation, Greene County, Alabama. Photograph by Alex Bush, 1935.

**7.6**

Granary at Northampton plantation, Prince Georges County, Maryland. Photograph by John O. Brostrup, 1936.

**7.7**
Barn at Belmont
plantation, Colbert
County, Alabama.
Photograph by
Alex Bush, 1936.

**7.8**
Barn at Pond Spring
plantation, Lawrence
County, Alabama.
Photograph by
Alex Bush, 1935.

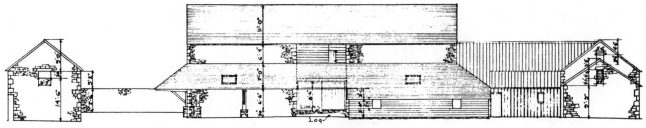

SOUTH ELEVATION

**7.9**

Elevation and
sectional view
of the barn at
Hayfields, Baltimore
County, Maryland.
Drawn by Robert E.
Lewis, 1936.

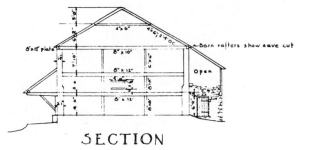

SECTION

**7.10**

Floor plan of the
barn at Hayfields.
Drawn by Robert E.
Lewis, 1936.

THE BIG BARN GROUP

SCALE 1/16" = 1'-0"

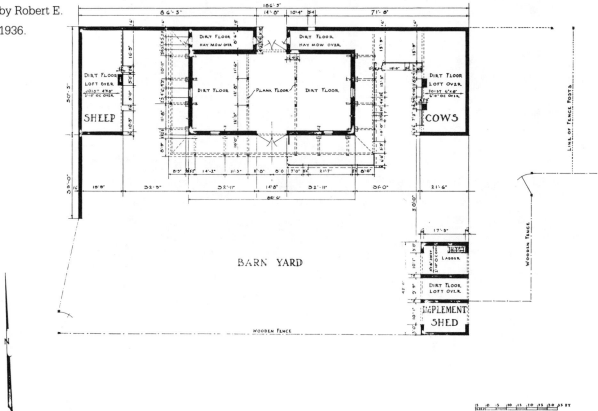

ROBERT E. LEWIS DEL.

**7.11**
View of joists
supporting the
pent roof along the
south wall of the
barn at Hayfields.
Photograph by E. H.
Pickering, 1936.

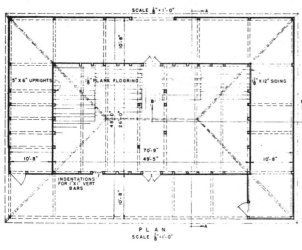

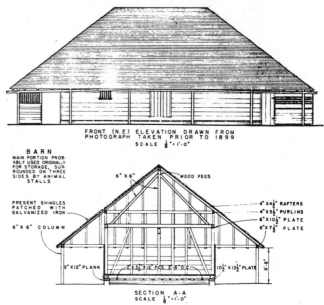

**7.12** [top]

Barn at the Homeplace plantation, St. Charles Parish, Louisiana. Photograph by Lester Jones, 1940.

**7.13** [above]

Front elevation, floor plan, and sectional view of the barn at the Homeplace. Drawn by Adolph H. Felder, 1940.

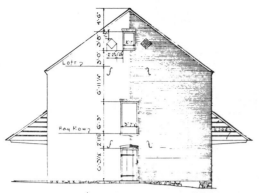

EAST & WEST ELEVATIONS

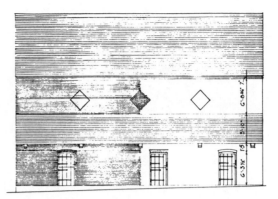

SOUTH ELEVATION

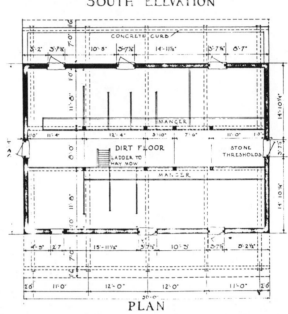

PLAN

**7.16**
Side and end elevations and floor plan of the stable at Hayfields. Drawn by Robert E. Lewis, 1936.

**7.17**
Stable at Hikes Place, Jefferson County, Kentucky. Photograph by Lester Jones, 1940.

# EIGHT

# Production Machinery and Buildings

Included among the structures on most plantation estates were the devices and machines needed to prepare the crop for market. On tobacco plantations, for example, a "prize" or press was considered an essential piece of equipment. One type of tobacco press consisted basically of a screw-operated ram set in a heavy timber frame large enough to hold a "hogshead," a barrel-shaped container four feet long and two-and-a-half feet in diameter. With other tobacco presses, long levers were used to force between 1,000 and 1,300 pounds of loose tobacco into a hogshead.[1] Only a few of these machines have been found at plantation sites, mainly because many tobacco planters, particularly those in the Chesapeake region, shifted to wheat and livestock production as early as the mid-eighteenth century. Moreover, after 1860 prizing was generally abandoned by tobacco farmers as they discovered that the process was harmful to the leaves and as the owners of tobacco factories complained that prized leaves were too hard to separate after they were removed from their barrels.[2]

Even examples of the mule-driven cotton press, another machine based on simple screw action that was once ubiquitous all across the South, had become rare by the first decades of the twentieth century. Fortunately, during the 1930s two presses were still in place at the C. L. Dunham plantation in Shelby County, Alabama, although both were by then already in ruins. Drawings of their surviving elements provide a trustworthy basis for a reasonable re-creation of these devices (figs. 8.1, 8.2).

A cotton press could stand as much as forty feet tall. Its sturdy timber frame supported a large, threaded wooden shaft more than a foot in diameter over a boxlike form in which bales were shaped. From the top of the screw, two long beams stretched outward and downward almost to the ground like arms. Mules harnessed to these beams, or "levers" as they were sometimes called, walked in a circular path, turning the screw and thereby compressing the loose cotton lint into a bale weighing between four hundred and six hundred pounds. Up until the 1830s, slaves had packed cotton into bags by stamping on it with their feet or by tamping it with wooden poles. With such techniques, it took one man fourteen days to pack fourteen bags. When the screw press was introduced in the 1840s, two men, a boy, and a pair of mules could do the same job in a single day.[3] It is not difficult to understand why the screw press became a standard piece of cotton plantation equipment.

One of the presses at the Dunham plantation had a screw fashioned from wood; the screw of the other was made of cast iron. Wooden screws, however, were preferred because they were less prone to break under the tremendous pressure exerted as a bale was topped off. Former slaves have reported that a cotton press would emit a high-pitched "cry" as the mules strained before the levers. Jim Martin, who worked on the Matthews plantation in Pike County, Mississippi, stated: "When dey put de press on it [the cotton], yer could hear it moren a mile."[4] The bases of the Dunham cotton presses, containing the boxlike forms in which the bales were shaped and then banded, were originally protected by pyramidal roofs supported on four cornerposts. Similar but smaller roofs covered the tops of the screws. Thus the critical junctions between the levers and the screw were protected from excessive weathering, and the slaves were provided with some degree of shelter from the sun as they loaded the press with lint and wrapped the bales in burlap and rope.[5]

By 1860 almost no cotton plantation was without a gin, a machine that removed the seeds from the plant fiber. Jacob Branch, a former slave at the Stevenson plantation in Double Bayou, Texas, recalled: "When I 'bout ten dey sets me ginnin' cotton. Old massa he done make de cotton with de hand crank. It built on a bench like. I gin de cotton by turnin' dat crank. When I gets a lapful I puts it in the de tow sack an dey take it to Miss Susan to make de twine with it. I warm the damp cotton before de fireplace before I start ginnin' it."[6] En route to her new plantation home in Georgia, Frances Kemble paid a visit to a "ginning house" on Edisto Island, South Carolina. Inside she found "about eight or ten stalls on either side, in which a man was employed at a machine, worked like a turner's or knife grinder's wheel, by the foot, which, as fast as he fed it with cotton, parted the snowy flakes from the little black first cause, and gave them forth soft, silky, clean, and fit to be woven."[7] Machines like the ones described by Branch and Kemble were, however, too small to handle the ever-increasing output of southern cotton planters. Beginning in the 1830s larger machines, driven first by mules and later by steam engines, replaced the hand- or foot-powered models. In 1860 there were fifty-four gin manufacturers in the South; most were small concerns employing fewer than ten workers. But at the largest factory, located in Prattville, Alabama, more than eight thousand gins were built between 1833 and 1860.[8]

The gin machinery, known specifically as a "gin stand," was commonly housed in a room raised about eight feet off the ground on wooden pillars. The gin at the L. A. Cliatt plantation in Russell County, Alabama, which dates from the middle of the nineteenth century, follows this pattern (figs. 8.3, 8.4). The upper room contained not only space for the gin stand but also holding areas for the harvested bolls and for the cotton seed that was separated from the lint. Once the fiber was ginned, it was thrown down into a "save room" located in shed attached to one side of the structure. Lizzie Fant Brown, a former slave on a plantation in Holly Springs, Mississippi, worked at the gin house, where she would "jump in the lint room and pack the cotton down tight. Then it was packed in hamper baskets and we toted it to the press."[9]

Underneath the gin room, mules were driven in a circular path while harnessed to bars connected like spokes to a vertical axle. The rotation of this shaft turned a large gear, which in turn furnished power to a drive wheel and belt connected to the gin machinery. The drawings of the Cliatt plantation gin provide clear views of this "running gear," showing how a large horizontal gear, levers or push bars, and seats for the mule drivers were all attached to the main axle. Their arrangement confirms Lizzie Brown's memory: "Ever place had a gin house then. Ours was run with levers and two mules. A child could run it by touching the mules with a long switch onc't in awhile."[10]

The work yards of rice plantations along the coastal fringes of South Carolina and Georgia were marked by distinctive winnowing houses. Typically, one of these structures consisted of a small, square room raised about ten feet off the ground on wooden posts and reached by an external stairway. A photo from the Mansfield plantation in Georgetown County, South Carolina, provides a good example of this type of building, although its stairway has fallen away (fig. 8.5). After the rice was harvested, it was brought into the plantation yard and placed on the "rice floor," a hardened surface about the size of football field. Here it was threshed with flails so that the heads of grain were separated from their stalks. Next the rice was pounded in wooden mortars with pestles in order to remove the tough outer husk that surrounded each kernel.

The rice was then carried up into the winnowing house and dropped through a grate in its floor; the heavier rice kernels fell to ground below while the chaff blew away in the wind. The rice was then gathered up, beaten again with mortar and pestle, and carried once more into the winnowing house. This sequence was repeated until the rice was judged to be clean; as many as three winnowings might be required. The pearly white grain was then shoveled into barrels or sacks to be shipped to market.[11] Even after steam-powered mills were in wide use throughout the region, winnowing houses were still important because seed rice still had to be cleaned with mortars and pestles. Rice kernels would not germinate if processed by mechanical means.[12]

The first mills along the Rice Coast were water powered. Large reservoirs were filled with the aid of the tidal lift; when the tide had dropped about five feet, the gates were opened and the machinery was set in motion until the reservoir was emptied. Later, when steam engines were used to drive the machinery, planters were freed from the restrictions of the tidal cycles and gained more control over their production schedules. Steam-powered mills made the rice plantations look more like factories than farms. Indeed, one could surmise from the descriptions of Frances Kemble that these mills were the distinctive emblem of the region. In 1838 she observed at Butler Island, Georgia: "Now on this estate alone there are three threshing mills—one worked by steam, one by tide, and one by horses; there are two private steam mills on plantations adjacent to ours, and one public one at Savannah, where the planters who have none on their own estates are in the habit of sending their rice to be threshed at a certain percentage."[13] One mill located on the Savannah River in Georgia, capable of refining 150 "tierces" or barrels a day, included seven brick buildings and three steam engines that burned 1,600 cords of wood a year.[14] South Carolinian Robert F. W. Allston described his mill at Waverly plantation thus:

> By steam power, the rough-rice is taken out of the vessel which freights it, up to the attic of the building—thence through the sand-screen to a pair of (five feet wide) heavy stones, which grind off the husk—thence into large wooden mortars, in which it is pounded by large iron-shod pestles (weighing 250 to 350 pounds), for the space of some two hours, more or less.
>
> The rice, now pounded, is once more elevated into the attic, whence it descends through a rolling-screen, to separate whole grains from the broken, and flour from both; and also through, wind-fans, to a vertical brushing screen, revolving rapidly, which polishes the flinty grain, and delivers it fully prepared into the barrel or tierce, which is to convey it to market.[15]

Clearly the buildings constructed to house such machinery had to be quite large. Frederick Law Olmsted described the rice mill at one Georgia plantation as a "monster barn."[16] Photographs taken at the Mansfield and Chicora Wood plantations in Georgetown County, South Carolina, convey some sense of the impressive dimensions of these mills as well as providing views of some of their machinery (figs. 8.6, 8.7; see also fig. 8.5).

Although rice mills reflected the technological orientation of the planter class and their desire to be up to date and in step with the latest industrial practices, milling was not exclusively a white enterprise. Olmsted reported that the rice mill in Georgia, where he had seen "more extensive and better machinery . . . than I have ever seen used for grain," was run by a slave:

> a respectable-looking, orderly, and quiet-mannered mulatto, who was called by his master, "the watchman." His duties, however, as they were described to me, were those of a steward, or intendant. He carried, by a strap at his waist, a very large number of keys, and had charge of all the stores of provisions, tools, and materials of the plantations, as well as of all their produce, before it was shipped to market. He weighed and measured out all the rations of the slaves and the cattle; superintended the mechanics, and made and repaired, as was necessary, all the machinery, including the steam-engine.[17]

South Carolina rice planter David Doar also noted the key role that slave craftsmen might play at the mill: "These men, many of them, were no mean artisans. Generally, there were some intelligent boys or sons of some favorite slave who were sent to the city and put to trade with such firms as Cameron and Mustard, where they served 6 to 7 years; on completing the term, they could do almost any kind of work in their line. They could make repairs and run the engine of the rice mill, and I have seen them patch a boiler, replace a cog broken out of a spur wheel and various other jobs."[18] Just as former slave Gabe Lance felt a proprietary claim over all the rice fields that had been created by "slavery people," the slave mechanics at the rice mills probably saw the machinery that they operated, maintained, and repaired as belonging more to them than to their masters.

On sugar plantations, the mill or sugar house was the dominant building. Usually a two-story structure measuring between 100 to 340 feet in length and 50 to 60 feet in width—although it was often larger—the mill sheltered the metal rollers that expressed juice from the cane and the boilers and cooling vats that converted the juice first into syrup and then into sugar. The sugar house was a large machine shed punctuated by tall chimneys spewing smoke and venting steam. The complexity of sugar-processing machinery is apparent from a nineteenth-century notice advertising the sale of the Bellegrove plantation in Iberville Parish, Louisiana: "A large Brick Sugar House, containing a superior steam engine (40 horse power); three boilers, 40 feet long; two small engines; a large sugar mill; two sets six sugar kettles each; one steam granulating pan; two purgeries, about 500 hhds. [hogsheads] capacity; bagasse burner, sugar coolers, and other appurtenances, which have proved capable of taking off and securing a crop of over 1,000 hhds."[19]

Visitors to southern Louisiana, a region then popularly known as the "sugar bowl," were consistently impressed by the size of the sugar mills. W. H. Russell wrote in 1863: "Rising up in the midst of the verdure are the white lines of the negro cottages and the plantation offices and sugar-houses which look like large public edifices in the distance."[20] Sixty years earlier Pierre de Lausatt had made similar observations as he sailed down the Mississippi River: "It is really interesting and picturesque to see this mass of furnaces succeeding one another, from which clouds of dense smoke constantly rise, sometimes red with flame. It is a spectacle providing us with great entertainment on our journey."[21]

Examples of these industrial structures can be seen in drawings of the remnants of the large brick sugar mill located at Chenango plantation along the Texas coast in Brazoria County, a sugar-producing region southwest of Houston (figs. 8.8, 8.9). Because much of the structure had been destroyed by the time the measured drawings were made—none of the engines, boilers, or kettles, for example, remained—it is difficult to describe exactly how the building was used. However, in 1843 there were twenty-nine sugar mills in the county, and because almost all of them were built with brick masonry, the Chenango mill can at least be seen as typical in its construction.

The mill was built under the direction of Monroe Edwards sometime after 1836 when he, with the financial backing of New Orleans merchant Christopher Dart, took over a 1,300-acre cotton plantation. He eventually expanded the estate to 3,800 acres. Soon after acquiring the land, Edwards made a trip to Cuba to purchase the slave work force needed to operate the plantation. These slaves, who were smuggled into the state, were alleged to have arrived recently from Africa, a claim substantiated by eyewitness testimony stating that many of these people had tribal marks on their cheeks.[22]

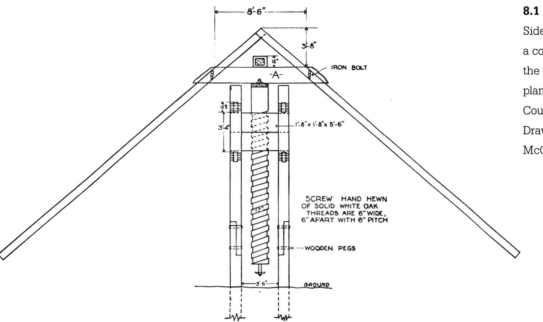

**8.1**

Side elevation of
a cotton press at
the C. L. Dunham
plantation, Shelby
County, Alabama.
Drawn by J. Wendell
McGee, 1936.

IRON BOLT

1'-8" x 1'-8" x 5'-6"

SCREW HAND HEWN
OF SOLID WHITE OAK
THREADS ARE 6" WIDE,
6" AFART WITH 6" PITCH

WOODEN PEGS

GROUND

SCALE 1"=2'-0"

**8.2**

Side elevation of the
remnants of a cotton
press with a cast-iron
screw at the C. L.
Dunham plantation.
Drawn by J. Wendell
McGee, 1936.

**8.3**

Elevations and plans
of the cotton gin
at the L. A. Cliatt
plantation, Russell
County, Alabama.
Drawn by J. Wendell
McGee, 1936.

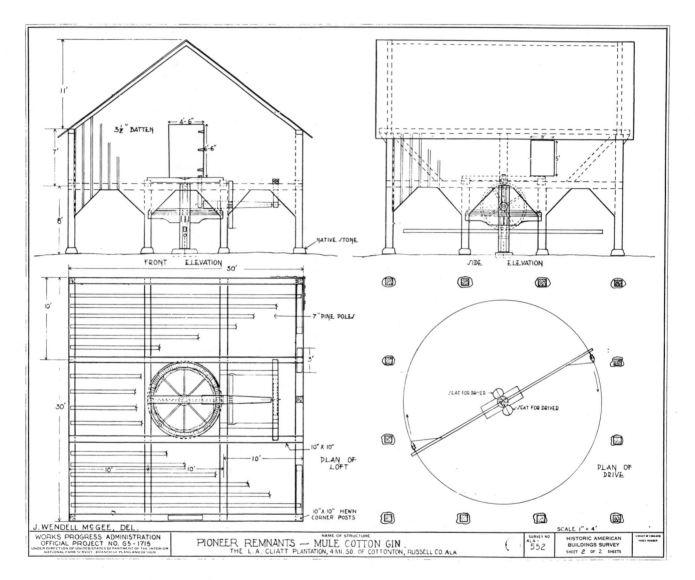

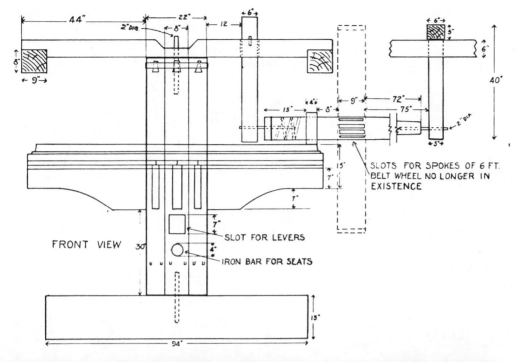

**8.4**

Drawing of the gear works of the cotton gin at the L. A. Cliatt plantation. Drawn by J. Wendell McGee, 1936.

FRONT VIEW

SLOT FOR LEVERS

IRON BAR FOR SEATS

SLOTS FOR SPOKES OF 6 FT. BELT WHEEL NO LONGER IN EXISTENCE

**8.5**

Winnowing house at Mansfield plantation, Georgetown County, South Carolina. The steam-powered rice mill stands in the distance. Photograph by Charles N. Bayless, 1977.

**8.6**

Rice mill at Chicora
Wood plantation,
Georgetown County,
South Carolina.
Photograph by
Charles N. Bayless,
1977.

**8.7**

Interior view of the
machinery in the
rice mill at Chicora
Wood. Photograph by
Charles N. Bayless,
1977.

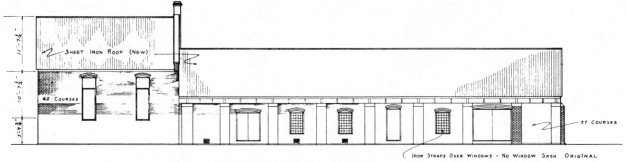

## SOUTH ELEVATION

SCALE ⅛" = 1'0"

**8.8**

Elevation of the sugar
mill at the Chenango
plantation, Brazoria
County, Texas. Drawn
by L. R. Porter, 1936.

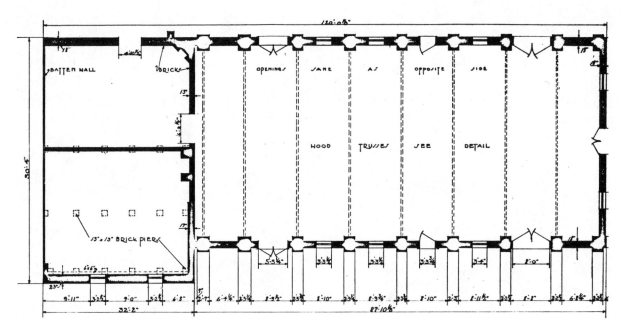

**8.9**

Floor plan of the sugar
mill at Chenango.
Drawn by L. R. Porter,
1936.

# NINE

# Overseers' Houses

**W**henever planters owned more than thirty slaves, work routines were usually supervised by overseers. The census of 1860 listed almost 38,000 men in such positions. This was an increase of almost 20,000 from the previous decade, reflecting the planter class's growing dependence on hired supervisors by the middle decades of the nineteenth century.[1] Although some overseers forged lasting associations with their employers, on the whole they tended to be highly mobile men who rarely held a position for more than a year. The short duration of their employment can be explained, to a great extent, by the nature of their work. Overseers were expected to coerce efficient, profitable labor from reluctant slave gangs while simultaneously adhering to their employers' warnings not to abuse the slaves by pushing them too hard. It is not so surprising, then, that they were routinely judged inept.

Although planters generally regarded overseers as a bothersome nuisance, they nonetheless found their services useful. According to historian Eugene D. Genovese, planters used their overseers to shield themselves psychologically from the harsher aspects of slavery. Because the overseer was the person most immediately responsible for the slaves' misery, when he was censured or fired the master of a plantation would appear to be concerned with the slaves' well-being. By disposing of a harsh overseer, particularly one prone to use the whip as his chief means of discipline, slaveholders might flatter themselves that they were benevolent and kindly masters. In the short run, their slaves might even have shared this perception.[2]

An overseer's paradoxical position as intermediary between a group of slaves and their owner was sometimes reflected in the layout of the plantation. At Hampton, Pierce Butler's cotton estate on St. Simons Island, Georgia, the overseer's house was placed literally halfway between Butler's house and the slave settlements.[3] At the neighboring Cannon's Point plantation belonging to John Couper, a similar arrangement was employed: the overseer's residence was located in the middle of the estate, well away from the Big House and in between two slave villages.[4] At Henry McAlpin's Hermitage plantation, an estate laid out with exact geometric precision on the banks of the Savannah River, all the primary buildings were set in a straight line, with the overseer's house poised in a grove of oak trees halfway between the owner's mansion and the houses of his slaves (see fig. 11.10). A similar expression of hierarchy was encountered by Frederick Law Olmsted in Mississippi, where on one plantation the slave quarter actually included the overseer's house, an arrangement that clearly signaled the overseer's subordinate relationship to the plantation owner. However, his authority over the slaves was still made clear by the fact that his cabin was bigger than the others and was positioned at the head of the "street."[5]

At Tower Hill in Sussex County, Virginia, the overseer's residence was initially placed amid a set of barns, craft shops, and storage houses, whereas the main house stood off by itself on a high ridge in the distance. After the mansion burned, however, the planter and his family took over the overseer's house, and a new and smaller house was built for the overseer.[6] These examples suggest that the overseers' social position was tenuous at best. Separated by class from the planters for whom they worked and by race from the slaves they supervised, they existed at the margins of the two groups both socially and spatially.

The separation of overseers and slaves within the plantation ensemble became more explicit over time. In Virginia during the eighteenth century, for example, slaves and overseers were often housed in the same types of structures. Planter Robert Wormley Carter wrote in his diary on February 1, 1768, "Guy & Jimmy [two slave carpenters] returned this day from Ring's Neck [a section of Carter's plantation] where they have been building two Negroes quarters 20 by 16 and an Overseer's house 20 × 16."[7] Eighteenth-century traveler J. F. D. Smyth even discovered one place in Virginia where an overseer and six slaves shared the same cabin: "That miserable shell, a poor apology for a house, consisted but of one small room, which served for the accommodation of the overseer and six negroes; it was not lathed or plastered, neither ceiled nor lofted above, and only very thin boards for its covering; it had a door on each side, one window but no glass in it; it had not even a brick chimney, and as it stood on blocks about a foot above the ground, the hogs lay constantly under the floor which made it swarm with flies."[8]

On eighteenth-century plantations, at least in Virginia, the owner of an estate took great pains to place himself far above all of his employees, black and white alike. Consequently, these two subordinate groups were actually drawn together, however unwittingly or reluctantly, by their mutual exploitation.[9] The architectural linkages between slaves and overseers continued to be most clearly manifested during the initial phases of setting up a plantation. In the winter of 1834, James K. Polk of Tennessee sent his overseer, Ephraim Beanland, and a gang of field hands south to Yalabusha County, Mississippi, to set up a cotton estate. After the first eighteen days, a Dr. Caldwell (one of Polk's partners in the venture) wrote to report that, in that brief period, they had been able to "put up a house for Beanland, four houses for the negroes, a smokehouse, and a kitchen, and made a lot for our stock."[10] Given the expediency with which they must have worked, these structures could not have been anything more than the roughest type of log cabins. Indeed, they all had to be replaced within five years' time. It is also probable that there was little difference between the house occupied by Beanland and the cabins of his slave charges. If there was a subsequent improvement to the overseer's quarters at Polk's plantation, it was never reported.

When a plantation had an absentee owner, or when a widow was left with a vast estate that included hundreds of slaves, an overseer's managerial services were definitely needed. And with the increase in the number of large plantations—by 1860 there were 2,292 estates holding more than one hundred slaves each—more planters found that they could use extra supervisory help.[11] As the value of overseers increased, their social status was elevated. One Virginia planter wrote in 1837: "On small farms, when the owner is an active and energetic man, he may manage his concerns well enough without aid, but on farms of 800 acres, or more, I think he will find it a difficult task to manage his negroes unless assisted by an overseer."[12] Even though this same writer found most overseers to be "vain, weak tyrants, 'dressed' in a little brief authority," overseers were gradually granted their own niche in the plantation system, one significantly above the slave work force.

Plantation owners who felt well served by their overseers provided them with both food allowances and servants. In 1861, for example, Arkansas planter Francis Leak provided to James Sergeant "all his bread, including 300 to 400 lbs of flour; 50 lbs sugar, 5 to 10 gall[ons] molasses; a negro boy to cut his wood, make his fires, feed his horse, & draw a bucket of water, night & morning; a negro woman to cook & wash for him whenever his wife is sick; and $350.00 wages."[13] Housing was also provided, sometimes in the planter's own house if the overseer was unmarried, or in a separate dwelling if, as was more often the case, he had a family. Census records for Hancock County, Georgia, indicate that, in 1860, 98 of 139 overseers were provided with their own cabins.[14] Former slave Richard Carruthers was vividly aware of the privileges granted to overseers at his Texas plantation toward the end of the antebellum period. "In them days," said Carruthers, "the boss men had good houses but the niggers had log cabins and they burned down oftentimes."[15] Implied in this description is an overseer's residence built of frame with a brick fireplace and chimney, and one that probably had glass windows as well—architectural refinements not found in the common types of slave houses. Surviving examples suggest, however, that there was no standard building type for overseers' quarters.

At Eyre Hall in Northampton County, Virginia, the overseer lived in a superior brick cabin that originally consisted of one large square room with a loft above (fig. 9.1; see also fig. 12.8).[16] The overseer's house at the Bacon Hall estate of Maryland planter Thomas Crauford consisted of a sturdy frame hall-and-parlor house (fig. 9.2). Perched on a low rise overlooking similarly constructed but significantly smaller slave houses, this house resembled the modest residence of a typical yeoman farmer. At Farintosh plantation in Durham County, North Carolina, the Cameron family provided their overseer with a T-plan house consisting of a double-unit cabin plus a rear addition. Although this house looked out across the yard toward a slave quarter, it was grouped with the plantation office, school, and teacher's house, a location that assured its occupant that he was in the "managerial" section of the estate.[17]

Other sources also confirm the variability of overseer housing. Martha Colquitt, a former slave from the Piedmont region near Milledgeville, Georgia, recalled that the "overseer lived in a four-room house up the road a piece from the Big 'Ouse."[18] Her testimony matches the archaeological findings at Cannon's Point plantation on the Georgia coast. The foundations unearthed at the site of the former overseer's residence there outlined a frame building raised on brick piers and containing four rooms. Equal in size to the home of a small planter, the house featured a central passage and two internal fireplaces located along the party walls dividing the front and back rooms. Further excavation also determined that the overseer's kitchen was located in a separate building.[19] Frances Kemble, who lived for a few months in the overseer's house on Butler Island, Georgia, found it an inadequate structure. But even though her account of the building is tinged with disgust, it is clear that she is describing a six-room house:

Of our three apartments, one is our sitting, eating, and *living* room, and it is sixteen feet by fifteen. The walls are plastered indeed, but neither painted or papered; it is divided from our bedroom (a similarly elegant and comfortable chamber) by a dingy wooden partition covered all over with hooks, pegs, and nails. . . . The third room, a chamber with sloping ceiling, immediately over our sitting room and under the roof, is appropriated to the nurse and my two babies. Of the closets, one is Mr. O——, the overseer's bedroom, the other his office or place of business; and the third adjoining our bedroom, and opening immediately out of doors, is Mr. Butler's dressing room and *cabinet d'affaires.*[20]

Frequently overseers were assisted by knowledgeable slaves known as "drivers." Indeed, on those plantations that had no overseer in residence, the driver filled the overseer's role. Eugene Genovese estimates that two-thirds of the slave population may have worked under black supervision.[21] That these black managers were highly regarded is indicated in the following discussion from a popular nineteenth-century plantation manual: "The head driver is the most important negro on the plantation. He is to be treated with more respect than any other negro both by the master and the overseer. He is on no occasion to be treated with any indignation calculated to lose the respect of other negroes without breaking him."[22]

Architecturally, the prestige of the slave driver was often reflected in the location of his cabin at the head of the slave row.[23] Occasionally this cabin was slightly larger than the other slave dwellings in tribute to the driver's favored status. An example of this sort of arrangement can be seen in the buildings at the Kingsley plantation in northern Florida, where the drivers' cabins were not only larger than the other cabins but occupied the central positions within the semicircle of slave houses (see figs. 12.30, 12.31). The drivers' cabins were located right next to the pathway connecting the slave village to the Big House. Not all drivers, however, were granted superior housing. Richard Macks, the son of a driver who was raised on a plantation in Charles County, Maryland, grew up in a one-room log cabin that had a dirt floor.[24]

**9.1**

Overseer's house
from Eyre Hall
plantation,
Northampton County,
Virginia. Originally
this building
consisted of one
room plus a loft. The
vertical seam in the
wall indicating the
addition of a second
room is clearly visible
in the photograph.
Photographer
unknown, 1960.

**9.2**

Overseer's house at
Bacon Hall plantation,
Prince Georges
County, Maryland.
The original two-room
structure stands to
the right; the wing
to the left is either
a late-nineteenth-
or early twentieth-
century addition.
Photograph by
John O. Brostrup,
1935.

# Buildings for Slave Welfare

**D**uring much of the nineteenth century, planters generally considered it economically prudent, if not an ethical obligation, to attend carefully to their slaves' physical well-being. In the 1840s, the average price of a top field hand hovered near $1,000, and by 1860 the figure was approaching $2,000 in some markets.[1] One contributor to the *American Farmer* cautioned as early as 1820: "The blacks constitute either absolutely, or instrumentally, the wealth of our southern states. If a planter, as it often happens, is deprived by sickness of the labour of one third, or one half, of his negroes, it becomes a loss of no small magnitude."[2] That such warnings were apparently heeded, at least on the larger estates, was demonstrated in part by the construction of two kinds of specialized buildings, dining halls and hospitals. These structures were intended chiefly to ensure that slaves were fed efficiently and provided with adequate health care. Eugene Genovese has noted that between 1831 and 1861 the treatment of slaves grew progressively better as planters attempted to improve the physical conditions of the daily plantation routine in hopes that slaves might become more inclined to accept their fates.[3] The new buildings constructed in the interests of slave welfare were intended, then, as a kind of propaganda aimed at convincing the slaves that they would not find better conditions elsewhere. Even freedman status, this argument claimed, would not match the plantation owners' promises of material benefits. Such contrived gestures were, however, decidedly ineffective instruments of propaganda. Even where the material circumstances of servitude were improved, slaves continued to break their tools, abuse livestock, work to their own pace, threaten to run away, and otherwise refine their tactics for resisting the demands placed upon them.

## Dining Halls

Annie Davis, a former slave from Eutaw, Alabama, described for Federal Writers' Project interviewers a special building in which the slaves' meals were served on the Pettigrew plantation: "The dinner for the slaves was cooked in the main kitchen which in those days on plantations was always separated from the house. Each slave came with his tin plate and received his or her portion. On clear days they ate out in the yard under the trees and they had a room attached to the kitchen for the slaves to eat in on rainy days, and in cold weather."[4] Similar arrangements were, according to former slave John Finnely, provided at his master's plantation in Jackson County, Alabama, where the meals for field hands were prepared in a specially designated "cookhouse" and consumed in "de eatin' shed."[5]

Photographs taken at the Jenkins plantation in Crenshaw County, Alabama, illustrate a related type of building (fig. 10.1). The plantation kitchen, which stood some distance behind the Big House, had a dining room attached to it. This cookhouse, built in the 1840s, was basically a square cabin with an extra room added to the end opposite the fireplace. That the building was not simply a large kitchen was clearly indicated by its two front doors, one leading to the cooking room and the other opening into the dining area. At Greenway, the plantation in Charles City County, Virginia, belonging to President John Tyler, the house slaves had not only their own dining hall but also their own kitchen (figs. 10.2, 10.3). The kitchen for Tyler's residence was positioned directly behind his modest house and was connected to it by a short colonnaded breezeway. The slaves' meals were prepared and served in another building located along the eastern edge of the partially enclosed yard behind the main house. As a site plan indicates, the slave dining hall at Greenway was essentially a low ell attached to the back of the slave kitchen.

A larger slave mess hall was described by William Dunwoody, a former slave who recalled his childhood in Alabama: "All the slaves ate together. They had a cook special for them. This cook would cook in a long house more than thirty feet long. Two or three women would work there and a man, just like the cooks would in a hotel now. All the working hands ate there and got whatever the cook gave them. . . . There was one woman in there cooking that was called 'Mammy' and she seed to all the chillen."[6] A structure on a similar scale still stands at Hayfields a few miles north of Baltimore, Maryland (fig. 10.4). This so-called slaves' mess hall was probably built in the 1830s, when Nicholas Bosley employed as many as fifteen slaves to help him run his stock and grazing farm. This building, like many of Bosley's other outbuildings, was a substantial stone masonry structure measuring twenty-four by sixty feet. The room and loft at the west end of the building, probably used as a slave residence, was completely separated from the adjacent dining room. This long room, well lighted by seven windows, was equipped with a fireplace in which the meals were cooked. Because there was a full cellar with eight feet of headroom beneath the mess hall and a sizable loft above, the structure also functioned as the plantation's storehouse.

## Hospitals

No topic of discussion among planters attracted more comment than the health of their slaves. Following a thoroughly racist line of reasoning, they argued that black people were simply incapable of taking adequate care of themselves. Without the intercession of a thoughtful master, it was presumed, the slaves would undoubtedly perish.

The lowcountry of South Carolina and Georgia was considered a particularly unhealthy region. Visitors to this area during the antebellum period regularly commented on the dangers of "marsh miasma, which engenders fevers of a dangerous nature," and they worried about their chances of escaping the "sickly season" that threatened "pestilence and death."[7] Responding to these perceptions, planters in the region made slave hospitals a standard feature of their estates. In 1828 Roswell King, Jr., overseer at a Georgia rice plantation, preached: "A hospital should be on each plantation, with proper nurses and apartments for lying-in women, for the men, and for a nursery; when any enter, they are not to leave the house until discharged."[8]

Hospital buildings varied widely in size, construction, and design. At one Georgia plantation, Frederick Law Olmsted found that the hospital, a building referred to as the "sick house," was nothing more than one of the slave dwellings that was reserved for people who were too ill to work.[9] This was the pattern followed at James Thornton's plantation in Greene County, Alabama (see fig. 12.33; compare with figs. 11.10, 12.45, and 12.46). The hospital at Robert F. W. Allston's Guendalos plantation, however, represented a more serious gesture of concern. Considerably larger than a slave cabin, it was described in 1858 as containing six bedrooms, "2 with fire places and piazza."[10] The Jehossee Island estate of William Aiken, Jr., a noted South Carolina rice planter, boasted three hospitals, which provided health care to more than seven hundred slaves; two were described as "common," while the third was a "lying-in hospital" or maternity ward.[11] To Frances Kemble the hospital at Butler Island, Georgia, seemed "a sad spectacle," a place where slaves "lay like brutes" in dark, dingy rooms. The building was, nevertheless, a larger-than-usual structure two-and-a-half stories high, containing four rooms plus a loft. Set at the end of a double row of slave cabins, it was the architectural focal point of the slave street.[12]

One of the most elaborate slave hospitals must have been the infirmary at Hopeton, the Georgia plantation owned by James Hamilton Couper. In 1833 he described this building for the *Southern Agriculturist*:

> The hospital is an airy and warm building, 80 feet by 24, with four wards, an entry which answers as an examining room, a medicine closet, a kitchen, and a bathing room. One ward is for lying-in women, another for women, and two others for men. The whole is heated with steam, supplied by two small copper boilers, and this mode has been in use for 14 years. The accommodations for the sick are a cot for each person with a straw mattress and pillar, a pillar case, 2 blankets and a coverlid, with benches. The beds are refilled with clean straw once a month, and the cases and blankets at the same time washed. The wards are swept every day and washed out once a week, and the whole building whitewashed twice a year.[13]

The slave hospital at Thomas Butler King's Retreat plantation on St. Simons Island, Georgia, rivaled the grand scale of the Hopeton infirmary. Although in ruins when it was photographed, the remnants of the surviving shell of tabby concrete were still impressive (fig. 10.5). They reveal that the building was once two-and-a-half stories tall and contained ten rooms, at least one of them heated by an internal fireplace. Further, the exterior walls were coated with stucco, which was scored to imitate the look of cut stone blocks. Built to care for the health needs of more than three hundred slaves, the hospital was considerably larger than the King family residence, a low story-and-a-half frame dwelling containing not more than four rooms.

## Chapels

Once planters decided that they needed to monitor the physical condition of their slaves, it was but a small step for some of them to attend to their slaves' spiritual well-being as well. In fact, it was widely accepted among the planter class that religion could have a calming influence on the slave population, significantly lowering the risk of potential rebellions and thus making slaves more compliant and productive workers.

Religion, in the minds of many slaveowners, was an instrument of social control.[14] This point of view is reflected in the testimony of Lucretia Alexander, whose former master hired ministers expressly to preach docility and obedience: "The preacher came and preached to them [the slaves] in their quarters. He'd just say, 'Serve your masters. Don't steal your master's turkey. Don't steal your master's chickens. Don't steal your master's hogs. Don't steal your master's meat. Do whatsomeever your master tell you to do.' Same old thing all de time."[15] Alexander also recalled that later in the same day her father would conduct a private service in the slave quarters that included "real preachin'," with a message of optimism and liberation that the slaves found more up-lifting and hence more valuable. Such services have been labeled as manifestations of an "invisible institution" because they were often conducted in secret.

There were, however, plantations where the overt practice of slave religion was ardently supported. In 1859 Tennessee minister Holland N. McTyerie called on planters "to make *special* provisions" for their slaves. What he recommended was the construction of houses of worship explicitly for slave use. He urged slaveowners to provide "a chapel—not the barn, the cotton-shed, the sugar-house; for these have a work-day association, and, especially when attendance is compulsory, the servants come to look upon religious services as a part of plantation police, and the preacher in the light of an overseer—on the roadside, where several plantations may be served at once, this will be economy in many particulars."[16] McTyerie may have had in mind a structure like the Methodist church at the Silver Bluff plantation in South Carolina built in 1845 by James Henry Hammond and named St. Catherine's in honor of his wife. Visitors to the estate in 1860 found the services held there "solemn and impressive."[17] According to former slave Litt Young, Martha Gibbs, mistress of a plantation near Vicksburg, Mississippi, "built a nice church with glass windows and brass cupola for the blacks."[18] This was an exceptional act; more often slave services were held in the quarters or in the yard of the master's house.

In the 1830s and 1840s, some southern ministers became increasingly concerned with what they perceived as the neglect of the spiritual needs of the slave population. The plantation missionary movement they advocated was hailed all over the South but was most actively pursued in the lowcountry of South Carolina and Georgia.[19] Given the fact that three-fourths of the population in this area were slaves, the coastal plantations were considered an opportune target for religious reform. Consequently it is in the lowcountry that buildings constructed explicitly for slave worship were most commonplace.

In 1858 South Carolina planter Benjamin Allston reported that many slaves had converted to orthodox faiths: "There are many communicants, and it is stated that there are more converts among the negroes of the South than all the other missions of the heathen can boast of. Chapels are provided on several places where they hold their services, thus affording them a place for the worship of God at home."[20] Along the Georgia coast, slaves were encouraged to build small structures they called "praise houses"—small, unpretentious wooden halls in which they held Sunday services and weeknight prayer meetings. Although most of these plantation chapels lacked the usual architectural trappings that would have indicated their sacred purposes, the church at Charles C. Jones's Montevideo plantation in Liberty County, Georgia, was apparently designed as an advertisement for religion, being a "neat plastered building with belfry and bell." That this building was more elaborate than most of the other praise houses is not surprising, seeing that Jones was one of the principal advocates of the plantation mission movement.[21]

Some idea of what these plantation chapels were like can be gained from the photograph of the slave church at Mansfield plantation in Georgetown County, South Carolina (fig. 10.6). This rice estate, belonging to Dr. Francis Parker, was in 1850 home to 121 slaves.[22] Their church strongly resembled the other cabins with which it was grouped. Like the dwelling houses, it was a frame building covered with horizontal clapboards. In size it was no larger than the other houses designed for occupancy by two families, and further, like the common slave cabin, its entrance was in the long side rather than in the gable end as might be expected of a chapel. Only a short "steeple" topped by a pyramidal roof and a bell hung in a nearby wooden frame signaled the building's sacred function.[23]

In such austere surroundings, slaves managed to fuse the Christian message preached at them with the emotional contexts of their African backgrounds and their experience of bondage. It is reported that at one plantation service, in response to the prayer led by a slave foreman named Jim Nelson, "The Negroes sobbed and shouted and swayed backward and forward, some with aprons to their eyes, most of them clapping their hands and responding in shrill tone: 'Yes, God!' 'Jesus!' 'Savior!' 'Bless de Lord, amen,' etc. . . . Jim Nelson when he rose from his knees trembled and shook as one in a palsy, and from his eyes you could see the ecstasy had not left him yet. He could not stand at all, and sank back on his bench."[24] Slaves turned Christian doctrine to their own purposes and created the ritual means by which they could find a spiritual release to compensate for their lack of personal liberty.

Planters built chapels for their slaves in the hopes of winning their cooperation; in this they were only partly successful. The slaves at Silver Bluff plantation, for example, soon resurrected their own services in defiance of the decorous formal liturgy promoted by their owner, even though he had provided them with a fine church building. "They are running the thing into the ground," he wrote in 1851, "by being allowed too much organization—too much power to the head men & too much praying and Church meeting on the plantation."[25] It is clear that slaves used their chapels, particularly the unpretentious structures like the building at Mansfield plantation, to worship in ways and for reasons their owners had never anticipated. The not-too-subtle message that emerged was that, although slaves might be manipulated, they were unlikely ever to be completely mastered.

**10.1**

Kitchen with dining
room at the Jenkins
plantation, Crenshaw
County, Alabama.
Photograph by E. W.
Russell, 1937.

**10.2**

Outbuildings at Greenway plantation, Charles City County, Virginia. From the left, these buildings include a structure housing both a laundry and a bakery, a slave dining hall, and a slave kitchen. Photograph by Albert S. Burns, 1934–35.

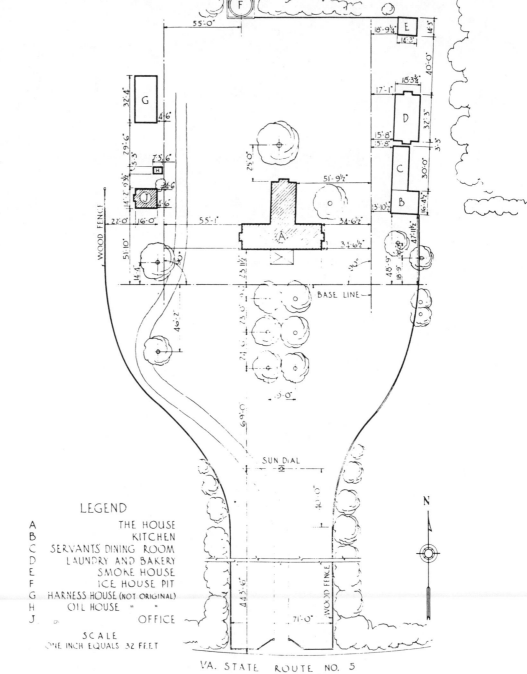

**10.3**

Site plan of Greenway. Drawn by Lyle Swiger and Philip Colavita, Jr., 1934.

LEGEND

A — THE HOUSE
B — KITCHEN
C — SERVANTS DINING ROOM
D — LAUNDRY AND BAKERY
E — SMOKE HOUSE
F — ICE HOUSE PIT
G — HARNESS HOUSE (NOT ORIGINAL)
H — OIL HOUSE  "  "
J — OFFICE

SCALE
ONE INCH EQUALS 32 FEET

**10.4**

Elevation and floor plan of a combined slave quarter and dining hall at Hayfields, Baltimore County, Maryland. Drawn by Robert E. Lewis, 1936.

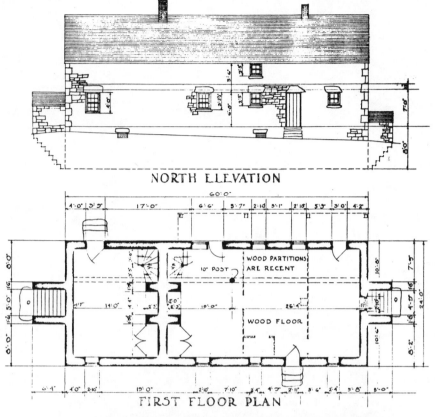

NORTH ELEVATION

FIRST FLOOR PLAN

**10.5**

Ruins of a slave hospital at Retreat plantation, Glynn County, Georgia. Photograph by Branan Sanders, 1934.

**10.6**
Chapel at Mansfield
plantation,
Georgetown County,
South Carolina.
Photograph by
Charles N. Bayless,
1977.

# ELEVEN

# Quarters for Field Slaves

The dwellings constructed to house field slaves were generally small, unpretentious cabins grouped together a significant distance away from the Big House. Viewed as emblematic features of the plantation environment as well as the miserable shacks where black people were kept, these buildings completed the social statement initiated by a planter's mansion. Any man of property might own fields, barns, sheds, equipment, and livestock, but only the most financially well off could own large numbers of human beings. In 1860 no more than 12 percent of all southerners owned enough slaves to be considered members of the planter class.

All across the Old South, the ideal plantation landscape was bracketed between a planter's house and the houses of slaves. Letitia Burwell, who enjoyed the benefits of being a planter's daughter, revealed how important the slave domain was to a white resident's sense of place when she wrote: "Confined exclusively to a Virginia plantation during my earliest childhood, I believed the world one vast plantation bounded by negro quarters."[1] Big Houses and slave quarters were significantly linked but located at the opposite ends of a scale of power. When Frederick Law Olmsted first entered the South in 1852, these were the two elements of the rural landscape that immediately commanded his attention. Passing through northern Virginia, he observed: "A good many old plantations are to be seen; generally standing in a grove of white oaks, upon some hill-top. Most of them are constructed of wood, of two stories, painted white, and have, perhaps, a dozen rude-looking little log-cabins scattered around them, for the slaves."[2] Although, in architectural terms, slave quarters were humble, almost inconsequential structures, they were nevertheless a public index of a planter's wealth and a proof of his or her right to be treated with deference.

For most of the seventeenth century, slave spaces in Virginia were largely devoid of the symbolism they would acquire during the antebellum period; there were few rows of cabins or "streets" like the ones Olmsted and other commentators so frequently remarked upon. Various kinds of documentary and archaeological evidence indicate that seventeenth-century slaves either were quartered in their owners' houses or slept in the lofts of nearby kitchens, sheds, and barns rather than in buildings expressly designated as slave residences. If a separate quarters house was built for servants, it was located close to the main residence.[3] These early slaves were treated more like indentured servants than like chattels who were owned outright. A 1681 court deposition from York County, Virginia, for example, suggests more social intimacy than might be expected between slaves and their owners when it reports that a slave named Frank was allowed into the parlor to share drinks with his mistress.[4] In a society where the behavioral boundaries between slave and owner were not always clearly maintained, there was also a discernible ambiguity regarding the use of domestic space. Toward the end of the seventeenth century, when the enslaved status of black people was more rigorously defined by legal codes and social practices, racial segregation was more strictly enforced.[5] The slaves who were not employed as house servants were then moved out of their owners' houses to cabins explicitly designated for their use.

In 1686 French traveler Durand de Dauphine witnessed the campaign of improvements to the rural environment. In addition to small hall-and-parlor structures—called "Virginia houses"—that the planters constructed for themselves, he observed, "They build also a separate kitchen, a separate house for the Christian slaves [white indentures], and one for the negro slaves, & several to dry the tobacco."[6] A new social regimen was being established in which the planter's house would become mainly a place for the master's rest and leisure. Most of the essential work activities and mundane domestic chores were pushed away from the house and, as those tasks were removed from the home, so were the slaves and servants who were expected to perform them.

At the beginning of the eighteenth century, as vast rural estates comprising thousands of acres were being acquired by members of the Virginia gentry, the practice arose of subdividing plantation land holdings into more manageable portions called "quarters." In 1701 planter Ralph Wormley of Middlesex County, Virginia, for example, listed six parcels of land: Pine Quarter, Loghouse Quarter, Quarter over the

Creek, Flemings Quarter, Quarter called Whitakers, and Black Walnut Quarter.[7] The term *quarter* was somewhat ambiguous, referring variously to a building in which slaves were housed, the place where their houses were located, and the lands that they worked. Apparently to clarify the meaning of the word, Edward Kimber, an eighteenth-century traveler, appended to his "itinerant jottings" the following note: "A Negro Quarter is a Number of Huts or Hovels, built some Distance from the Mansion-House; where the Negroes reside with their wives and Families and cultivate at vacant times the little Spots allow'd them."[8] As the rules of the "peculiar institution" became more restrictive, slaves found themselves increasingly confined to spaces set aside exclusively for them. By the middle of the eighteenth century, sets of slave cabins—located out of a planter's sight, though never very far from his or her thoughts—had become definitive features of southern plantations.

The circumstances of slave housing were significantly different in South Carolina, the other major beachhead for chattel slavery. There, very soon after their arrival, African slaves were directed to build segregated quarters. Their status as a separate population was further emphasized by the fact that often their dwellings were actually African-style dwellings, small rectangular huts constructed with mud walls and thatched roofs. Some of this difference can be accounted for by the fact that the settlement of Virginia began more than sixty years earlier than that of the Carolinas. When a strong plantation economy based on the cultivation of rice finally emerged in the lowcountry in the 1690s, South Carolina planters had almost half a century's worth of Virginian precedents to follow. Further, these planters imported many more African laborers than did their Virginian counterparts—so many that by 1737 a Swiss newcomer would remark that the region "looks more like a negro country than a country settled by white people." The early South Carolina rice plantation, requiring as it did a large labor force, featured separate residential zones reserved exclusively for slaves even during its pioneer period.[9]

The dwelling houses used as field quarters frequently were only one-room structures. By the 1850s Olmsted found these minimal buildings in use all across the South. As he ranged beyond Richmond, Virginia, he discovered that: "The houses of the slaves are usually log-cabins, of various degrees of comfort and commodiousness. At one end there is a great open fire-place, which is exterior to the wall of the house, being made of clay in an inclosure, about eight feet square and high, of logs. The chimney is sometimes of brick, but more commonly of lath or split sticks, laid up like log work and plastered with mud." Later, as he followed the course of the Pee Dee River through South Carolina, he was shocked to find that the houses built for slaves were so small:

> The negro-cabins, here, were the smallest I had seen—I thought not more than twelve feet square, inside. They stood in two rows, with a wide street between them. They were built of logs, with no windows—no opening at all, except the doorway, with a chimney of sticks and mud; with no trees about them, no porches, or shades, of any kind. Except for the chimney . . . I should have conjectured that it had been built for a powder-house, or perhaps an ice-house—never for an animal to sleep in.

Consequently, by the time he reached eastern Texas, Olmsted was somewhat prepared for the even meaner conditions that he would discover: "The negro-quarters here, scattered irregularly about the [planter's] house, were of the worst description, though as good as local custom requires. They are but a rough inclosure of logs, ten feet square, without windows, covered by slabs of hewn wood four feet long. Great chinks are stopped with whatever has come to hand—a wad of cotton here, and corn shuck there."[10]

The testimony of former slaves confirms Olmsted's observations. Bill Homer recalled the one-room cabins near Shreveport, Louisiana, where he had grown up: "De cabins was built of logs and had dirt floors and a hole where a window should be and stone fireplace for de cookin' and de heat." In Georgia, Robert Shepard remembered log cabins with "chimblies made out of stick and red mud. Dem chimblies was all de time catchin' fire. Dey didn't have no glass windows. For a window dey just cut a openin' in a log." John Finnely gave a minimalist portrayal of Alabama slave housing: "Us have cabins of logs with one room and one door and one window hole." His account matches J. T. Tims's memory of slave dwellings in Mississippi: "Before the War, we lived in a old log house. It had one window, one door, and one room."[11]

The single-pen cabins described by former slaves were often so poorly constructed that they had little chance of surviving into the twentieth century. Indeed, from all accounts, many of these structures were falling apart even while slaves were living in them. However, if a slave cabin chanced to be built of durable materials like stone or if it had been constructed with a measure of diligence, it probably outlasted the institution that gave rise to it.

A log cabin from the Sotterly plantation in St. Mary's County, Maryland, consisting of one room measuring approximately eighteen by sixteen feet, plus a loft space, provides an example of the most minimal house type used as a slave quarter (fig. 11.1). This particular cabin was, however, slightly larger and better built than most. Its log walls were actually sawn planks held in place by three joinery systems: keyed notches at the ends of the planks, dowels that pinned each plank together edge to edge, and log buttresses pegged to the cabin's exterior walls. The exceptionally skillful carpentry found in this house follows eighteenth-century techniques and certainly accounts for the building's longevity.[12] Closer in appearance to the quarters described by most slaves is the cabin built in 1836 in Robertson County, Texas, on the Cavitt place (figs. 11.2, 11.3). The logs were roughly hewn, and the wide spaces between them were filled with mud. However, because the dwelling measures almost twenty feet on a side, its four hundred square feet of floor space was four times greater than the cabins from east Texas noted by Olmsted during the same period.

Many one-room slave cabins were built of frame. A house from the William Gaines farm in Hanover County, Virginia, provides an example believed to date from the mid-eighteenth century (figs. 11.4, 11.5, 11.6). In plan, the building consisted principally of one rectangular room plus a loft. Next to the chimney, two small sheds extended beyond the main section of the house. Constructed with rather large posts and finished on the inside with lath and plaster, the structure is reminiscent of a slave cabin built by Joseph Ball in 1754 at Morattico plantation in Lancaster County, Virginia, for a privileged bondsman named Aron Jameson. Ball, after carefully specifying how the structure was to be framed, directed that "the whole house must lathed and filled [i.e., plastered]."[13] It seems likely that the Gaines farm quarter was also built either for a similarly favored slave or as the residence for an overseer.

A photograph taken at Roseberry plantation in Dinwiddie County, Virginia, shows a row of clapboard-covered slave houses (fig. 11.7). These dwellings, probably built in the nineteenth century, represent updated and improved examples of the single-pen cabin. Over the course of the nineteenth century, many planters gradually came to the conclusion that plank-covered frame houses were superior to log cabins. If they deemed it prudent to provide healthier and more comfortable homes for their slaves, they usually opted for frame cabins.[14] Litt Young, who lived on a plantation near Vicksburg, Mississippi, confirmed this supposition when he declared: "Old Missy Gibbs had so many niggers she had to have lots of quarters. They was good houses, weatherboarden with cypress."[15] However, the writings of many planters, as well as the testimony of former slaves, indicate that log buildings continued to be used as slave housing throughout the South until the 1860s.

Even more substantial than well-covered frame houses were the stone cabins found at several sites in Maryland. An example from the Darnell farm in Montgomery County had a relatively large loft, making the cabin almost a full two stories tall (fig. 11.8). Although this configuration was not commonplace, it was nevertheless reported at other Maryland sites. Former slave James Deane described the house he grew up in Charles County as "two rooms, one up and one down." According to Annie Henson, who lived downriver from Deane on a plantation in Northumberland County, Virginia, her cabin and those of her fellow slaves also contained two rooms, "one over one."[16]

Slightly larger than cabins of the single-pen type were hall-and-parlor houses, buildings with rectangular floor plans divided into two rooms. These rooms, one slightly larger than the other, were assigned specialized functions. The bigger of the two rooms, the "hall" entered directly from the outside, served as the kitchen and workroom. The smaller room, or "parlor," served mainly as a bedroom and was entered from the kitchen.[17] Buildings of this type were constructed in the 1830s by Henry McAlpin at the Hermitage, a Georgia rice plantation in Chatham County near Savannah, to house his almost four hundred slaves. Two long rows of brick cabins with almost pyramidal roofs, symmetrically arranged window-door-window facades, and exterior brick fireplaces and chimneys lined the road leading up to the mansion. The use of sturdy building materials represented no extra cost to McAlpin because he operated a large brickworks on his estate. In fact, most of the outbuildings on the plantation were made of bricks. In an 1864 description of the Hermitage, a northern journalist wrote: "There are about 70 or 80 Negro houses, all built of brick and white-washed so they look very neat, and rows of live oaks between, making it the handsomest plantation in Georgia."[18] By the 1930s, only thirty-six of these cabins were still standing. A photograph, taken as these remaining cabins were being pulled down, shows six of them set along a pathway just off to the side of the main approach to the mansion (figs. 11.9, 11.10).

Another common type of slave quarter during the antebellum period was a two-unit building, which was essentially two single-pen cabins joined under one roof, with either a single chimney placed between the two rooms or a chimney located at each gable end.[19] Lining the approach to one plantation along the banks of the James

River, Olmsted found "well-made and comfortable log cabins, about thirty feet long by twenty wide, and eight feet tall, with a high loft and shingle roof. Each divided in the middle, and having a brick chimney in the wall at either end, was intended to be occupied by two families."[20] John Roles, the former overseer at a Louisiana estate, wrote of the homes of his human charges: "Their quarters consisted of small one-story frame tenements of two rooms each, to accommodate two families, with a chimney in the center."[21] These observations from opposite ends of the plantation region are confirmed by slave testimony, ranging from North Carolina to Texas, certifying that double-pen houses were in wide use as quarters.[22]

A surviving slave cabin from the Singleton plantation, an estate located south of Wedgefield in Sumter County, South Carolina, is representative of the center-chimney or saddlebag plan (fig. 11.11). Constructed around 1830, it was a frame structure built with timbers and boards that were probably produced at the plantation's own sawmill. Seeing that John Singleton controlled almost three thousand acres and, according to the 1830 federal census, owned 310 slaves, including 200 capable of picking cotton, he may have had as many as sixty buildings like this one on his plantation.[23] Although slaves like Anne Broome from nearby Fairfield County recalled that they too had lived in "two-room plank houses," the overwhelming majority of field quarters were constructed of logs.[24] Josephine Stewart, who lived on a plantation near Blackstock, South Carolina, describes the prevailing circumstances in that area at midcentury: "Dere was a row of log houses, 'bout ten I think. Mammy and me lived in one dat had two rooms. De chimney was made of sticks and mud, but de floor was a good plank floor."[25]

Although the more representative slave dwellings were built with corner-notched logs, some saddlebag cabins were constructed of stone (fig. 11.12), but perhaps the most exotic construction technique was employed at Bremo plantation in Fluvanna County, Virginia, where John Cocke built several houses using rammed earth or mud for the walls (fig. 11.13). One of his earth-walled cabins was a two-room saddlebag house. Cocke extolled the virtues of his experiment in a letter to the *American Farmer* in 1821, claiming that after a period of five years, his pisé buildings had "stood perfectly, affording the warmest shelter in winter and the coolest in the summer of any buildings their size I ever knew."[26] Even though most plantations had ample supplies of dirt with which to shape cabin walls, few planters were adventuresome enough to follow Cocke's lead.

Double-pen slave cabins with gable-end chimneys were recorded in Henrico

County, Virginia, and Montgomery County, Maryland (figs. 11.14, 11.15). That such buildings were sometimes created by adding on to an existing structure rather than in a single construction campaign is demonstrated by a cabin north of Hunstville, Alabama (fig. 11.16). The first section of this double-pen cabin at the Mastin place was built in 1835 as a single-pen log house, and at a later date another log pen was added to the end opposite the fireplace. As this new room had no exterior door, the cabin probably was occupied by only one family.

In plan, the colorfully labeled dogtrot house type consists of two rooms separated by an open breezeway, a layout that is the spatial equivalent of a center-passage house.[27] Former slave Perry Sid Jamison, who grew up in the cotton lands of central Alabama, remembered living in such a house: "When we [his family] wuz all together we lived in a log hut. Der wuz a porch in between and two rooms on each side."[28] Two different families usually occupied the two halves of a dogtrot cabin but shared the shaded common space in the middle, the area Perry Jamison called the porch. When the same house was built by white yeoman farmers, the doors into the rooms usually opened off the passageway, so that building was seen by passers-by as one dwelling rather than as two cabins under one roof.[29] The dogtrot house built in 1828 at Belmont plantation in Colbert County, Alabama, shows how the house type might be modified when used as a slave quarter (fig. 11.17). Each log pen had its own front door, immediately indicating that the small structure was intended for double-family rather than single-family occupancy.

Designs for slave housing were, for the most part, based on an Anglo-American architectural tradition that employed square or rectangular room units.[30] Single-pen cabins, either as detached units or arranged in one of several paired configurations, formed the core of most slave quarters. Another type of slave dwelling, one apparently used more often on large rice and sugar plantations, differed significantly from pen-derived structures. Built first in the 1830s, these buildings were probably inspired by a reform movement calculated to appeal as much to planters' interest in making a profit as to their sense of duty toward their slaves.[31] Although the type is not mentioned in any of the narratives of former slaves, planters' accounts and travelers' descriptions provide a clear picture of these innovative buildings. In 1838 James Sparkman, master of Birdfield plantation in Georgetown County, South Carolina, wrote that his slave houses were "well framed buildings 18 by 22 feet," and he noted that he used sawn frames, milled weatherboarding, and cypress shingles—only "the best material." He also added: "Each house contains a hall and 2 sleeping apartments and is intended to accommodate an average of *five* people, or one family."[32]

The same asymmetrical three-room configuration was also used in the design of the slave houses at William Aiken's Jehossee Island estate, except that the plan was doubled. Solon Robinson, who visited the island in 1850, found seven hundred slaves "occupying 84 double frame houses, each containing two tenements of three rooms to a family, besides the cockloft."[33] At one Georgia rice plantation, Olmsted found the slaves quartered in several different villages. At the largest of these black settlements, he observed that

> [the] cabin was a framed building, the walls boarded and whitewashed on the outside, lathed and plastered within, the roof shingled; forty-two feet long, twenty-one feet wide, divided into two family tenements, each twenty-one by twenty-one; each tenement divided into three rooms—one, the common household apartment, twenty-one by ten; each of the others (bedrooms), ten by ten. There was a brick fire-place in the middle of the long side of each living room, the chimneys rising in one, in the middle of the roof. Besides these rooms, each tenement has a cock-loft, entered by steps from the household room.[34]

Olmsted also noted larger-than-usual slave quarters on the sugar plantations of southern Louisiana, writing that they "were exactly like those I have described on the Georgia Rice Plantation, except that they were provided with broad galleries in front."[35]

In plan, the double-tenement house type described by Olmsted and others was more complex than any other buildings used as dwellings for slaves. Examples from Georgetown County, South Carolina, and Prince Georges County, Maryland, might at first glance resemble large, center-chimney, double-pen houses, but these buildings were both longer and deeper than the usual two-unit cabin (figs. 11.18, 11.19). The tenement houses were four rooms long and two rooms deep. If the loft spaces are counted, they each contained eight rooms. Using Olmsted's measurements, each slave family was provided with 441 square feet of ground floor space. Although the larger examples of single-pen houses measuring twenty feet on a side might have afforded almost the same amount of space, the room arrangement in the tenement cabins offered their occupants a greater degree of privacy. Reported figures suggest that, as a rule, five people slept in three different rooms while the housekeeping tasks were performed in yet another room. To Frances Kemble, however, these buildings seemed cramped and "wretched in the extreme." She described the two bedrooms that were divided off from the main room by rough wooden partitions as "a couple of closets smaller and closer than the staterooms of a ship."[36] Her negative assessment of the tenement cabins on Butler Island suggests that the new and allegedly improved dwelling house type did not necessarily lead to improved living conditions for their enslaved occupants.

The cabins built for slaves in the French-settled areas of Louisiana sometimes differed from slave houses in other parts of the South. At the Barbarra plantation in St. Charles Parish, a sugar estate established in 1820 just upriver from New Orleans, a surviving slave house followed French precedents in both its form and its construction (fig. 11.20). The building was an example of the creole house type, a one-story structure two rooms wide and two rooms deep, with a central chimney between the two front rooms.[37] This plan can be traced back to northwestern France, as can the house's steeply pitched hipped roof with a slight kick at the eaves, its *poteaux sur solle* (post on sill) construction, and its *bousillage* (mud) plaster.[38] The Barbarra plantation slave house shows that the pen-based design system dominant across the South might occasionally be displaced where other local, ethnic building traditions remained vital.

Slave quarters that survived long enough to be photographed represent exceptional buildings of their kind, houses constructed well enough to last, in some instances, for almost two hundred years. Considering only the most durable examples of these cabins can collectively obscure the more representative experiences of former slaves like Rose Holman from Choctaw County, Mississippi, who reported, "We lived in little log houses daubed wid mud an' didn't have no beds—slept on de ground on pallets. We eat out o' troughs down at Marsa's back doo'."[39] Nevertheless, the selection presented here does confirm the exploitive social hierarchy upon which the design of all slave houses was based, regardless of whether their mode of construction was solid or flimsy.

The slave quarters depicted in this book are, without exception, bare geometric expressions—square or rectangular boxes with roofs. Few of them had porches or shed additions that might indicate attempts by former slave occupants either to exercise a degree of choice in their houses' design or to personalize the buildings. The walls, often left unpainted, were pierced only by a door and a few square holes for windows, if there were any windows. Dark both inside and out, these buildings would only on rare occasions be taken for homes. They were clearly slave quarters, a type of outbuilding that in size, form, construction, and finish closely resembled a kitchen, dairy, smokehouse, or tool shed. Quarters were meant to function chiefly as shelters for people who, by definition, were not allowed to own homes.

During the nineteenth century, agricultural reformers encouraged planters to pay more attention to the houses of their slaves, pointing out that "leaky roofs and airy floors, in addition to shocking chimneys and walls, are too often met with." One commentator even labeled slave houses "laboratories of disease."[40] Some planters, however, seem to have been more concerned with the appearance of the quarters than with the health and comfort of the slaves living in them. In an 1850 essay detailing procedures for the efficient management of slaves, one planter concluded: "The negroes should be required to keep their houses and yards clean, and in case of neglect, should receive such punishment as will be likely to insure more cleanly habits in the future." A Mississippi planter, who worried particularly about what he termed his slaves' "propensity" to accumulate "dirty rags, old shoes, coon skins, chicken feathers and every other description of trash," similarly agreed that slave dwellings should be frequently inspected by the overseer "to see that all is right within—that they keep a clean house."[41]

In an article in the *Southern Planter* written in 1856, the master of a large Virginia plantation suggested that it was the ugliness of old log houses that made it necessary to place "the negro cabin out of sight of the mansion." Plank-covered frame houses, decorated with "some cheap ornamental cornice," were his recommended improvement.[42] The main reason for painting or whitewashing slave houses, stated another planter, was that "it adds very much to the neat and comfortable appearance of the buildings." Although this writer noted that whitewash also had a "cleansing and purifying effect, conducive to health," its chief virtue, he concluded, was that "the cost is almost nothing."[43] Planters' urgent advice on how to keep their estates neat and tidy reflected their deep-seated, almost fearful need to maintain control over their physical environments. Toward this end, they paid particular attention to the visual order of their holdings. The stark, elemental geometry of the buildings in which they housed their slaves signaled that a strict hierarchical order was in force.

Small houses, similar to slave quarters, were also built beyond the fence lines of plantations. These houses were, however, "read" very differently, even if they still were taken as indications of poverty or inferiority. No matter how ramshackle its condition, the cabin of a white yeoman farmer was usually seen as the lively core of a free and independent homestead. Rarely was a free person's household confined to four walls and a roof. Lean-to sheds and jerry-built additions, reflecting a sequence of personal decisions regarding the house's design or the owner's use of resources, gave each house its own slightly idiosyncratic character. Front porches were particularly important features that allowed the tasks performed in the house to flow easily into public view. J. H. Ingraham, observing the commotion at a nineteenth-century Mississippi homestead, cataloged the contents of its porch. He found, hung up on antlers or tossed on the floor: hats, coats, harnesses, guns, shot pouches, brogans, and shoes.[44] As Frederick Law Olmsted moved through the piney woods of South Carolina, he encountered many of the "lone houses" built by white farming folk. One of them, he reported, had a front porch with "a wide shelf at the end, on which a bucket of water, a gourd, and a hand-basin, are usually placed. There are chairs, or benches, in the porch, and you often see women sitting at work in it, as in Germany."[45] Clearly he was struck by the feeling of domesticity, a sentiment that was rarely stirred by the sight of a slave quarter. Viewing a row of slave houses, from the outside at least, the sense of regimentation and imposed authority could be palpable.

Little of the innate uniqueness of a slave household was physically apparent when each dwelling was a replica of every other one. The social routines upon which slaves based their important familial identities were severely crimped in Spartan settings consisting of one room, one door, and one window. Even when substantially constructed with bricks and mortar, freestanding slave dwellings were still seen first as a collection of buildings, as "the quarter" or "the street." Although North American planters are sometimes considered more humane than their Caribbean and South American counterparts because they housed their slaves in individual cabins rather than in large barracks, a row of single- or double-pen houses was simply a barracks spread out over a greater distance.[46] To dwell in a box on a line is no more dignified than being gathered nightly into a large building divided into many compartments.[47] The double houses that planters thought such an improvement over older single-unit slave cabins were actually more oppressive structures, because the slaves occupying them found themselves confined to half a building and thus had even less physical independence than when they were provided with freestanding one-room dwellings.

Planters were determined to keep their slaves under control by treating them as a collective population rather than as individuals. Most slaves worked in gangs, and they were gathered en masse into a designated area at the end of each day. Given the fact that they were treated little differently from cattle herded into a corral from the open pasture, it is not surprising that, in most property inventories, slaves are listed after domestic possessions and just before the livestock. Using houses as one of the primary means by which they marked their slaves as a captive people, planters managed to leave a broad signature of their intentions on the southern landscape. It is important to understand that slave quarters were only incidentally meant as residences; they were, foremost, the planters' instruments of social control.

Slaves did not, however, passively acquiesce to their owners' architectural designs or to their social imperatives. Okra, a slave living on James Couper's Hopeton plantation near Darien, Georgia, went so far as to build himself an African house. Former slave Ben Sullivan recalled that this structure "wuz bout twelve by foeteen feet an it hab dut flo an he buil du side lak basket weave wid clay plastuh on it. It hab a flat roof wut he make frum bush an palmettuh an it hab one doe an no winduhs." This dwelling was clearly at odds with the order of the plantation and thus was torn down soon after it was discovered.[48]

In some cases the minimal housing provided by planters may have encouraged slaves to retain their African identities. Susan Snow, a former slave raised on a plantation in Jasper County, Mississippi, reported that most of the slave cabins had wooden floors, except the one that was assigned to her African-born mother: "My ma never would have no board floor like de rest of 'em, on 'count she was a African—only dirt."[49] By rejecting an apparent material "improvement," this women re-created in her house an aspect of African domestic life with which she was more comfortable. Whereas her master probably thought he was saving lumber and his carpenter's time, she was subtly resisting his ownership. In fact, Susan Snow recalled that her mother never took orders from the overseers but "worked without no watchin'." It is not too hard to believe that her independent behavior was nurtured, in part, by what she perceived as the African quality of her cabin. The example of Susan Snow's mother suggests that many other slaves, particularly those recently arrived from Africa, may also have viewed their dirt-floored cabins more positively than we have previously imagined. Further, a packed earthen floor can, if properly maintained, become as hard and smooth as concrete; being made of dirt does not necessarily mean that such a floor is actually dirty.

The small slave houses seen by Olmsted in South Carolina—buildings so small that at first he did not think that they could even be dwellings—might also have reminded slave occupants of their African roots. The traditional building units in much of West and Central Africa frequently measure ten feet by ten feet or less, and many freestanding houses have no openings other than a single doorway.[50] The dark, tight enclosure provides adequate shelter in a tropical environment where most living is done out-of-doors and a house is used mainly for sleeping. An eighteenth-century account of the Congo region in Africa describes buildings very similar to those discovered by Olmsted: "The houses, with respect to their dimensions, may be compared to the tiny cells of monks. Their height is such that when you stand up your head touches the roof, so to speak. The doors are very low. . . . The houses receive no other light than that which comes in through the door. There are no windows."[51]

Given the fact that a sizable portion of the slaves imported into South Carolina from Africa came from the Congo area (70 percent of the total imported up to 1740 and 40 percent of those imported between 1740 and 1808), the similarities between Central African houses and the windowless cabins of South Carolina are probably not just coincidental.[52] By building log cabins that were low, dark, and small, planters unwittingly abetted the perpetuation of African proxemic traditions.[53] Indeed, those dwellings closely resembled the African house built at Hopeton; only the building materials and roof form were different. Because planters saw expediently constructed buildings mainly as an economical way to provide shelter, it is unlikely that they ever would have guessed that such meager structures might allow their slaves to recall their African homeland.

Although photographs of slave quarters reveal little of the slaves' attempts to transform their cabins into more serviceable, if not more comfortable, dwellings, verbal testimonies indicate that they did try to modify and improve their houses. Nelson Cameron, who labored on the Brice plantation near Blackstock, South Carolina, recalled that his cabin was dressed up with flowers: "Us live in log house wid a little porch in front and de mornin' glory vines use to climb 'bout it. When they bloom, de bees would come a hummin' 'round and suck the honey out de blue bells on the vines. I 'members dat well 'nough, dat was a pleasant memory."[54] Any traces of such floral decoration would, of course, not last without constant maintenance, and so it is difficult to know how many of the slave cabins that survived into the twentieth century might at some time in the past have been similarly graced. Certainly the possibility exists that other slaves experienced the same pleasure in colorful blossoms that Nelson Cameron did and used them to blunt the harsh edge of slavery.

There is still more testimony illustrating how slaves tried to improve the interiors of their cabins. Former slave Cora Gillam from Desha County, Arkansas, recalled that slaves "made cupboards, and women that was smart would make covers for them. They would make home-made tables and everything."[55] George Fleming, a former slave from Laurens County, South Carolina, also remembered how slaves fixed up their quarters. In addition to "good beds," he claimed: "We had shelves and hooks to put our clothes on. We had benches and tables made wid smooth boards."[56] Similarly, Mandy Morrow from Burnet County, Texas, bragged: "Grandpappy am a cahpentah.'Cause ob dat, weuns quatahs am fixed fine. Co'se dat am compared wid de udder nigger quatahs 'roun' dere. Weuns have reg'lar windahs, an' han' made chaiahs, an' a wood flooah. Gran'pap spen' his extra time, fixin' up de quatahs."[57] The slaves' conscious efforts to decorate their quarters when possible were recalled by Martha Stuart, a former slave from the Black Creek plantation in Louisiana. Slave houses had "pictures on the wall," she said, colorful prints of scenery obtained from traveling salesmen, "picture men who come through the country."[58]

The simple beds, benches, and tables fashioned by slaves during their little bits of free time, together with a few cheap pictures and other trinkets, may not seem like much of an improvement, but within the context of servitude these items represented significant achievements. They suggest that slaves wanted more than the bare necessities their owners supplied, and that they would carefully husband their resources to obtain an occasional luxury item. Most planters only provided their slaves with cell-like rooms, rude holding pens from which the field hands might be called forth to work each day. Because slave-made furnishings helped to make the austere quarters more tolerable, such artifacts should be seen as part of the slaves' adaptive strategies that helped them cope with difficult and painful circumstances.

Slave initiative was further manifested in the gardens they sometimes planted near their quarters. Former slave Olin Williams recalled that, in the Piedmont region of Georgia, the cabins were "in long rows wid gyarden space 'twixt 'em an' evvy family had deir own gyarden jes' like Marster had." He added that they were "big gyardens and [we] growed all de vegetables us could use."[59] At one Georgia rice plantation, according to Olmsted, the slaves also raised most of their food: "Between each tenement and the next house, is a small piece of ground, inclosed with palings, in which are coops of fowl with chickens, hovels for nests, and for sows with pig. There are a great many fowls in the street. The negroes' swine are allowed to run in the woods, each owner having his own distinguished by a peculiar mark. In the rear of the yards were gardens—a half-acre to each family."[60]

In Louisiana Thomas Bangs Thorpe observed equally impressive gardens grown by the slaves on large sugar plantations. He noted that these well-tended plots not only were fenced to keep out intruding animals but also featured numerous birdhouses made from hollowed gourds; while protecting their nests, the birds also kept the vegetables from being attacked by insects and other pests.[61] The extra care displayed in the maintenance of these gardens serves as evidence of their importance to their slave "owners." Charlie Fraser, a Mississippi slave alleged to be an African, was apparently able to use his allotted garden space to re-create the foodways remembered from his homeland. According to Fraser's fellow captive Callie Gray: "His house wus seperate from the other niggers and he had his own garden. He raised rice 'cause he been use to living on it. They told him it wouldn't grow here but he showed 'em. And he fixed it nice too." Not only did he grow the relatively exotic food that he preferred, but he then fashioned the tools required to prepare the grain for cooking. Callie Gray recalled how Fraser made a wooden mortar: "He would cut down a tree and hollow out a section, then he would pour rice in and maul off the chaff."[62]

Throughout the antebellum period, planters debated the virtues of encouraging slaves to plant gardens and raise livestock. Although opinion was divided, there can be no doubt that the practice was widespread.[63] When slaves were allowed to have gardens, planters were spared the expense of providing rations, but gardening was also considered dangerous because it gave the slaves a significant opportunity to claim a degree of autonomy. Northern visitor Richard Soule was struck by the "manorial attitude" that South Carolina slaves displayed toward their garden plots.[64] Having been given an acre of land on which to raise his own cotton, Scott Hooper's father made enough money to buy his own horse and saddle, possessions generally allowed only to white men.[65] Clearly Olin Williams saw his garden as a device by which he might compare his master's household with his own. Moreover, when slaves were capable of feeding themselves, they were also able to develop their own market economy. Henry Barnes, a former slave from Mobile County, Alabama, recalled "De only money de slaves ebber had wuz from selling de corn or tobaccy dey raised on de li'l patch dy had to wuk."[66] The space around the slave cabins was highly charged with social symbolism. In their gardens, the part of the quarters for which they were most responsible, slaves were most effective in establishing a territorial claim within the plantation's confines.

Novelist Ralph W. Ellison observes that people without power are not without nobility. Reflecting on the black experience in America, he astutely notes that "any people who could undergo such dismemberment and resuscitate itself, and endure until it could take the initiative in achieving its own freedom is obviously more than the sum of its brutalization."[67] When viewed from the outside, slave quarters can be seen as instruments of control, as material devices used by planters to demean and brutalize their slaves. Ellison's comment reminds us, however, that the degree of control achieved by the planters was nowhere near as absolute as they imagined. Slaves sometimes found in their assigned quarters features beyond their masters' comprehension. In other cases, they subtly modified their cabins and the spaces around them to serve needs of their own.

**11.1**

Slave quarter at
Sotterly plantation,
St. Mary's
County, Maryland.
Photograph probably
by H. Bevile, 1953.

WEST ELEVATION

SOUTH ELEVATION

FEET 1/2" = 1'-0"
METERS 1:24

**11.2**
Side and front
elevations of a slave
quarter at the Cavitt
plantation, Robertson
County, Texas. Drawn
by Barbara Rottler
and Alan Hohlfelder,
1980.

**11.3**
Floor plan of the slave
quarter at the Cavitt
plantation. Drawn by
Barbara Rottler, 1980.

**11.4**

Quarters house at the William Gaines farm, Hanover County, Virginia. Photograph by Albert S. Burns, 1934–35.

**11.5**

Front elevation and floor plan of the quarters house at the Gaines farm. Drawn by A. A. Davis, 1941.

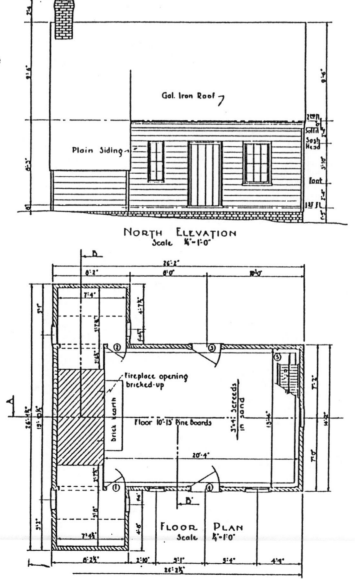

Gal. Iron Roof

Plain Siding

NORTH ELEVATION
Scale ¼"=1'-0"

Fireplace opening bricked-up

Floor 10"-13" Pine Boards

Brick hearth

FLOOR PLAN
Scale ¼"=1'-0"

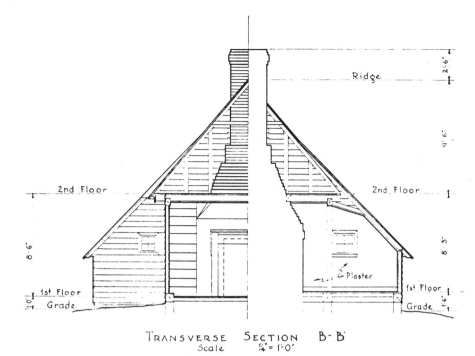

**11.6**
Sectional view of the quarters house at the Gaines farm. Drawn by A. A. Davis, 1941.

**11.7**
Row of slave quarters at Roseberry plantation, Dinwiddie County, Virginia. Photograph by [?] Beckstrom, 1936.

**11.8**

Slave quarter at the Darnell farm, Montgomery County, Maryland. Photograph by John O. Brostrup, 1936.

**11.9**

Row of slave quarters at the Hermitage plantation, Chatham County, Georgia. Photograph by Charles E. Peterson, 1934.

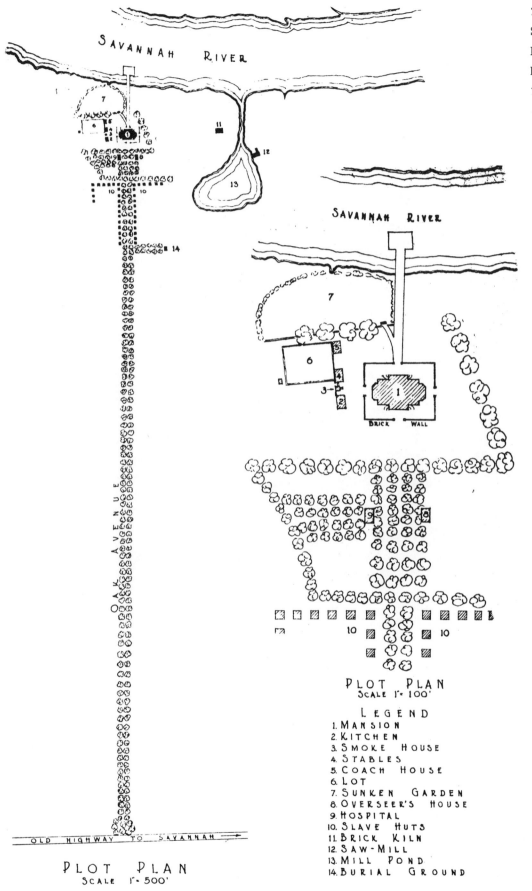

SAVANNAH RIVER

SAVANNAH RIVER

BRICK WALL

OAK AVENUE

OLD HIGHWAY TO SAVANNAH

PLOT PLAN
SCALE 1" = 500'

PLOT PLAN
SCALE 1" = 100'

LEGEND
1. MANSION
2. KITCHEN
3. SMOKE HOUSE
4. STABLES
5. COACH HOUSE
6. LOT
7. SUNKEN GARDEN
8. OVERSEER'S HOUSE
9. HOSPITAL
10. SLAVE HUTS
11. BRICK KILN
12. SAW-MILL
13. MILL POND
14. BURIAL GROUND

**11.11**
Slave quarter at the
Singleton plantation,
Sumter County, South
Carolina. Photograph
by Frederick D.
Nichols, 1940.

**11.12**
Slave quarter at the
Beauregard ranch,
Wilson County,
Texas. Photograph by
Arthur W. Stewart,
1934.

**11.13**
Slave quarter at
Bremo plantation,
Fluvanna County,
Virginia. Photograph
by C. O. Greene,
1940.

**11.14**
Slave quarter from
Henrico County,
Virginia. Photograph
by Thomas T.
Waterman, 1940.

**11.15**

Slave quarter at Mt.
Carmel, Montgomery
County, Maryland.
Photograph by
John O. Brostrup,
1936.

**11.16**

Slave quarter at
the Mastin place,
Madison County,
Alabama. Photograph
by Alex Bush, 1935.

**11.17**

Slave quarter at
Belmont plantation,
Colbert County,
Alabama. Photograph
by Alex Bush, 1936.

**11.18**

Slave quarter at
Mansfield plantation,
Georgetown County,
South Carolina.
Photograph by
Charles N. Bayless,
1977.

**11.19**
Slave quarter
at Northampton
plantation,
Prince Georges
County, Maryland.
Photograph by
John O. Brostrup,
1936.

**11.20**

Slave quarter at
Barbarra plantation,
St. Charles
Parish, Louisiana.
Photograph by
Richard Koch is an
enlargement of a 1927
photograph.

# TWELVE

# Plantation Landscape Ensembles

**A**n antebellum plantation was fundamentally a place of work. This is, however, not the usual image associated with plantation estates. Grand mansions and elegant grounds have, at least since the early twentieth century, come to be regarded as emblematic of the plantation as a place. Generally overlooked is the fact that a planter's house was only the centerpiece of a holding that necessarily included fields, pastures, and woodlots. Moreover, these holdings would not have existed at all were it not for the sizable profits amassed through the unrelieved labor of enslaved workers. Because it is often the case that only the mansion houses remain, the impression conveyed by plantation sites today is exclusively one of wealth and easy comfort. Because the slave quarters and various work spaces are frequently missing, how such splendor and comfort were sustained remains something of a mystery. It is said that visitors to historic properties will often remark at the conclusion of their tours, "Nice place! Do you suppose they had any help?" Although this story is doubtless apocryphal, it indicates the sort of confusion that can arise when a built environment is shorn of its mundane, but vitally necessary, structures.

Fortunately, there are quite a few sites at which a considerable number of the cabins and outbuildings were photographed and mapped. Amazingly, there are even some places where large clusters of original slave and work buildings are still standing today. The images presented in this chapter provide us with the opportunity to examine some of these places. Moving beyond the analysis of individual examples of standard building types to look at groups of related buildings brings us considerably closer to the environmental experience of slavery. Because the sites examined here extend over a broad geographical area—from Maryland to Texas—and include plantations that produced most of the commodities characteristic of the nineteenth-century plantation economy, they provide a useful and representative overview of the region.

Consider first the photographs and drawings of the surviving buildings of Hampton, a plantation located in Towson, Maryland, due north of Baltimore (figs. 12.1, 12.2, 12.3). The first phase of construction at Hampton was undertaken between 1783 and 1790. It was during this period that Charles Ridgely built his impressive mansion (fig. 12.4). The house, elaborately decorated with what were originally sneered at as "new-fangled notions," was from a design based on several houses that Ridgely had visited in England, Philadelphia, and Virginia. Located around the perimeter of the mansion's gardens are several service buildings that were probably built at the same time. These include sheds, a privy, a cider cellar, a smokehouse, and an extremely large icehouse (see fig. 12.2).

Because Ridgely had no direct heir, he willed his plantation and adjacent lands, which by then encompassed more than twelve thousand acres, to his nephew, Charles Carnan, who changed his surname to Ridgely in accordance with the requirements of the will. Charles Carnan Ridgely, the first of Hampton's owners actually to live on the estate, eventually served as Maryland's governor from 1815 to 1818.[1] Most of Ridgely's 196 slaves, who were kept at four different locations within his vast land-holdings, were housed in log cabins.[2] Still standing within the remaining forty-two acres of the plantation is a double-pen log cabin built in the 1850s, allegedly with logs from two older cabins. Two additional double-pen slave quarters, both standing two stories high, were constructed with stone masonry at the same time (figs. 12.5, 12.6, 12.7). All of these slave houses—together with an overseer's house (fig. 12.8), now greatly enlarged beyond its initial one-room log cabin—define the edges of a square yard measuring approximately sixty feet on each side. Set almost a third of a mile down the hill from the Big House, this domain was probably reserved for the slaves' domestic activities.[3]

Because wheat and livestock had, by the late eighteenth century, displaced tobacco as Hampton's primary agricultural product, its granary, barns, and dairy were particularly prominent. Constructed with stone masonry, like most of the other outbuildings on the plantation, they survive in good shape today (figs. 12.9, 12.10, 12.11, 12.12, 12.13, 12.14, 12.15, 12.16). The use of such a durable building material is an obvious sign of the plantation's economic success. Although the barns, stables, workshops, and corncribs at Hampton might seem exceptional, comparable buildings can be found at Hayfields, a slave-run stock farm only a few miles away (see figs. 7.9, 7.10). Other surviving slave quarters in nearby Howard and Montgomery counties (see fig. 11.15) were also constructed with stone.[4] Perhaps nothing should be made of this concentration of masonry buildings other than to note that stone outlasts wood. However, the persistent use of stone could also be taken as an index of local identity, seeing that this material was more commonly used in the mid-Atlantic than in the Deep South. The buildings at Hampton reveal a combination of northern and southern traits frequently encountered in this and other border states; the idea of the plantation traveled north from the Chesapeake, whereas the choice of building technology may reflect a northern or mid-Atlantic orientation.[5]

When Henry Tretham, a former slave from Camden, South Carolina, was asked about his days of servitude, he recalled: "Marster's plantation was a awful big plantation with 'bout four hundred slaves on it. It was a short distance from the Wateree River. The slave houses looked like a small town and there wus grist mills for corn, cotton gin, shoe shops, tanning yards, and lots of looms for weavin' cloth. Most of de slaves cooked at dere own houses, dat dey called shacks. . . . Dere wus a jail on the place for to put slaves in, and in de jail dere wus a place to put your hands in called stocks."[6]

Slave "towns" of an equivalent scale were also created at the Green Hill plantation in southern Campbell County, Virginia. This plantation was developed by Samuel Pannill, who purchased an initial six hundred acres in 1797 and by the time of his death in 1864 had increased his holdings to almost five thousand acres. Green Hill, located on a high plateau overlooking the Staunton River, consisted, in fact, of two "towns." The cluster of buildings on top of the bluff, including Pannill's residence and at least twelve other structures, was dubbed "Upper Town," while a set of slave cabins and workshops located near the river's edge was called, as might be expected, "Lower Town."

A drawing of the property made in 1960 indicates that even at that late date the locations of the two original "towns" were still discernible (fig. 12.17). It shows that much of the original Upper Town was still in place, but only the ruins of a mill and a miller's house marked the former river site of Lower Town. In addition to raising tobacco and wheat, Pannill also developed something of an industrial village. He not only milled grain but operated a fleet of keelboats that carried the flour downriver to markets in North Carolina. Among his slaves were carpenters, coopers, blacksmiths, shoemakers, weavers, and sawyers. Their workshops and dwellings were all located in Lower Town, along with a stone church for their own use.[7] The 1860 federal census indicates that Pannill owned eighty-one slaves, who were kept in seventeen houses. Most of these buildings were probably in Lower Town.

Dominating Upper Town was a rectangular boxwood garden surrounded by a low stone wall; all of the buildings were arranged around the edges of this enclosure. The main residence (fig. 12.18) was located at the northwest corner of the garden and flanked by an office, icehouse, servants' house, loom house, laundry, and duck house (later used as a pigsty). These structures defined a rectangular space that served as a work yard for activities related to the domestic routines of Pannill's residence (figs. 12.19, 12.20). The barns, granaries, stables, and the carriage house, all structures related to farm work, were arranged along the southern edge of the garden. All of the outbuildings, except for the tobacco barn, were ordinary examples of their respective types (figs. 12.21, 12.22, 12.23, 12.24, 12.25, 12.26, 12.27, 12.28). Even Pannill's Big House, although built of brick, was only an I-house, the commonplace residence of a middle-class yeoman.[8] What most distinguished Green Hill was its cluster of outbuildings, which provide a reminder that once almost one hundred people lived and worked there.

A 1967 plan of Cedar Grove, the tobacco plantation established by Cary Whitaker in 1792 in Halifax County, North Carolina, effectively portrays some of the dynamics involved in determining the best location for slave houses (fig. 12.29). Whitaker had the quarters for his forty-eight slaves aligned with the main house, but they were set slightly more than a hundred yards away from his residence. These buildings were within earshot of the house, but because they were screened by intervening barns and sheds (and possibly by trees, too), they were out of constant sight. Plantation owners were concerned about the behavior of their slaves and thus wanted them close at hand. However, as Frederick Law Olmsted discovered at one Virginia plantation, the close proximity of slaves could also prove bothersome. The planter's advice, Olmsted reported, was so frequently sought by his bond servants that, "During the three hours, or more, in which I was in company with the proprietor, I do not think ten consecutive minutes passed uninterrupted by some of the slaves requiring his personal direction or assistance. He was even obliged three times to leave the dinner-table."[9]

Some planters thus elected not only to allow the slaves to run their own households, but to let them do so without much supervision. Basil Hall noted, during his observations of plantation routines in the coastal regions of South Carolina, that masters frequently left their slaves alone for long periods and even instructed their overseers to interfere "as little as possible with their domestic habits, except in matters of police." [10] At Cedar Grove, Whitaker apparently was hoping to achieve an optimal positional balance, so that his slaves' houses would be neither too near nor too far away. From his perspective, the slaves could readily be called for work while presumably they were not so close that they would bring their every problem to him.

Some of the largest plantations of the antebellum era were located along the Rice Coast of South Carolina and Georgia. Not only were the landholdings of these estates extensive, but the average number of slaves on a rice-producing plantation was slightly more than two hundred.[11] Rice plantations were thus distinguished by the great number of slave dwellings required to house such large work forces. Frequently set miles away from the planter's residence, the quarters were sizable villages where slaves developed social routines of their own. According to Olmsted, who meandered through several of these slave villages in Georgia: "I rode in, by a private lane, to one of these. It consisted of some thirty neatly whitewashed cottages, with a broad avenue, planted with Pride-of-China trees between them." Once within the settlement, he observed adjacent to each house gardens and pig yards enclosed by substantial wooden fences, evidence of an independent slave-operated trade network in livestock and vegetables.[12]

The estate belonging to Zephaniah Kingsley is representative of plantations along the southeastern coast—at least in scale, even if some aspects of its layout are unique. Kingsley acquired this property, located on Fort George Island off the Florida coast in Duval County, in 1813 and proceeded to raise sugar cane and cotton until his death in 1843. Like his fellow planters in the adjacent southeastern lowcountry, he owned a large number of slaves. An 1814 document lists him as having more than 70 bond servants, and the 1830 census records him as the owner of 220 slaves. Kingsley kept such large numbers of field hands, however, for other than agricultural purposes; he was actually using his plantation as the base for a slave-trading operation. Although the importation of African slaves remained legal in Florida until the territory became part of the United States in 1821, Kingsley is best described as a smuggler. His slaves were trained on Fort George Island to perform field tasks and then sold within a year's time to plantation owners throughout the adjacent lowcountry of South Carolina and Georgia. Ardently sought by planters who needed large labor gangs to develop their rice lands, the so-called Kingsley Niggers were considered to be excellent workers, and thus buyers were willing to pay a premium for them.[13]

The Kingsley slave settlement consisted of thirty-two cabins arranged in a distinctive arc (fig. 12.30). Trees were planted in front of each house in this semicircular village, and wells reportedly were placed between every two cabins. The dwellings were all constructed with tabby. Cabins measured approximately sixteen by twenty feet or less and thus, even though their substantial mode of construction made them both fire and hurricane resistant, they were very cramped.[14] Two slightly larger structures were located at the midpoint of the curving row of slave houses. These two-room houses, measuring close to twenty-five by nineteen feet, were reserved for the slave drivers—black foremen who supervised the daily operations of the plantation (fig. 12.31). The larger dimensions of their dwellings may have been intended as a signal to the other slaves of the superior status of these men.

Kingsley's own residence, a building two stories tall with a wide veranda, stood about a thousand feet from the slave village. It was clearly the largest building on the plantation and was made to seem even larger when Kingsley linked it to a second two-story house built for one of his common-law wives (fig. 12.32). Although this move might at first seem to be motivated by Kingsley's desire to establish his status as well above that of his slaves, the paired houses actually signal a more complex message. The occupant of the second house, Anna Madagegine Jai (also called Ma'am Anna), was a free black woman, allegedly a princess of mixed African and Arabian ancestry from Madagascar. It was further claimed that she had saved Kingsley's life when he was attacked during one of his African voyages. Clearly Kingsley was bucking the rules of the white social establishment by having a black woman for his wife. The linking of the two houses suggests that he was trying to find a successful compromise between his personal behavior and the demands of social protocol. Anna Jai and her children were kept, like house slaves, close at hand in an adjacent building. That the social censure eventually became increasingly burdensome is indicated by the fact that in 1835 Anna Jai and her children were sent to Haiti, which was by then an independent black republic. Kingsley did, however, leave much of his estate to these children in his will, and Jai returned to the plantation in 1865 and lived there until her death in 1870.[15]

After the invention of the cotton gin by Eli Whitney in 1793, cotton became the dominant commodity produced in the South. The owners of great plantations and small farms alike became obsessed with raising cotton. So intense was the mania for this crop that one southern journalist even referred to it as a "plague" and said that its growers were "as thick as locusts in Egypt."[16] Throughout the first half of the nineteenth century, the southern frontier and cotton moved westward together from the

Carolina backcountry to the prairies of central Texas. Although much of the South's cotton was grown on relatively small, nonslaveholding farms, the planter class still managed to dominate the region.[17]

Because cotton lands were developed quickly in a land-rush spirit, and because cotton had relatively few requirements for its successful cultivation, there was considerable variation in the layout of cotton-producing plantations. William Henry Townes, who worked on a plantation in Tuscumbia, Alabama, recalled that his master ran a highly organized operation. The formal order of the plantation layout reflected a disciplined approach to farming. According to Townes: "The Big House was a two-story house; white like mos' houses endurin' that time. On the north side of the Big House set a great, big barn, where all de stock an' stuff dat was raised was kep'. Off to de southwes' of de barn, wes' of de Big House, set 'bout five or six log houses. These house was built facin' a space of ground in de center of a squa'e what de house make. Anybody could stan' in his front do' an' see in at the front of de yuther houses."[18] The contrast between this plantation and the one belonging to the Toom family of Simpson County, North Carolina, was quite pronounced. Manus Robinson, one of the Tooms' former slaves, remembered: "Ole Mars has his slave cabins scattered all 'round over his plantation, he lacked 'em dat way, he wanted 'em convenient to der different parts. Some ob 'em wuz clos' ter de barn an' stables, den dey wuz two or three close ter de big house fer de servents an' maid ter live, uders wuz near de fields an' pastures."[19] Each cotton planter generally followed an individual pattern. What linked one cotton plantation to another was mainly the crop produced.

Thornhill, the cotton plantation in Greene County, Alabama, developed by James Thornton between 1833 and 1835, still retains many of its original structures (fig. 12.33). The site plan shows that the main house, a large building based on a Georgian plan and graced by six Ionic columns (fig. 12.34), is located near the passing roadway. All the other buildings and structures, except for a small temple-form schoolhouse, are set behind it. Placed close to Thornton's residence are five structures that surround a service yard for the Big House. These include the kitchen, dairy, smokehouse, two wells, and a cistern (figs. 12.35, 12.36, 12.37). Just beyond this cluster of buildings once stood two dwellings for house slaves, the smaller one reserved for the cook (figs. 12.38, 12.39). A hundred feet further on, a row of houses for more slaves extends along a road running back to a twentieth-century barn. The first of these cabins was used as a slave hospital. The four other cabins were dwellings of the dogtrot type (figs. 12.40, 12.41).[20] In 1860 Thornton owned 156 slaves, 89 of them aged fifteen or older. About a third of them lived in the quarters behind the Big House. Others were kept at two other locations on the plantation close to the cotton fields.

From several photographs of the plantation, one can form a reasonable impression of the daily routine in slavery times. As late as 1934, the bell that had called the slaves to their tasks was still in place (fig. 12.42). A photograph of a section of the yard known as the "wash place" depicts huge cast-iron vessels that were once used to do the laundry (fig. 12.43). There is even a picture of the interior of one of the cabins (fig. 12.44). Its meager furnishings are a poignant reminder that the Spartan conditions endured under slavery lasted well into the twentieth century.[21]

Thornton, who served as Alabama's first secretary of state from 1824 to 1834, was clearly a prominent person. The scale of his plantation matched his social position; at 2,600 acres, his holdings were extensive. However, he did not cultivate all of his land. Because each full field hand could not be expected to harvest more than five acres of cotton, in any year not much more than five hundred acres, less than a fifth of Thornton's acreage, was committed to this popular cash crop. Family documents show that some of his land was used for gardens and orchards. Thornton also raised corn and kept some land for pasturing horses. Other sections probably were left as woodlots to provide firewood as well as the building materials with which his slave cabins were constructed, and another section of his woods was enclosed with a rail fence and maintained as a deer park. However, the main reason Thornton acquired so much land was that intensive single-crop farming soon depleted the soil, dramatically lowering its yield. Rather than fertilize the spent fields in order to restore their capacity, it was the custom of cotton planters simply to clear new ground. The surplus acres that went unplanted were basically a hedge against the calamity of crop failures.[22]

Although some sugar cane was grown along the southeastern coast and near the Gulf Coast of Texas, the majority of sugar plantations were found in the so-called Sugar Bowl of southern Louisiana. By 1853 there were almost 1,300 of them, and collectively they accounted for one-fourth of the world's sugar production.[23] Sugar tracts were usually quite extensive, consisting of cleared, leveled, and ditched fields stretching out to the horizon. Nineteenth-century visitors pronounced them "superb beyond description"; one writer found a Louisiana sugar plantation to be so large that he began to "doubt his senses."[24]

Estates of such great size required large work forces of slaves. Thus Louisiana sugar plantations, like the plantations along the Rice Coast, were marked by large slave villages as well as the specialized structures required for the processing of the cane and the maintenance of the planting operations. The 1868 bill announcing the sale of Bellegrove, an estate located just south of Baton Rouge in Iberville Parish, describes a typical sugar plantation. Besides the planter's mansion, the property included a slave settlement consisting of twenty two-room slave cabins and a six-room brick house arranged in two rows on either side of a long street. Included among the other buildings were a large brick sugar mill, a two-story overseer's house, a slave hospital, blacksmith's and cooper's shops, a steam-powered sawmill, a warehouse, a stable, and smoke and meat houses.

Uncle Sam plantation in St. James Parish was, during the 1930s, still comparable in scale to what Bellegrove had been almost a century earlier. An aerial view and site plan show that the plantation was divided into at least four different domains (figs. 12.45, 12.46). The territory reserved for planter Samuel Faggot was close to the river. His residence, thought to be the largest mansion house in Louisiana (fig. 12.47), was flanked by two *garçonnières* (dormitories for the young men of the household) as well as two plantation offices and two dovecotes (fig. 12.48), plus the carriage house and stable (fig. 12.49). Immediately to the south of the planter's compound, a row of six double-unit slave houses with front galleries extended back from the river to the site of the former sugar works. About two hundred yards south of the mill site was a second slave quarter consisting of three rows of frame buildings. Twenty-four workers' houses were counted, three reserved for white employees and twenty-one said to be for slaves. As many as 165 slaves toiled in the fields at Uncle Sam plantation in 1850. As their dwellings were generally double-unit creole houses consisting of four rooms, these slaves seem to have lived more comfortably than the bond servants on other plantations. At Uncle Sam, slave accommodations averaged between three and four people to a dwelling unit, a significant departure from the testimony of many former slaves who reported that they shared a room with ten or twelve others.[25]

Geographer John B. Rehder has identified three ideal layouts for the Louisiana sugar plantation: the linear plan, the block plan, and the nodal-block plan. In the linear arrangement, as the name suggests, the major buildings are strung out in a line from the river's or bayou's edge to the swampy backlands, generally following the property lines of lots that are narrow but quite deep. Plantations that follow a block organization cluster their structures together near the planter's residence; the nodal-block plan groups buildings together at separate locations on the plantation property.

The linear scheme is thought to have French West Indian antecedents, whereas the block plans are found in areas dominated by Anglo-American settlers.[26] Features of all three plans are found in the layout of Uncle Sam plantation. The residential, work, and slave domains are clustered together in a typical block plan, whereas the slave quarters are arranged in a linear pattern. Further, the division of the slave quarters into two widely separated sets suggests a degree of nodal planning. Perhaps the Uncle Sam plantation illustrates a synthesis of the various nineteenth-century strategies for sugar cultivation, a fusion of French and American plantation ideals.

As one moves westward across central Texas, the look of the land changes rather abruptly as the black-soil prairie zone gives way to hills dotted with scrub cedar and live oak trees. This physical divide is a cultural boundary as well; to the east one finds farms, to the west there are mainly cattle ranches.[27] The estate of E. Sterling C. Robertson, Jr., located near Salado in southern Bell County, was clearly in ranching territory.[28] Although not a plantation in the usual sense, Robertson's property was laid out in plantation mode. Most important is the fact that in 1860 he owned thirty slaves, all of whom were above the age of fifteen. Consequently, Robertson certainly qualified as a member of the planter class.

A map of his ranch illustrates that Robertson divided his estate into zones reserved for Big House routines, slave life, and ranching activities (fig. 12.50). Construction on the main house was started in 1854 and completed in 1864. The dwelling, apparently inspired by Louisiana plantation houses, had open verandas on its front and rear facades and was topped by a tall hipped roof (fig. 12.51). Its plan featured a standard Georgian scheme of four rooms with a central passage, but it also had small square rooms at each of the corners, spaces known in Louisiana as *cabinets*. Robertson's residence sat in its own fenced yard at the end of a tree-lined drive. The slaves were quartered in one long stone building consisting of three two-room units (figs. 12.52, 12.53). Each of these units alone would have been nothing other than a commonplace double-pen house, which was used widely across the South as a farmhouse by nonslaveholding yeomen.[29] However, by tripling this standard unit and placing all three under one roof, Robertson created a structure that resembled a barracks, a type of slave quarter more common to the West Indies and South America and rarely encountered in the United States.

The occupants of this quarters building were physically positioned between two worlds of work. Some of them, most likely the women, toiled in the service wing of the Big House, an L-shaped structure containing a kitchen and dining room, meat room and dairy, and the laundry and cistern (fig. 12.54). The frame hyphen that links this building to the main house is a twentieth-century addition; the structure originally was seen as a place apart from the residence and thus was considered primarily as a slave work space. To the west of the slave quarter, roughly the same distance from the house, was the barn. This building, a stone structure surrounded on three sides by wooden sheds, sheltered horses and other equipment (fig. 12.55). Following the local custom of the region, the cattle were allowed to roam free for most the year, finding bits of feed wherever they could. Ranching required much open land (particularly in central Texas, where range fodder was sparse) and relatively few buildings.

The drawings and photographs of the Robertson property remind us that slave labor was utilized in many different agricultural pursuits. Robertson's buildings describe a context in which a slave would more often be found on horseback than hoeing in the fields. They are a reminder that African Americans, too, worked as cowboys and took part in the taming of the West.[30]

The seven ensembles reviewed here collectively illustrate the considerable variation in the antebellum southern landscape. Wheat, cotton, tobacco, sugar, and cattle— the commodities produced on these plantations—all had different requirements, leading ultimately to the creation of distinct vistas. The appearances of plantations could vary considerably. A sugar estate, for example, was largely industrial in character, whereas cotton plantations often resembled nothing more than oversized farms. If the work force was large (say, more than fifty slaves), then the quarters would be spread in clusters across the fields, while a smaller group might be quartered in the backyard of the owner's house. Local traditions in vernacular design and technology might determine the choice of barn type. All plantations reflected the willful order imposed on the land by slaveowners, but clearly all slaveholders were not equally rigorous in making their imprint. Thus some plantations seem to have been laid out with a strict adherence to geometry, whereas the buildings on others are more randomly arranged.

By looking at plantations as ensembles, we come to realize that it is more correct to speak of southern plantation*s* rather than of *the* southern plantation. That there was not a single, unifying plantation style should not surprise us. After all, a region as large as the South encompasses not only a number of distinct ecological zones but an array of ethnic and subregional identities as well. After factoring in the variables of class and wealth, one realizes that any semblance of unity among southern planters would have to have been based more on ideological grounds than on material means. It has been suggested that during the antebellum period a widespread plantation ideal linked well-to-do planters and small, independent farmers with shared goals. "Yeomen," says historian John Boles, "looked up to their 'betters,' admired and took local pride in the occasional mansion, and may have longed for self-advancement to the slave-owning class."[31] A big plantation was a clear symbol of economic success to which all white southerners could aspire. The enslaved occupants of those estates had, of course, different hopes and thought about the plantations in different terms.

**12.1**

Site plan for Hampton plantation, Baltimore County, Maryland. Drawing by Herbert L. Banks, 1959.

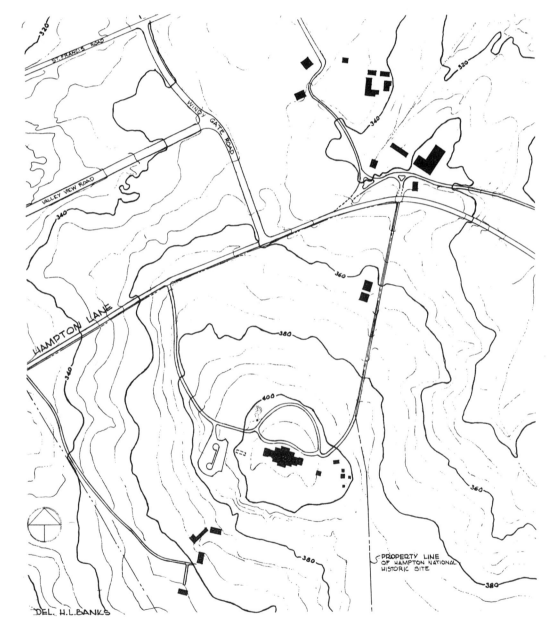

**12.2**

Enlarged section
of the site plan of
Hampton, showing
mansion house
and adjacent
grounds. Drawn by
Charles C. Boldrick
and Herbert L. Banks,
1959.

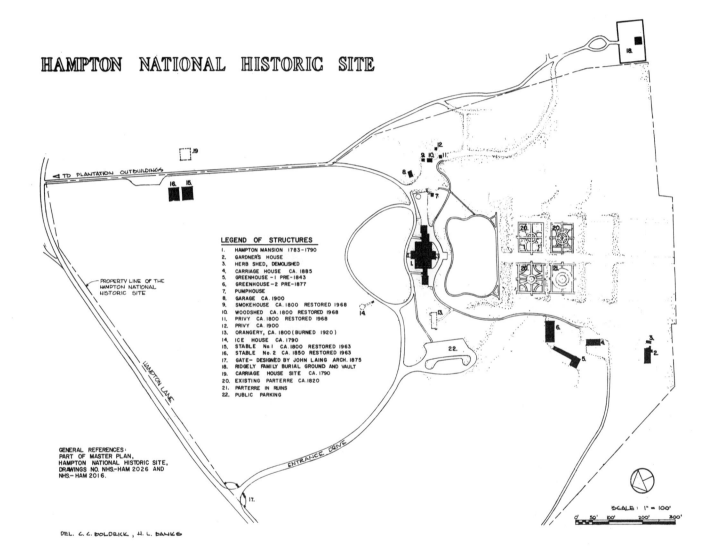

HAMPTON NATIONAL HISTORIC SITE

LEGEND OF STRUCTURES

1. HAMPTON MANSION 1783-1790
2. GARDNER'S HOUSE
3. HERB SHED, DEMOLISHED
4. CARRIAGE HOUSE CA. 1885
5. GREENHOUSE-1 PRE-1843
6. GREENHOUSE-2 PRE-1877
7. PUMPHOUSE
8. GARAGE CA. 1900
9. SMOKEHOUSE CA. 1800 RESTORED 1968
10. WOODSHED CA. 1800 RESTORED 1968
11. PRIVY CA. 1800 RESTORED 1968
12. PRIVY CA. 1900
13. ORANGERY, CA. 1800 (BURNED 1920)
14. ICE HOUSE CA. 1790
15. STABLE No.1 CA. 1800 RESTORED 1963
16. STABLE No.2 CA. 1850 RESTORED 1963
17. GATE- DESIGNED BY JOHN LAING ARCH. 1875
18. RIDGELY FAMILY BURIAL GROUND AND VAULT
19. CARRIAGE HOUSE SITE CA. 1790
20. EXISTING PARTERRE CA.1820
21. PARTERRE IN RUINS
22. PUBLIC PARKING

— TO PLANTATION OUTBUILDINGS

— PROPERTY LINE OF THE
HAMPTON NATIONAL
HISTORIC SITE

HAMPTON LANE

ENTRANCE DRIVE

GENERAL REFERENCES:
PART OF MASTER PLAN,
HAMPTON NATIONAL HISTORIC SITE,
DRAWINGS NO. NHS-HAM 2026 AND
NHS-HAM 2016.

SCALE: 1" = 100'

0'  50'  100'    200'      300'

DEL. C.C. BOLDRICK, H.L. BANKS

# HAMPTON OUTBUILDINGS

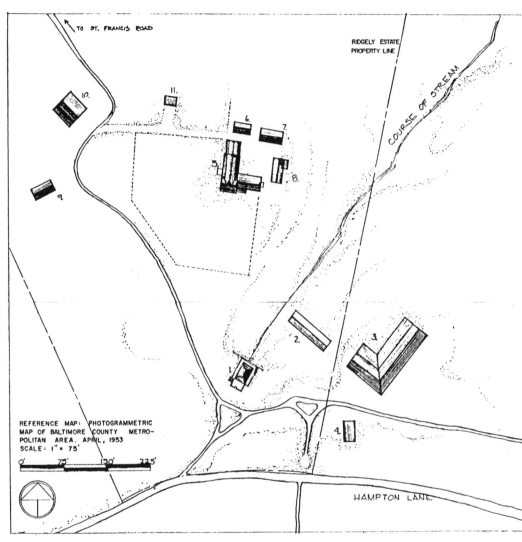

**12.3**

Enlarged section of the site plan of Hampton, showing the location of the plantation's major outbuildings. Drawn by Richard C. Mehring and Herbert L. Banks, 1959.

**12.4**

Mansion at Hampton. Photograph by Lanny Miyamoto, 1959.

**12.5**

Slave Quarter No. 2 at Hampton. Just visible at the left is the edge of the one remaining log quarter. Also visible is a small stone structure with a gable door where ashes used in the manufacture of soap were stored until needed. Photograph by E. H. Pickering, 1936.

**12.6**
Slave Quarter No. 3 at
Hampton. Photograph
by Lanny Miyamoto,
1959.

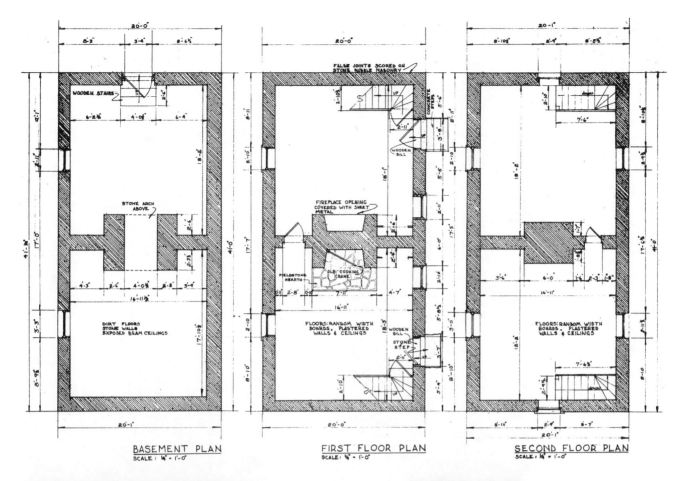

BASEMENT PLAN
SCALE: ¼" = 1'-0"

FIRST FLOOR PLAN
SCALE: ¼" = 1'-0"

SECOND FLOOR PLAN
SCALE: ¼" = 1'-0"

**12.7**

Floor plans for Slave Quarter No. 2 at Hampton. Drawn by Charles C. Boldrick, 1959.

**12.8**

Overseer's house at Hampton. The original segment of this building, which was much expanded over the years, is the portion standing to the right of the door. This portion of the building was constructed with logs and once contained just one room plus a loft. Photograph by E. H. Pickering, 1936.

**12.9**

Granary at Hampton.
Photograph by E. H.
Pickering, 1936.

**12.10**

Dairy at Hampton.
Photograph by E. H.
Pickering, 1936.

**12.11**
Cow barn at
Hampton. Photograph
by E. H. Pickering,
1936.

**12.12**
Horse stables
at Hampton. The
older of the stables
stands to the left.
Photograph by Lanny
Miyamoto, 1959.

**12.13**

A mule barn at Hampton. Photograph by E. H. Pickering, 1936.

**12.14**

Blacksmith shop at Hampton. Photograph by Lanny Miyamoto, 1959.

**12.15**

Corncrib at Hampton.
Photograph by Lanny
Miyamoto, 1959.

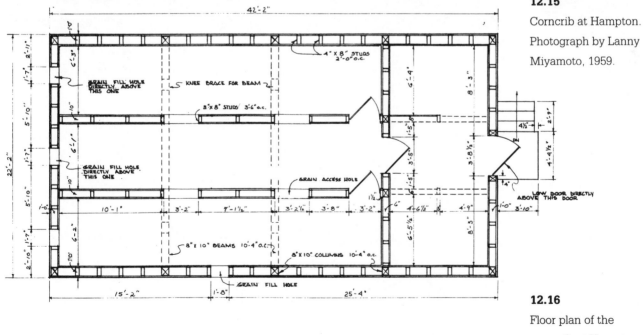

PLAN
SCALE : 1/4" = 1'- 0"

**12.16**

Floor plan of the
corncrib at Hampton.
Drawn by Richard C.
Mehring, 1959.

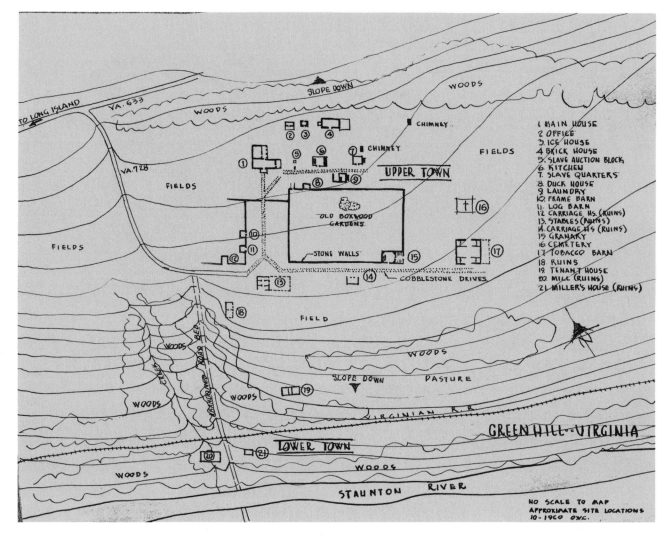

Map legend:
1 MAIN HOUSE
2 OFFICE
3 ICE HOUSE
4 BRICK HOUSE
5. SLAVE AUCTION BLOCK
6 KITCHEN
7. SLAVE QUARTERS
8 DUCK HOUSE
9 LAUNDRY
10. FRAME BARN
11. LOG BARN
12 CARRIAGE HS. (RUINS)
13. STABLES (RUINS)
14. CARRIAGE HS (RUINS)
15 GRANARY
16 CEMETERY
17 TOBACCO BARN
18. RUINS
19. TENANT HOUSE
20. MILL (RUINS)
21 MILLER'S HOUSE (RUINS)

**12.17**

Site plan of Green Hill
plantation, Campbell
County, Virginia.
Drawn by Orville W.
Carroll, 1960.

**12.18** [opposite]
Main house at Green
Hill. Photograph by
Jack E. Boucher,
1960.

**12.19**
Upper Town at Green
Hill, as seen from the
fields. Photograph
by Jack E. Boucher,
1960.

**12.20**

Upper Town at
Green Hill, as seen
from the main house.
Photograph by
Jack E. Boucher,
1960.

**12.21**
Brick dependency
at Green Hill.
Photograph by
Jack E. Boucher,
1960.

**12.22**
Slave quarter
at Green Hill.
Photograph by
Jack E. Boucher,
1960.

**12.23**
Kitchen at Green
Hill. Photograph by
Jack E. Boucher,
1960.

**12.24**
Laundry at Green
Hill. Photograph by
Jack E. Boucher,
1960.

**12.25**
Duck house at Green
Hill. Photograph by
Jack E. Boucher,
1960.

**12.26**
Granary at Green
Hill. Photograph by
Jack E. Boucher,
1960.

**12.27**
Tobacco barn
at Green Hill.
Photograph by
Jack E. Boucher,
1960.

**12.28**
Log barn at Green
Hill. Photograph by
Jack E. Boucher,
1960.

**12.29**

Site plan of Cedar
Grove plantation,
Halifax County, North
Carolina. Drawn by
Charles D. Harris,
1967.

LEGEND

1. EAST PORCH
2. NORTH PORCH
3. SOUTH PORCH
4. DINING WING
5. NECESSARY HOUSE
6. KITCHEN
7. SMOKE HOUSE
8. GUEST HOUSE (J. B. WHITAKER HOUSE)
9. SLAVE HOUSES
10. FARM BUILDINGS
11. STABLES
12. WELL

RECONSTRUCTED SITE PLAN

SCALE

**12.30**

Site plan of the
Kingsley plantation,
Duval County,
Florida. Drawn by
George G. Cellar,
1934.

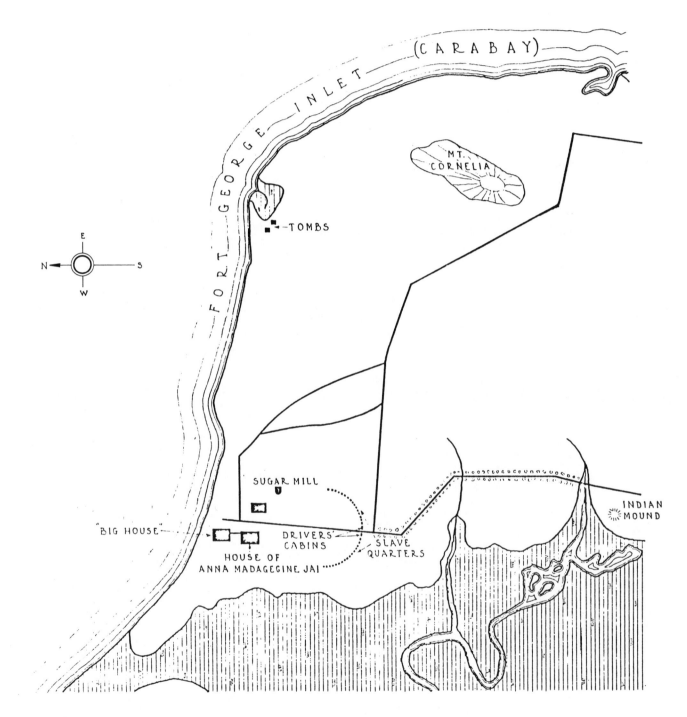

**12.31**

Elevation, plan, and section of a slave driver's cabin at the Kingsley plantation. This structure was slightly larger than the other cabins. Drawn by H. C. Dozier, W. C. Vaughn, and George G. Cellar, 1934.

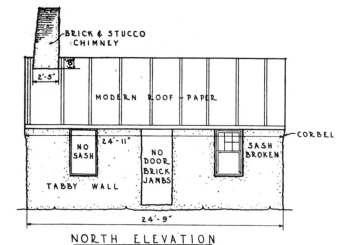

NORTH ELEVATION

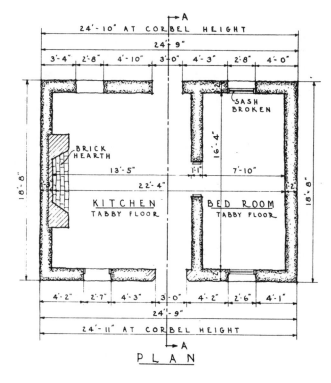

PLAN

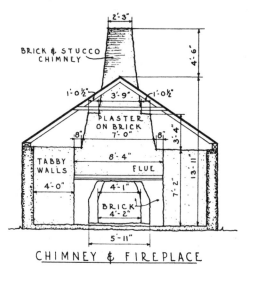

CHIMNEY & FIREPLACE

**12.32**

House of Anna
Madagegine Jai
at the Kingsley
plantation.
Photograph by
unknown HABS
photographer, 1934.

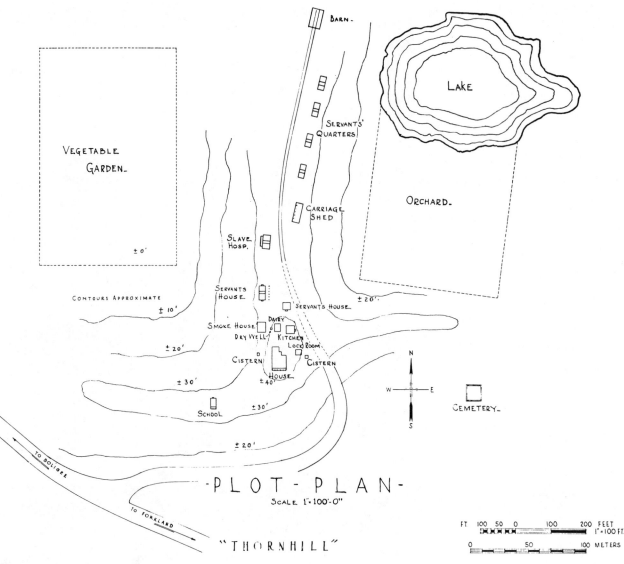

VEGETABLE GARDEN.

± 0'

CONTOURS APPROXIMATE

± 10'

BARN.

LAKE

SERVANTS' QUARTERS

ORCHARD.

CARRIAGE SHED

SLAVE HOSP.

SERVANTS HOUSE

± 20'

SMOKE HOUSE

DRY WELL

DAIRY

SERVANTS HOUSE

KITCHEN

LOCK ROOM

± 20'

CISTERN

HOUSE

± 40'

CISTERN

N

W · E

± 30'

S

CEMETERY.

SCHOOL

± 30'

± 20'

TO BOLIGEE

TO FORKLAND

· P L O T · P L A N ·

SCALE 1"=100'-0"

"THORNHILL"

FT 100 50 0   100   200 FEET
1"=100 FT.

0   50   100 METERS

**12.33**

Site plan of Thornhill
plantation, Greene
County, Alabama.
Drawn by W. A.
Hotchkiss, 1934–35.

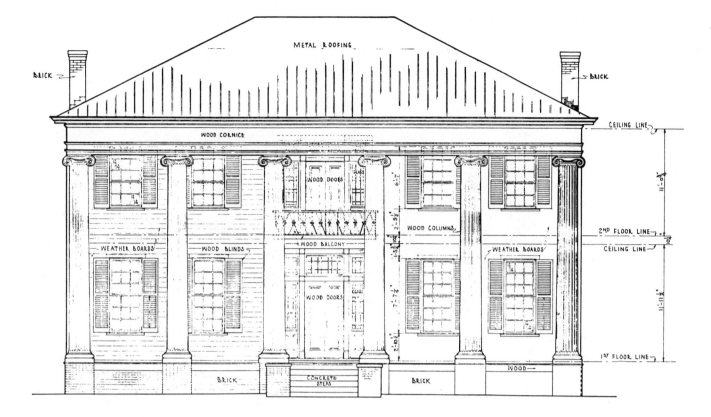

Labels visible on the drawing:

METAL ROOFING

BRICK

BRICK

WOOD CORNICE

CEILING LINE

WOOD DOORS

WEATHER BOARDS

WOOD BLINDS

WOOD COLUMNS

WOOD BALCONY

WEATHER BOARDS

2ND FLOOR LINE

CEILING LINE

WOOD DOORS

BRICK

CONCRETE STEPS

BRICK

WOOD

1ST FLOOR LINE

·SOUTH·FRONT·ELEVATION·

SCALE - ¼"=1'-0"

**12.34**

Front elevation of the
mansion at Thornhill.
Drawn by Carl Edins,
Frederick Utting, and
Clive Richardson,
1934–35.

**12.35** [top l.]
Well at Thornhill.
Photograph by Alex
Bush, 1934.

**12.36** [top r.]
Cistern at Thornhill.
Photograph by Alex
Bush, 1934.

**12.37** [below]
Plans and elevations
of the well and cistern
at Thornhill. Drawn
by Clive Richardson,
1934–35.

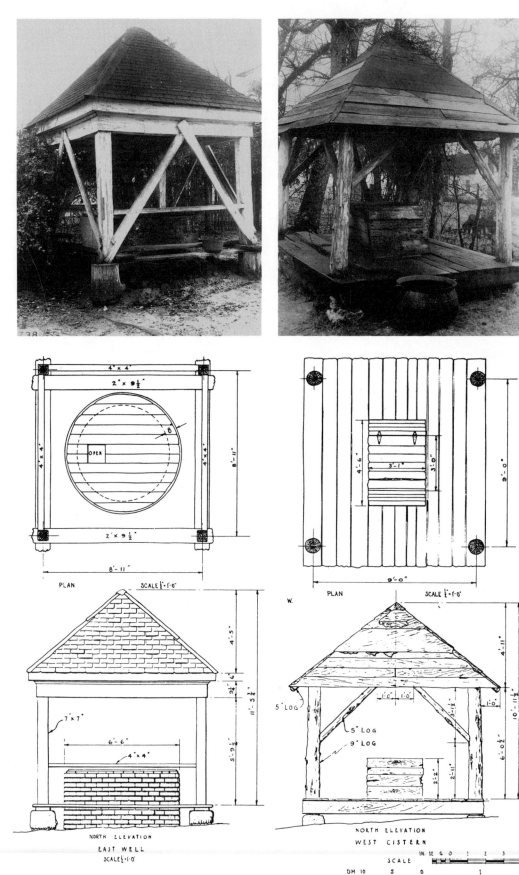

**12.38**
Cook's cabin at
Thornhill. Photograph
by Alex Bush, 1934.

**12.39**
Plan and front
elevation of cook's
cabin at Thornhill.
Drawn by Willis E.
Jordan and W. A.
Hotchkiss, 1934–35.

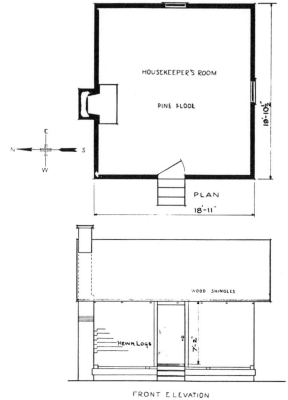

HOUSEKEEPER'S ROOM

PINE FLOOR

19'-10"

PLAN

18'-11"

WOOD SHINGLES

HEWN LOGS

7'-2"

FRONT ELEVATION

**12.40**

Slave house at
Thornhill. Photograph
by Alex Bush, 1934.

**12.41**

Elevations and
floor plan of a slave
quarter at Thornhill.
Drawn by Kent W.
McWilliams, 1934–35.

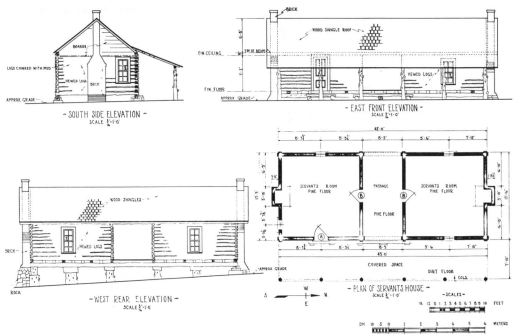

**12.43**

The "wash place" at Thornhill. Photograph by Alex Bush, 1934.

**12.42**

Plantation bell at Thornhill. Photograph by Alex Bush, 1934.

**12.44**

The interior of a slave cabin at Thornhill. Photograph by Alex Bush, 1934.

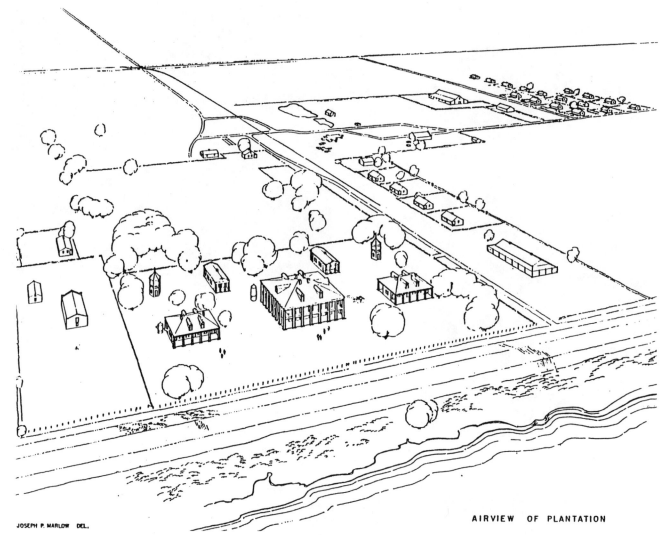

JOSEPH P. MARLOW DEL.

AIRVIEW OF PLANTATION

**12.45**
Aerial view of
Uncle Sam plantation,
St. James Parish,
Louisiana. Drawn by
Joseph P. Marlow,
1940.

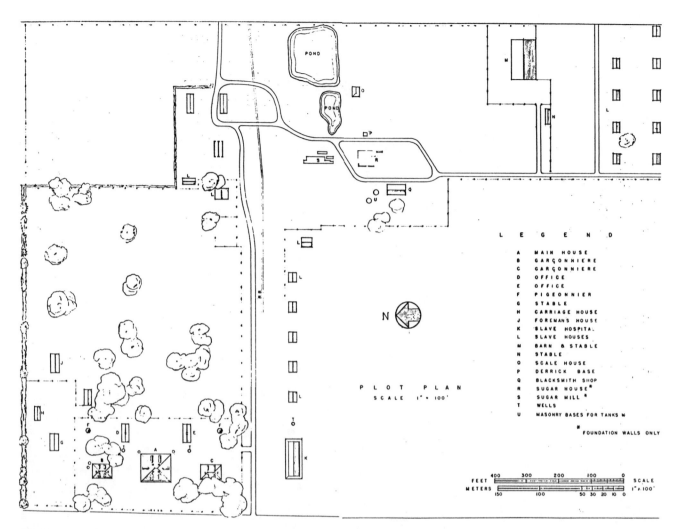

**12.46**

Site plan of Uncle
Sam. Drawn by F. H.
Manger and Joseph P.
Marlow, 1949.

**12.47**

Front elevation of the mansion at Uncle Sam. Drawn by F. H. Manger and Joseph P. Marlow, 1940.

**12.48**

Dovecote at Uncle Sam. Note as well the row of slave houses in the background. Photograph by Thomas T. Waterman, 1937.

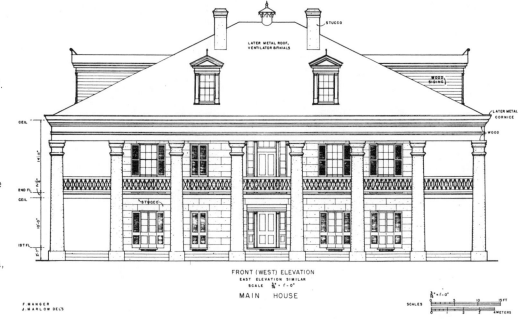

FRONT (WEST) ELEVATION
EAST ELEVATION SIMILAR
SCALE

MAIN HOUSE

**12.49**

Stable at Uncle
Sam. Photograph by
Richard Koch, 1936.

**12.50**

Site plan of the
E. Sterling C. Robert-
son, Jr., ranch, Bell
County, Texas. Drawn
by Mark E. Adams,
1936.

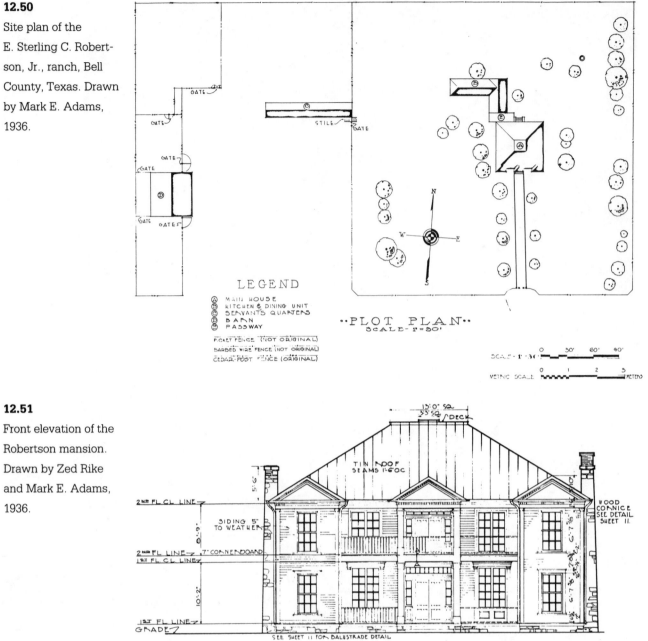

**12.51**

Front elevation of the
Robertson mansion.
Drawn by Zed Rike
and Mark E. Adams,
1936.

**12.52**

Slave quarter at the Robertson ranch. Photograph by Arthur W. Stewart, 1936.

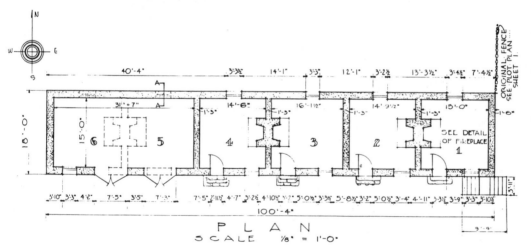

**12.53**

Floor plan of the slave quarter at the Robertson ranch. Drawn by Mark E. Adams, 1936.

**12.54**

Plan and elevation
of the service wing
of the Robertson
mansion. Drawn by
Mark E. Adams, 1936.

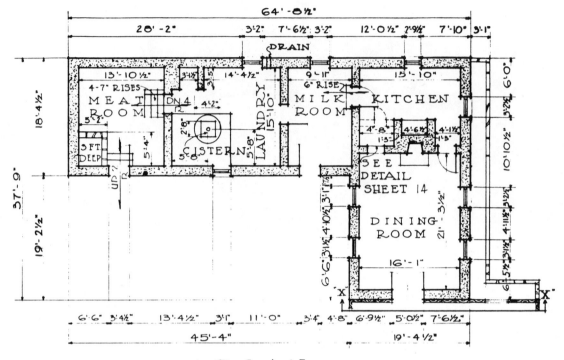

·P L A N·
SCALE ·· ⅛" = 1'-0"

"NOTE:" CEILING ONLY IN DINING
ROOM & KITCHEN · · EXPOSED RAF-
TERS ARE IN ALL OTHER ROOMS

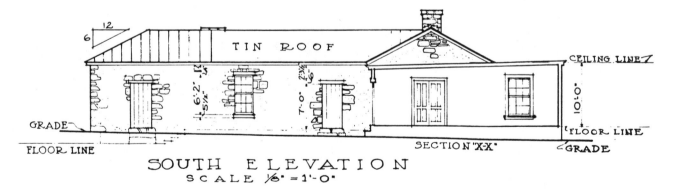

SOUTH ELEVATION
SCALE ⅛" = 1'-0"

**12.55**

Elevations and plan
of the barn at the
Robertson ranch.
Drawn by Truett H.
Coston, 1936.

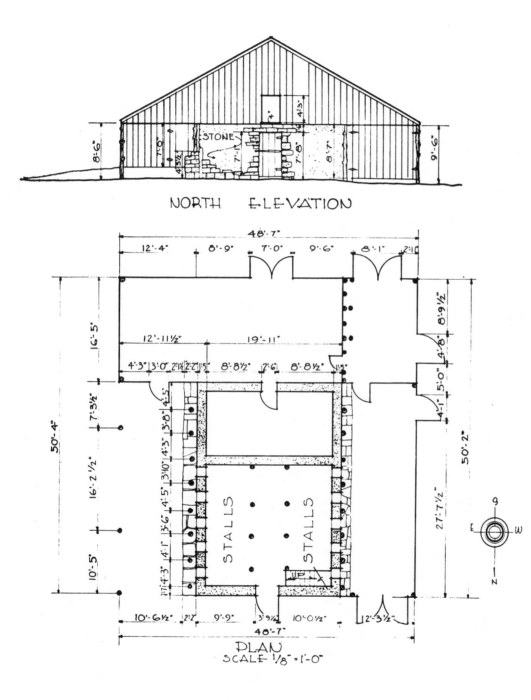

NORTH ELEVATION

PLAN
SCALE 1/8" = 1'-0"

# Conclusion

**P**lantation landscapes were most overtly marked by the architectural choices made by their white creators. At every turn in "the world the slaveholders made," one encountered the results of their decisions. By selecting the types of structures to be built, their locations, size, mode of construction, and style of decoration, planters were able to determine not only the look of the land around them but also, to a great extent, the conditions and circumstances under which their bondsmen and bondswomen lived and worked. The physical settings that they established can be regarded, then, as a direct material expression of their social power.

The social eminence of planters was, however, never as secure as they liked to believe. Fretful that their authority might be challenged, particularly by slaves, they felt that no aspect of a plantation's daily routine, however minor, could be overlooked. Success, according to one planter, required "taking into consideration everything, slaves, land, horses, stock, fences, ditches and farming utensils; all of which must be kept up and improved in value."[1] In an 1851 article describing how best to run a plantation, one Mississippi planter listed sixteen rules, the first of which he spelled out in bold capital letters: "THERE SHALL BE A PLACE FOR EVERY THING AND EVERY THING SHALL BE KEPT IN ITS PLACE."[2] The ideal order among planters was a rigorous order intended to confirm their final authority in all matters. It was important that their domains be planned with care, defined with clear and certain boundaries, and run on efficient, unwavering schedules. Striving constantly toward this goal, planters used every means—but especially the manipulation of the built environment—to convince themselves that they were both physically and symbolically above their slaves and other less wealthy whites as well.[3]

Anchoring their claims to social power to their visible ownership of sizable land-holdings, gangs of slaves, and numerous buildings, planters used a strategy of contrasts to draw attention to themselves. Their houses were almost always the largest, if not the most elaborately decorated, buildings on a given site. Their residences, when compared to the surrounding outbuildings, would always be seen as the Big Houses. Frederick Douglass recalled that all the slaves living at Tuckahoe, the plantation in eastern Maryland where he grew up, referred to their owner's mansion as the "*great house*," in recognition of both its physical dimensions and the authority of the man who lived there.[4] A planter further emphasized his social significance by situating his house either on high ground or close to the main thoroughfare. His house was thus "up" while the other buildings were "down," or at the "front" while the other structures were set to the "rear." If a planter's abode was not literally at the center of his estate, it was at least the symbolic center. The size and visual prominence of his residence expressed, in positional terms, a desired social order. Slaves were assigned to their appropriate place below or behind their master. He was at the center of their world, whereas they were consigned to the margins of his.

Within the landscapes created by slaveowners, however, absolute social power was an ideal that was asserted more often than it was achieved. Much to their chagrin, planters came to realize that their systems of architectural manipulation could be easily frustrated if one simply refused, as many slaves did, to acknowledge or take notice of it. Thus they turned to the public spectacles of whippings and other punishments to make their point. These open displays of brutality were intended as a warning to slaves who constantly ignored or resisted their owners' demands. From the earliest times, slaves had proved to be a "troublesome property." Consequently, slave-holders' claims to absolute social power were widely known to be a pretense invented to reinforce the faltering image of the slave system.[5]

Slaveowners knew that their directions would be, at best, only partially followed. Complete acquiescence was rarely expected even if it was constantly demanded. Only tasks performed close at hand—say, inside the Big House or in its adjacent yard, where slaves could be carefully watched—were certain to be completed according to their masters' wishes or even done at all. Even then slaves might follow their own schemes. The goings-on in the slave quarters, on the other hand, were always, from the master's point of view, mysterious and seemingly charged with mischief. South Carolina planter James Henry Hammond was so perplexed by his slaves' behavior that he accused them of maintaining a "system of roguery."[6] Deviations from the slaveowners' desired routines were so commonplace, argues historian John W. Blassingame, that they were only able to maintain their sense of command by being "selectively inattentive to rules infractions."[7] Slaveholders who owned hundreds of slaves—those masters who had to be most concerned about maintaining slave discipline—in fact undercut their ability to be completely in charge by assigning their bond servants to marginal locations beyond immediate scrutiny. They then had to depend on overseers, a bothersome solution that was generally found wanting. Out in the field quarters, slaves were unwittingly provided with residential contexts in which they could be relatively free from their masters' constant intrusion, a condition that encouraged slaves' hopes for greater autonomy, if not for liberty itself.

A feeling of autonomy was usually more pronounced on plantations worked by large groups of slaves, groups large enough to foster a sense of community. This feeling was so strong among the 174 slaves at Silver Bluff plantation in South Carolina that even at the conclusion of the Civil War they preferred to remain on the estate as a group rather than go their separate ways as individuals; in fact, they refused to leave.[8] Communities like this one seem to have drawn their coherence from the deep wellspring of a shared African American culture and its inventory of expressive forms. However, among the many distinctive behaviors credited to slaves, the creation of their own residential domains has been an achievement that has consistently been overlooked. Leslie Howard Owens, one of the few scholars to recognize that a vigorous slave culture was necessarily tied to a readily identifiable slave space, explains that "the Quarters, sometimes partially, sometimes entirely, and often mysteriously, encompassed and breathed its own special vitality into these experiences, frequently assuring that bondage did not snuff out the many-sided existence slaves created for themselves."[9]

Slaves overturned the logic that their owners used to place themselves well up in the social landscape. Employing mainly behavioral strategies, slaves privately remapped the domains designed by planters, reconceptualizing their various assigned landscapes in ways that they found more suitable. Ignoring the obvious symbols of supremacy that slaveowners had impressed on the land, slaves focused instead on their own sense of self-worth. Some slaves clearly recognized that their masters' fortunes were unquestionably dependent on their labor and their achievements, as revealed in the testimony of a South Carolina woman known as Aunt Phyllis. Although she was confined to her bed by illness at the time that she was interviewed, one question provoked her to sit up suddenly with great indignation. When asked where her former owner got the money to build his new house, she pushed up her sleeve, pointed to her arm and exclaimed, "You see dat . . . ? Dat's whar he got he money—out o' dat black skin he got he money." [10]

In the quarters, slaves looked to their cabins, even if they were meager or decrepit, as the centers of their own domains, and they did what they could to transform these buildings into homes. The plots of ground where they were allowed to raise the food and livestock that sustained their families were also highly valued. Other buildings, such as dining halls, hospitals, and churches, that were intended to promote the slaves' well-being were also enfolded into a slave community, whereas the fields and farm buildings, but most especially their owner's house, were relegated to the margins of the slave domain. For slaves these places generally held negative connotations. The hinterland surrounding a planter's estate, on the other hand, symbolized liberty, and slaves developed a detailed knowledge of its features so they could run away to it, either to find temporary refuge from abusive treatment or, in some cases, to escape captivity entirely. [11] According to Frederick Douglass, the woods surrounding a plantation provided effective cover for rebellious acts: "crimes, high-handed and attrocious," that "could be committed there with strange and shocking impunity." [12]

Whereas slaveowners designed their plantations so that all of their features would refer inwardly toward themselves, slaves used subtle behavioral means to structure alternative landscapes with different spatial imperatives. They would simply ignore the ritual obeisance of a plantation's carefully marked "processional landscape" and move across its fields, gardens, and grounds more or less as they pleased. They took shortcuts across lawns and through gardens and entered parlors and bedrooms without always asking permission. Because they were seen as part of the inventory of an estate, they were expected to be everywhere and thus did not have to adhere to the scripted movements the planters expected of visitors. Because slaves were, while within a plantation's boundaries, free to move about pretty much as they pleased, they soon realized that they had privileges of access that were denied to white visitors. They eventually used this level of access to inscribe plantations with their own meanings and associations. Because discrete slave domains were, for the most part, established beyond the slaveholders' immediate sight and in ways that did not obviously rearrange their hierarchical schemes, such places could be easily and reassuringly dismissed. Thus the planters' sense of control over their slaves remained, in theory, unchallenged—but only in theory.

Apparently inspired by the protective sense of place that they experienced in their quarters communities, some slaves asserted even bolder claims over the fields, livestock, and various work buildings belonging to their masters, using gestures of appropriation calculated to surprise, and even disturb, their owners. Such assertions might have alerted some planters that their slaves actually possessed a keen understanding of the rules they were using to determine status, rank, and prestige. Slaves found, like any worker might, that the skillful completion of assigned tasks could be very satisfying. Many of them developed a strong sense of personal worth, confident that respectability could be achieved by working well. Slave artisans, numbering roughly 10 percent of all bond servants, were particularly mindful of the fact that their skills assured them a certain level of social power. British traveler Charles Lyell noted this at a Georgia rice plantation, where he observed that, when the slave carpenters conversed with their owner, "their manner of speaking to him is quite as independent as that of English artisans to their employers."[13]

One detects a similar confidence in John Hemmings, one of Thomas Jefferson's slave carpenters. Hemmings had prolonged his stay at a neighboring plantation, where he was engaged in a demanding series of repairs. Jefferson wanted him back at Monticello, but Hemmings deflected his demand, writing at the end of a lengthy description of the work that he was doing simply: "I hope by the nex to Let you no when I shul finech and when to send for me."[14] In other words, he told Jefferson, "I'll be back when *I'm* ready." Because work done well confers a sense of achievement, it was but a simple step for a diligent slave to claim a well-plowed field as hers or a well-packed bale as his. Personal pride was converted into a pride of place. Because the actual ownership of a sizable estate by an African American was highly unlikely (although it did occur in a few cases), the claim to fictional ownership was a reasonable ploy.[15] It not only provided slaves with a safe way to oppose their masters' control over their lives, but it also gave them a means by which to compensate psychologically for the litany of indignities they were often forced to endure. One Georgia slave woman, when asked if she was owned by a particular family, responded without hesitation, "Yes, I belong to them and they belong to me."[16] Wherever a strong sense of community was in place among slaves, they could turn the tables on their owners almost without the owners' knowing it.

Slaves, however, must have keenly sensed that their claims to autonomy were tenuous and likely to be shattered at any moment by an expected, yet unpredictable, violent outburst. John Glover, a former slave from Timmonsville, South Carolina, characterized his master, Elijah Carson, as a very kind man and yet could recall the sadistic tortures that Carson used to keep his slaves in line: "Some of de time, dey put em in de screw box what dey press bales of cotton wid. Put em in dere en run press right down whe' can crush en dey couldn' move till dey take em out in the mornin en whip em en put em back to work."[17] Viewed in the context of such cruelty, attempts by slaves to define their own territories take on an even more heroic dimension.

Closer to the Big House, slave claims to territory were made less often and usually as individual rather than collective acts. The master's house was unquestionably seen as his or hers, even if some of its back or basement rooms were set aside for slaves. Because the outbuildings located near the main house were frequently designed, painted, or otherwise decorated in a manner that complimented the main house, they too were seen as immediate extensions of the master's space. In much the same way that these dependencies were tied to the Big House, the slaves who worked at the master's house were also blended into the household. One Georgia slaveholder went so far as to suggest that domestic slaves should develop a special visual demeanor that he labeled a "house look."[18] Not only was there little room within the confines of the Big House or its grounds for slaves to carve out spaces of their own, but the desire among house slaves to have their own space was less insistent. According to the testimony of former slaves, field hands were considerably more rebellious, being twice as likely as house servants to run away and four times more likely to have a verbal confrontation with their master or mistress.[19]

The familiarity between planters and their house slaves could, however, breed contempt as easily as sincere regard. Louisiana plantation mistress Clarissa Town complained that she had no influence over her house servants, writing, "When I reprimand them, they only say they don't mean to do anything wrong, or they wont do it again, all the time laughing as though it were all a joke."[20] Other house slaves responded more directly with acts of terror and mayhem. A North Carolina slave, for example, poisoned her master, mistress, and two others living in the household. Arson was another terrorist option employed by slaves, and many cases are reported from all over the South.[21] If they could not abide the strict regimen of around-the-clock service, house slaves could oppose their owners with acts of individual defiance: sassing, running away, theft, assault, suicide. A slave's claim over the kitchen, the laundry, or some other outbuilding should be seen as yet another means of personal resistance. If the grounds adjacent to the Big House contained numerous work buildings, as was the case on the manorial estates in Tidewater Virginia, the slaves living or working near their owner might collectively lay claim to those spaces as their own. However, the creation of an alternate society equipped with the spatial means to buffer the oppression of slavery remained chiefly the prerogative of the quarters communities of field hands. Usually house servants were too few in number and were kept too close to their owners to be able to create discrete, separate places for themselves.

Throughout the South, within the world the slaveholders made, there were sizable slave communities: places in which slaves had a sense, however fleeting, of security and protection. It is important to remember that in 1860 there were over 46,000 plantations run with the labor of at least twenty slaves; that over 11,000 of them were run with more than fifty slaves; and that almost 2,300 planters owned more than one hundred slaves. Within a typical southern county, there might be one large plantation surrounded by a network of several smaller estates. This pattern gave rise not only to a slave community within a given plantation's fence lines, but also to a much larger one that included people living miles apart.

Given their even spatial distribution across large segments of the South, plantations served as the meeting grounds where a regional African American identity was formed. On special occasions, many slaves from neighboring farms and villages would visit the prominent plantations, their numbers doubling or tripling, for the moment, the size of the resident slave community. Green Cumby, a former Texas slave, recalled the annual corn shuckings at which "all de marsters and dere black boys from plantations from miles 'round would be dar."[22] At similar events, Tanner Spikes remembered, "they put the corn in long piles and called the folkes from the plantations nigh round to shuck it. Sometimes four or five hunnert head of niggers 'ud be shukin corn at one time . . . . We started shuckin' corn 'bout dinnertime and tried to finish by sundown so we could have the whole night for frolic. Some years we 'ud go to ten or twelve corn shuckins in one year."[23] Slaves found in such activities more than an evening's worth of celebration. Through such routine festivities they were also able to forge the crucial social bonds needed to maintain families, friendships, and racial solidarity.

At the center of the slaves' plantation landscapes was the black family, an extensive social unit understood to contain a large assortment of kin, both biological and fictive. Indeed, quarters communities had been created, in large measure, to provide spaces where black families could be established and nurtured. So important was the family that, if it was threatened by a planter's exercise of power, slaves were sure to resist.[24] Because owners frequently threatened to break up families as a way to force their slaves to comply with their demands, the slaves developed a large repertoire of protest tactics to oppose them, on this as well as on other matters. Their forms of day-to-day resistance included: feigned sickness, shirking, foot dragging, feigned ignorance, stealing, lying, sabotage, deception, running away, and arson.[25] Slaves learned that the nuisance value of these actions would likely dissuade slaveholders from making good on most of their threats. Furthermore, because most of these strategies could be hidden behind a mask of seeming compliance, they provided relatively safe ways to oppose the brutality of inhumane masters and overseers.

These mundane forms of everyday resistance, "the weapons of the weak," are increasingly understood to be effective means of winning small skirmishes within the larger battles of class conflict. "These practices," writes anthropologist James C. Scott, "which rarely if ever called into question the system of slavery *as such*, nevertheless achieved far more in their unannounced, limited, and truculent way than the few heroic and brief armed uprisings about which so much has been written."[26] Frederick Douglass counseled that although resistance might be met with harsh penalties, it also promised significant rewards: "The doctrine that the submission to violence is the best cure for violence did not hold good as between slaves and overseers. He was whipped oftener who was whipped easiest. That slave who had the courage to stand up for himself against the overseer, although he might have many hard stripes at first, became while legally a slave virtually a free man."[27]

Slaves who claimed their masters' land as their own similarly found that it virtually *was* theirs. Acts of territorial appropriation were exceedingly clever because they were carried out, in the main, simply by the slaves' occupying the spaces to which they were assigned. Slaves gradually identified these spaces as theirs through a routine of innumerable domestic acts. Once the quarters were defined as a black place, further claims were made to other spaces and buildings such as fields, barns, and workshops. Their owner was unlikely to resist these assertions because the outbuildings were spaces that the slaves were supposed to occupy anyway, at least during the daylight hours. Thus, by steady increments, the official order set out by the planter on maps, documents, calenders, and schedules and expressed in the forms and locations of buildings, fields, fences, and roads was subtly but certainly turned aside.

Acts of landscape appropriation constituted an important means of day-to-day resistance with far-reaching consequences. In the process of laying claim to significant portions of their owners' land and buildings, slaves established defensible social boundaries for their communities in both pragmatic and symbolic terms. By 1860 planters had generally been induced into making significant concessions regarding work schedules and the physical treatment of their slaves. Moreover, the spaces that slaves claimed and modified for their own domestic purposes provided them with their own sense of place. In these locations they were able to develop a stronger sense of social solidarity, a feeling of community that would serve as a seedbed not only for further resistance but also for the invention and maintenance of a distinctive African American culture.

# Notes

## PREFACE

1. Leon F. Litwack, *Been in the Storm So Long: The Aftermath of Slavery* (New York: Alfred A. Knopf, 1979), pp. 307, 208; Claude F. Oubre, *Forty Acres and a Mule: The Freedmen's Bureau and Black Land Ownership* (Baton Rouge: Louisiana State University Press, 1978), p. 53; Eric Foner, *Nothing But Freedom: Emancipation and Its Legacy* (Baton Rouge: Louisiana State University Press, 1983), p. 82.

2. Quoted in Eric Foner, *Reconstruction: America's Unfinished Revolution: 1863–1877* (New York: Harper and Row, 1988), p. 105.

3. Quoted in Eugene D. Genovese, *Roll, Jordan, Roll: The World the Slaves Made* (New York: Random House, 1972), p. 137.

4. Charles Joyner, *Down by the Riverside: A South Carolina Slave Community* (Urbana: University of Illinois Press, 1984), pp. 42–43.

5. Julia Floyd Smith, *Slavery and Rice Culture in Low Country Georgia, 1750–1860* (Knoxville: University of Tennessee Press, 1985), p. 33.

6. Rhys Isaac, *The Transformation of Virginia, 1740–1790* (Chapel Hill: University of North Carolina Press, 1982), p. 53.

7. See Charles E. Peterson, "Memo to the National Park Service, 1933," *Journal of the Society of Architectural Historians* 16, no. 3 (1957): 30 (emphasis added).

8. All quotes, even those rendered in obviously caricatured versions of black dialect, have been quoted exactly as they appear in their original sources. In so doing, I follow the advice of historian Lawrence W. Levine, who writes, "Any attempt to standardize [dialect spellings of black English] into some ideal form of Afro-American dialect would have the effect of distorting it even more, since there was no standard black dialect covering all sections of the country and all periods from the antebellum South through the 1940s" (*Black Culture and Black Consciousness: Afro-American Folk Thought from Slavery to Freedom* [New York: Oxford University Press, 1977], pp. xv–xvi).

9. C. Vann Woodward, *American Counterpoint: Slavery and Racism in the North-South Dialogue* (Boston: Little, Brown, 1971), pp. 5–6.

## CHAPTER ONE

1. Edmund S. Morgan, *American Slavery, American Freedom: The Ordeal of Colonial Virginia* (New York: W. W. Norton, 1975), p. 94.

2. Quoted in Rhys Isaac, *The Transformation of Virginia, 1740–1790* (Chapel Hill: University of North Carolina Press, 1982), p. 33.

3. Quoted in Morgan, *American Slavery, American Freedom*, p. 220.

4. John R. Stilgoe, *Common Landscape of America, 1580 to 1845* (New Haven, Conn.: Yale University Press, 1982), pp. 75–76.

5. Louis B. Wright, *The First Gentlemen of Virginia: Intellectual Qualities of the Early Colonial Ruling Class* (San Marino, Calif.: The Huntington Library, 1940), pp. 158, 190, 286, 346.

6. Thomas Tileston Waterman, *The Mansions of Virginia, 1706–1776* (Chapel Hill: University of North Carolina Press, 1946), pp. 22–25; Nicholas Luccketti, "Archaeological Excavations at Bacon's Castle, Surry County, Virginia," in William M. Kelso and Rachel Most, eds., *Earth Patterns: Essays in Landscape Archaeology* (Charlottesville: University Press of Virginia, 1990), pp. 24, 27, 32, 35.

7. W. G. Hoskins, *The Making of the English Landscape* (London: Pelican, 1970), pp. 167, 170.

8. Gregory A. Stiverson and Patrick H. Butler III, eds., "Virginia in 1732: The Travel Journal of William Hugh Grove," *Virginia Magazine of History and Biography* 85 (1977): 26.

9. Louis Morton, *Robert Carter of Nomini Hall: A Virginia Tobacco Planter of the Eighteenth Century* (Williamsburg, Va.: Colonial Williamsburg, Inc., 1941), p. 207, n. 4.

10. Wright, *First Gentlemen of Virginia*, p. 330.

11. Waterman, *Mansions of Virginia*, pp. 108–9.

12. Quoted in Anne Leighton, *"For Use or for Delight": American Gardens in the Eighteenth Century* (Boston: Houghton Mifflin, 1976), p. 269; see also Clement Eaton, *The Growth of Southern Civilization, 1790–1860* (New York: Harper and Row, 1966), pp. 3–4.

13. Samuel Gaillard Stoney, *Plantations of the Carolina Low Country* (Charleston: South Carolina Art Association, 1955), pp. 59, 61–62, 119, 170–75.

14. Dell Upton, "White and Black Landscapes in Eighteenth-Century Virginia," *Places* 2, no. 2 (1985): 66.

15. Fraser D. Neiman, "Domestic Architecture at the Clifts Plantation: The Social Context of Early Virginia Building," in Dell Upton and John Michael Vlach, eds., *Common Places: Readings in American Vernacular Architecture* (Athens: University of Georgia Press, 1986), p. 311.

16. Roger G. Kennedy, *Greek Revival America* (New York: Stewart, Tabori, and Chang, 1989), p. 286.

17. Eugene L. Schwaab, ed., *Travels in the Old South Selected from Periodicals of the Times* (Lexington: University Press of Kentucky, 1973), 2:292, 295.

18. Quoted in Eaton, *Growth of South Civilization*, pp. 122–23.

19. John Burkhardt Rehder, "Sugar Plantation Settlements of Southern Louisiana: A Cultural Geography," Ph.D. diss., Louisiana State University, 1971, pp. 84–86, 100–103, 109; Schwaab, *Travels in the Old South*, 2:495.

20. Ulrich B. Phillips, *Life and Labor in the Old South* (Boston: Little, Brown, 1929), p. 339; John B. Boles, *Black Southerners, 1619–1869* (Lexington: University Press of Kentucky, 1983), p. 75.

21. Harold D. Woodman, ed., *Slavery and the Southern Economy: Sources and Readings* (New York: Harcourt, Brace and World, 1966), p. 15.

22. See Isaac, *Transformation of Virginia*, p. 21, for a discussion of figures on mid-eighteenth-century plantation ownership.

23. Upton, "White and Black Landscapes," p. 66.

24. Quoted in James C. Bonner, "Plantation Architecture of the Lower South on the Eve of the Civil War," *Journal of Southern History* 11 (1945): 372.

25. Ibid., p. 374.

26. Frederick Law Olmsted, *The Cotton Kingdom: A Traveller's Observations on Cotton and Slavery in the American Slave States*, edited by Arthur M. Schlesinger (New York: Alfred A. Knopf, 1953), p. 280.

27. The small plantation in northern Louisiana described by Olmsted can profitably be compared to the profile of a slaveowning farm in Yell County, Arkansas, detailed by John Solomon Otto in "Slaveholding General Farmers in a Cotton County," *Agricultural History* 55 (1981): 167–78.

28. Norman R. Yetman, ed., *Life Under the "Peculiar Institution": Selections from the Slave Narrative Collection* (New York: Holt, Rinehart, and Winston, 1970), pp. 61, 144.

29. Olmsted, *Cotton Kingdom*, p. 249. See also John Michael Vlach, "Plantation Landscapes of the Antebellum South," in Edward D. C. Campbell, Jr., and Kym S. Rice, eds., *Before Freedom Came: African-American Life in the Antebellum South* (Charlottesville: University Press of Virginia, 1991), p. 41, fig. 43.

30. Olmsted, *Cotton Kingdom*, p. 181.

31. Quoted in J. Carlyle Sitterson, *Sugar Country: The Cane Sugar Industry in the South, 1753–1950* (Lexington: University Press of Kentucky, 1953), p. 47.

32. Bonner, "Plantation Architecture of the Lower South," p. 375.

33. Boles, *Black Southerners*, p. 107.

34. George P. Rawick, ed., *The American Slave: A Composite Autobiography* (Westport, Conn.: Greenwood Press, 1972), 3 (pt. 4): 177, 15 (pt. 2): 364.

35. Yetman, *Life Under the "Peculiar Institution,"* p. 168.

36. See Vlach, "Plantation Landscapes of the Antebellum South," p. 28, fig. 30.

37. Dell Upton, "Imagining the Early Virginia Landscape," in Kelso and Most, *Earth Patterns*, p. 74.

38. Isaac, *Transformation of Virginia*, pp. 52–53.

39. J. L. Dillard, *Black English: Its History and Usage in the United States* (New York: Vintage, 1972); Eileen Southern, *The Music of Black Americans* (New York: W. W. Norton, 1971); Lynne Fauley Emery, *Black Dance in the United States from 1619 to 1970* (Palo Alto, Calif.: National Press Books, 1972).

40. See Mechal Sobel, *The World They Made Together: Black and White Values in Eighteenth-Century Virginia* (Princeton, N.J.: Princeton University Press, 1987), pp. 105, 109.

41. Quoted in Eugene D. Genovese, *Roll, Jordan, Roll: The World the Slaves Made* (New York: Random House, 1972), p. 534.

42. Charles Joyner, "The World of the Plantation Slaves," in Campbell and Rice, *Before Freedom Came*, p. 79, fig. 70.

43. Edward Kimber, "Observations in Several Voyages and Travels in America," *William and Mary Quarterly*, 1st ser., vol. 15 (1906–7): 148.

44. James O. Breeden, ed., *Advice among Masters: The Ideal of Slave Management in the Old South* (Westport, Conn.: Greenwood Press, 1980), p. 31.

45. See Herbert G. Gutman, *The Black Family in Slavery and Freedom, 1750–1925* (New York: Vintage, 1976); John Michael Vlach, *The Afro-American Tradition in Decorative Arts* (Cleveland, Ohio: Cleveland Museum of Art, 1978); Lawrence W. Levine, *Black Culture and Black Consciousness: Afro-American Folk Thought from Slavery to Freedom* (New York: Oxford University Press, 1977).

46. Frances Anne Kemble, *Journal of a Residence on a Georgian Plantation in 1838–39* [1863], edited by John A. Scott (Athens: University of Georgia Press, 1984), p. 63.

47. Philip D. Morgan, "The Ownership of Property by Slaves in the Mid-Nineteenth-Century Low Country," *Journal of Southern History* 49 (1983): 399–420.

48. Olmsted, *Cotton Kingdom*, p. 185.

49. Upton, "White and Black Landscapes," p. 70.

50. Elizabeth Fox-Genovese, *Within the Plantation*

Household: Black and White Women of the Old South (Chapel Hill: University of North Carolina Press, 1988), p. 142 (emphasis in original).

51. Charles Joyner, *Down by the Riverside: A South Carolina Slave Community* (Urbana: University of Illinois Press, 1984), pp. 42–43.

52. Genovese, *Roll, Jordan, Roll*, pp. 602–3.

## CHAPTER TWO

1. Eugene Genovese, *Roll, Jordan, Roll: The World the Slaves Made* (New York: Random House, 1972), p. 328.

2. Charles Joyner, *Down by the Riverside: A South Carolina Slave Community* (Urbana: University of Illinois Press, 1984), pp. 61, 81.

3. Quoted in C. W. Harper, "Black Aristocrats: Domestic Servants on the Antebellum Plantation," *Phylon* 46 (June 1985): 128.

4. Elizabeth Fox-Genovese, *Within the Plantation Household: Black and White Women of the Old South* (Chapel Hill: University of North Carolina Press, 1988), pp. 137–38.

5. Genovese, *Roll, Jordan, Roll*, p. 337.

6. Norman R. Yetman, ed., *Life Under the "Peculiar Institution": Selections from the Slave Narrative Collection* (New York: Holt, Rinehart, and Winston, 1970), p. 312.

7. Joyner, *Down by the Riverside*, p. 84.

8. John Michael Vlach, "Afro-American Domestic Artifacts in Eighteenth-Century Virginia," *Material Culture* 19 (1987): 6, 10.

9. Yetman, *Life Under the "Peculiar Institution,"* p. 66.

10. George P. Rawick, Jay Hillegas, and Ken Lawrence, eds., *The American Slave: A Composite Autobiography*, supp. ser. 1 (Westport, Conn.: Greenwood Press, 1977), 12: 109.

11. Yetman, *Life Under the "Peculiar Institution,"* p. 307.

12. See Dell Upton, "White and Black Landscapes in Eighteenth-Century Virginia," *Places* 2, no. 2 (1985): 59, 62.

13. Samuel Gaillard Stoney, *Plantations of the Carolina Low Country* (Charleston: South Carolina Art Association, 1955), pp. 82–83.

14. See John Linley, *The Georgia Catalog: Historic American Buildings Survey—a Guide to the Architecture of the State* (Athens: University of Georgia Press, 1982), pp. 72–73.

15. For other versions of the southern double-pen house, see Henry Glassie, *Pattern in the Material Folk Culture in the Eastern United States* (Philadelphia: University of Pennsylvania Press, 1968), pp. 101–6.

16. This residential pattern was employed at the Stagville plantation seven miles north of Durham, North Carolina, in a row of four two-story slave houses built in 1851.

17. For the creole cottage, see Fred B. Kniffen, "Louisiana House Types," reprinted in Philip L. Wagner and Marvin W. Mikesell, eds., *Readings in Cultural Geography* (Chicago: University of Chicago Press, 1969), pp. 159, 160 (fig. 3), 163 (fig. 13); and Kniffen's article, "Folk Housing: Key to Diffusion," reprinted in Dell Upton and John Michael Vlach, eds., *Common Places: Readings in American Vernacular Architecture* (Athens: University of Georgia Press, 1986), p. 25. See also *The Buildings of Biloxi: An Architectural Survey* (Biloxi, Miss.: City of Biloxi, 1976), p. 123, for plans and elevations of the Vance House dependencies.

18. Robert Gamble, *The Alabama Catalog: Historic American Building Survey, a Guide to the Early Architecture in the South* (University: University of Alabama Press, 1987), p. 237, suggests that Gracey's house was patterned after Waldwic Cottage, the plan of which was published in *The Architect* in 1851.

19. See David C. Driskell, *Two Centuries of Black American Art* (New York: Alfred A. Knopf, 1976), p. 28.

20. Susan Denyer, *African Traditional Architecture* (New York: Africana Publishing, 1978), pp. 42–46, 61, 74–90.

21. Richard T. Couture, *Powhatan: A Bicentennial History* (Berryville, Va.: Virginia Book Company, 1980), pp. 111–18.

## CHAPTER THREE

1. George P. Rawick, Jay Hillegas, and Ken Lawrence, eds., *The American Slave: A Composite Autobiography*, supp. ser. 1 (Westport, Conn.: Greenwood Press, 1977), 12: 283.

2. Quoted in Kate Mason Rowland, *The Life of George Mason, 1725–1792* (New York: G. P. Putnam's Sons, 1892), 1:99.

3. Cited in Dell Upton, "White and Black Landscapes in Eighteenth-Century Virginia," *Places* 2, no. 2 (1985): 70.

4. Norman R. Yetman, ed., *Life Under the "Peculiar Institution": Selections from the Slave Narrative Collection* (New York: Holt, Rinehart, and Winston, 1970), p. 200.

5. Rawick, Hillegas, and Lawrence, *The American Slave*, supp. ser. 1, 2:231–32.

6. Ibid., 3 (pt. 1): 101.

7. Charles L. Perdue, Jr., Thomas E. Barden, and Robert K. Phillips, eds., *Weevils in the Wheat: Interviews with Virginia Ex-Slaves* (Charlottesville: University Press of Virginia, 1976), p. 105.

8. Rawick, Hillegas, and Lawrence, *The American Slave*, supp. ser. 1, 9:1655–56.

9. Ibid., 8:1195.

10. Yetman, *Life Under the "Peculiar Institution,"* p. 264.

11. For another example of a well operated by a sweep, see the HABS files on the Cliatt plantation near Cottonton in Russell County, Alabama.

12. For other examples of Louisiana cisterns, albeit urban ones, see Samuel Wilson, Jr., and Bernard Lemann, *New Orleans Architecture,* vol. 1, *The Lower Garden District* (Gretna, La.: Pelican Publishing Co., 1971), pp. 37, 77. Many of the plans included in this volume indicate the presence of cisterns.

**CHAPTER FOUR**

1. Quoted in Mechal Sobel, *The World They Made Together: Black and White Values in Eighteenth-Century Virginia* (Princeton, N.J.: Princeton University Press, 1987), p. 121.

2. Fraser D. Neiman, "Domestic Architecture at the Clifts Plantation: The Social Context of Early Virginia Building," in Dell Upton and John Michael Vlach, eds., *Common Places: Readings in American Vernacular Architecture* (Athens: University of Georgia Press, 1986), p. 308.

3. For more on the architecture of segregation, see two articles by Cary Carson: "Segregation in Vernacular Buildings," *Vernacular Architecture* 7 (1976): 24–29, esp. p. 28; and "Doing History with Material Culture," in Ian M. G. Quimby, ed., *Material Culture and the Study of American Life* (New York: W. W. Norton, 1978), pp. 41–64, esp. pp. 52–54.

4. Robert Q. Mallard, *Plantation Life before Emancipation* (1892; reprint, Detroit: Negro History Press, 1969), p. 17.

5. George P. Rawick, ed., *The American Slave: A Composite Autobiography* (Westport, Conn.: Greenwood Press, 1972), 12 (pt. 1): 255.

6. Mallard, *Plantation Life,* p. 18.

7. For a detailed account of hole-set post buildings in the South, see Cary Carson, Norma F. Barka, William M. Kelso, Gary Wheeler Stone, and Dell Upton, "Impermanent Architecture in the Southern Colonies," *Winterthur Portfolio* 16 (1981): 135–96. The smoke bay is a feature with medieval antecedents, and its survival in a nineteenth-century American building is nothing short of remarkable; see Margaret Wood, *The English Mediaeval House* (New York: Harper and Row, 1965), pp. 258–59.

8. Henry Glassie, "The Types of the Southern Mountain Cabin," in Jan Harold Brunvand, *The Study of American Folklore: An Introduction* (New York: W. W. Norton, 1986), pp. 535–37.

9. See Howard W. Marshall, "Dog Trot Comfort: A Note on Traditional Houses and Energy Efficiency," in *Festival of American Folklife Program Book* (Washington, D.C.: Smithsonian Institution, 1980), pp. 29–31, for a discussion of the cooling effects of the breezeway through a dogtrot house.

10. George P. Rawick, Jay Hillegas, and Ken Lawrence, eds., *The American Slave: A Composite Autobiography,* supp. ser. 1 (Westport, Conn.: Greenwood Press, 1977), 8 (pt. 3): 1193.

11. For further examples of semidetached southern kitchens, see Henry Glassie, *Pattern in the Material Folk Culture of the Eastern United States* (Philadelphia: University of Pennsylvania Press, 1968), pp. 105–6.

12. *Arlington House* (Washington, D.C.: U.S. Department of the Interior, 1985), pp. 14–15, 24–25; see also Murray Nelligan, "The Building of Arlington House," *Journal of the Society of Architectural Historians* 10, no. 2 (1951): 11–15. On the social distance between house servants and field hands, see C. W. Harper, "House Servants and Field Hands: Fragmentation in the Antebellum Slave Community," *North Carolina Historical Review* 55 (1978): 42–59.

13. Rawick, Hillegas, and Lawrence, *The American Slave,* supp. ser. 1, 3 (pt. 1): 179.

14. Rawick, *The American Slave,* 12 (pt. 1): 255.

15. Norman R. Yetman, ed., *Life Under the "Peculiar Institution": Selections from the Slave Narrative Collection* (New York: Holt, Rinehart, and Winston, 1970), p. 265.

**CHAPTER FIVE**

1. Quoted in Sam Bowers Hilliard, *Hog Meat and Hoecake: Food Supply in the Old South, 1840–1860* (Carbondale: Southern Illinois University Press, 1972), p. 43.

2. Ibid., p. 42.

3. Ibid., p. 92.

4. Ibid., pp. 111, 105. See also Frederick Law Olmsted, *The Cotton Kingdom: A Traveller's Observations on Cotton and Slavery in the American Slave States,* edited by Arthur Schlesinger (New York: Alfred A. Knopf, 1953), p. 447; *Twelve Years a Slave: Narrative of Solomon Northrup,* in Gilbert Osofsky, ed., *Puttin' On Ole Massa* (New York: Harper and Row, 1969), p. 316.

5. George P. Rawick, Jay Hillegas, and Ken Lawrence, eds., *The American Slave: A Composite Autobiography,* supp. ser. 1 (Westport, Conn.: Greenwood Press, 1977), 2:216.

6. Charles Joyner, *Down by the Riverside: A South Carolina Slave Community* (Urbana: University of Illinois Press, 1984), p. 52.

7. Drew Gilpin Faust, "Culture, Conflict, and Community: The Meaning of Power on an Ante-bellum Plantation," *Journal of Social History* 14, no. 1 (1980): 88.

8. Eugene D. Genovese, *Roll, Jordan, Roll: The World the Slaves Made* (New York: Random House, 1972), pp. 599–604.

9. John W. Blassingame, ed., *Slave Testimony: Two Centuries of Letters, Speeches, Interviews, and Autobiographies* (Baton Rouge: Louisiana State University Press, 1977), p. 652.

10. *Narrative of William Wells Brown*, in Osofsky, *Puttin' On Ole Massa*, p. 184.

11. Rawick, Hillegas, and Lawrence, *The American Slave*, supp. ser. 1, 11:54.

12. James Oakes, *The Ruling Race: A History of American Slaveholders* (New York: Alfred A. Knopf, 1982), p. 53.

13. Quoted in Leon Litwack, *Been in the Storm So Long: The Aftermath of Slavery* (New York: Alfred A. Knopf, 1979), p. 112.

14. See Howard Wight Marshall, *Folk Architecture in Little Dixie: A Regional Culture in Missouri* (Columbia: University of Missouri Press, 1981), pp. 5–6, for a discussion of western migration of Virginia planters.

15. See Dell Upton, "Traditional Timber Framing," in Brooke Hindle, ed., *Material Culture of the Wooden Age* (Tarrytown, N.Y.: Sleepy Hollow Press, 1981), pp. 51–61.

16. Henry Glassie, *Pattern in the Material Folk Culture of the Eastern United States* (Philadelphia: University of Pennsylvania Press, 1968), p. 9. See also Donald A. Hutslar, *The Log Architecture of Ohio* (Columbus: Ohio Historical Society, 1972), p. 49; Terry G. Jordan, *Texas Log Buildings: A Folk Architecture* (Austin: University of Texas Press, 1978), pp. 177–79; Norbert F. Riedl, Donald B. Ball, and Anthony P. Cavender, *A Survey of Traditional Architecture and Related Material Folk Culture Patterns in the Normandy Reservoir, Coffee County, Tennessee*, Report of Investigations No. 17 (Knoxville: University of Tennessee Press, 1976), pp. 224–29.

17. Howard Wight Marshall, "Meat Preservation on the Farm in Missouri's 'Little Dixie,'" *Journal of American Folklore* 92 (1979): 408–10.

18. George W. McDaniel, *Hearth and Home: Preserving a People's Culture* (Philadelphia: Temple University Press, 1982), p. 212.

19. Quoted in James C. Bonner, "Plantation Architecture of the Lower South on the Eve of the Civil War," *Journal of Southern History* 11 (1945): 373.

## CHAPTER SIX

1. Quoted in Ulrich B. Phillips, *Life and Labor in the Old South* (Boston: Little, Brown, 1929), p. 332.

2. Quoted in Elizabeth Fox-Genovese, *Within the Plantation Household: Black and White Women of the Old South* (Chapel Hill: University of North Carolina Press, 1988), p. 105.

3. Benjamin H. Latrobe, *The Journal of Latrobe* (New York: D. Appleton, 1905), p. 23.

4. Henry Glassie, *Folk Housing in Middle Virginia: A Structural Analysis of Historic Artifacts* (Knoxville: University of Tennessee Press, 1975), p. 144. See also Henry Chandlee Forman, *Tidewater Maryland Architecture and Gardens* (New York: Architectural Book Publishing Co., 1956), p. 18, for a plan of Burley Manor, a nineteenth-century plantation on Maryland's Eastern Shore. Consult as well Forman's *Old Buildings, Gardens, and Furniture in Tidewater Maryland* (Cambridge, Md.: Tidewater Publishers, 1967), p. 61.

5. Dell Upton, "White and Black Landscapes in Eighteenth-Century Virginia," *Places* 2, no. 2 (1985): 59, 64. See also Jessie Thompson Krussen, "Tuckahoe Plantation," *Winterthur Portfolio* 11 (1976): 121, fig. 18.

6. Camille Wells, "The Eighteenth-Century Landscape of Virginia's Northern Neck," *Northern Neck of Virginia Historical Magazine* 37 (1987): 4232. For examples of dairies in an urban context, see *Legacy from the Past: A Portfolio of Eighty-eight Original Williamsburg Buildings* (Williamsburg, Va.: Colonial Williamsburg Foundation, 1971), pp. 53–56. For early dairies, see Cary Carson, Norman F. Barka, William M. Kelso, Gary Wheeler Stone, and Dell Upton, "Impermanent Architecture in the Southern American Colonies," *Winterthur Portfolio* 16 (1981): 180, 185.

7. John Martin Robinson, *Georgian Model Farms: A Study of Decorative and Model Farm Buildings in the Age of Improvement, 1700–1846* (London: Oxford University Press, 1983), p. 97.

8. George P. Rawick, Jay Hillegas, and Ken Lawrence, eds., *The American Slave: A Composite Autobiography*, supp. ser. 1 (Westport, Conn.: Greenwood Press, 1977), 1:157.

9. Forman, *Tidewater Maryland Architecture and Gardens*, pp. 67–68.

10. Sam Bowers Hilliard, *Hog Meat and Hoe Cake: Food Supply in the Old South, 1840–1860* (Carbondale: Southern Illinois University Press, 1972), pp. 132–33, 135.

11. For examples, see Norbert F. Riedl, Donald B. Ball, and Anthony P. Cavender, *A Survey of Traditional Architecture and Related Material Culture Patterns in the Normandy Reservoir, Coffee County, Tennessee*, Report of

Investigations No. 17 (Knoxville: University of Tennessee Press, 1976), pp. 245–46; Eric Sloane, *An Age of Barns* (New York: Ballantine Books, 1967), pp. 74–75; Amos Long, Jr., "Springs and Springhouses," *Pennsylvania Folklife* 11 (1960): 40–43; Henry Glassie, "Smaller Outbuildings of the Southern Mountains," *Mountain Life and Work* 40 (1964): 21–25; Henry Glassie, *Pattern in the Material Folk Culture of the Eastern United States* (Philadelphia: University of Pennsylvania Press, 1968), p. 10.

12. Rawick, Hillegas, and Lawrence, *The American Slave*, supp. ser. 1, 1:157.

13. Ibid., 5:296.

14. Cited in Joseph C. Jones, *America's Icemen: An Illustrative History of the United States Natural Ice Industry, 1665–1925* (Humble, Tex.: Jobeco Books, 1984), p. 75.

15. Ibid., pp. 75–76.

16. Richard O. Cummings, *The American Ice Harvests: A Historical Study in Technology, 1800–1918* (Berkeley: University of California Press, 1949), p. 2.

17. For the most elemental type of icehouse, a cave dug out of a hillside, see Forman, *Tidewater Maryland Architecture and Gardens*, p. 161, which shows Forman's sketch of the icehouse at Furley Hall on the outskirts of Baltimore.

18. Norman R. Yetman, ed., *Life Under the "Peculiar Institution": Selections from the Slave Narrative Collection* (New York: Holt, Rinehart, and Winston, 1970), p. 15.

19. Jones, *America's Icemen*, p. 123.

20. Hilliard, *Hog Meat and Hoe Cake*, p. 54, provides the menu for a meal served at the Alston plantation, Georgetown County, South Carolina, in 1832 that included a "high glass dish of ice cream."

21. Ibid., p. 144.

22. Cited in ibid., p. 147.

23. Jack P. Greene, ed., *The Diary of Colonel Landon Carter of Sabine Hall, 1752–1778* (Charlottesville: University Press of Virginia, 1966), 1:484.

24. Frances Anne Kemble, *Journal of a Residence on a Georgian Plantation in 1838–1839* [1863], edited by John A. Scott (Athens: University of Georgia Press, 1984), p. 83.

25. Rawick, Hillegas, and Lawrence, *The American Slave*, supp. ser. 1, 1:296–97.

26. John Linley, *The Georgia Catalog: Historic American Buildings Survey—a Guide to the Architecture of the State* (Athens: University of Georgia Press, 1982), p. 171.

27. Frederick Law Olmsted, *The Cotton Kingdom: A Traveller's Observations on Cotton and Slavery in the American Slave States*, edited by Arthur Schlesinger (New York: Alfred A. Knopf, 1953), p. 249.

28. Gerald W. Mullin, *Flight and Rebellion: Slave Resistance in Eighteenth-Century Virginia* (New York: Oxford

University Press, 1972), pp. 12, 10.

29. A. Lawrence Kocher and Howard Dearstyne, *Shadows in Silver: A Record of Virginia, 1850–1900, in Contemporary Photographs Taken by George and Huestis Cook with Additions from the Cook Collection* (New York: Charles Scribner's Sons, 1954), pp. 108–10.

30. Yetman, *Life Under the "Peculiar Institution,"* p. 15.

31. Ibid., p. 62.

32. "Inventory of the Estate of Landon Carter, February, 1779," Landon Carter Papers, Alderman Library, University of Virginia, Charlottesville.

33. George P. Rawick, ed., *The American Slave: A Composite Autobiography* (Westport, Conn.: Greenwood Press, 1972), 5 (pt. 4): 47.

34. Rawick, Hillegas, and Lawrence, *The American Slave*, supp. ser. 1, 7 (pt. 2): 602.

35. Greene, *Diary of Colonel Landon Carter*, 2:1043.

36. Olmsted, *Cotton Kingdom*, p. 187.

37. "Carter Papers," *Virginia Magazine of History and Biography* 7 (1899): 65. See also Wells, "Eighteenth-Century Landscape of Virginia's Northern Neck," pp. 4232–34.

38. J. Harold Easterby, Jr., ed., *The South Carolina Rice Plantation as Revealed in the Papers of Robert F. W. Allston* (Chicago: University of Chicago Press, 1945), p. 452; Charles Joyner, *Down by the Riverside: A South Carolina Slave Community* (Urbana: University of Illinois Press, 1984), p. 31.

39. Gary B. Mills, *The Forgotten People: Cane River's Creoles of Color* (Baton Rouge: Louisiana State University Press, 1977), p. 70.

40. W. Darrell Overdyke, *Louisiana Plantation Homes: Colonial and Ante-Bellum* (New York: Architectural Book Publishing Co., 1965).

41. Mills, *Forgotten People*, p. 132, illustrations between pp. 54 and 55, pp. 3–4.

42. Quoted in James C. Bonner, "Plantation Architecture of the Lower South on the Eve of the Civil War," *Journal of Southern History* 11 (1945): 381.

## CHAPTER SEVEN

1. Camille Wells, "The Eighteenth-Century Landscape of Virginia's Northern Neck," *Northern Neck of Virginia Historical Magazine* 37 (1987): 4234.

2. George P. Rawick, ed., *The American Slave: A Composite Autobiography* (Westport, Conn.: Greenwood Press, 1972), 6 (pt. 1): 385.

3. Fiske Kimball, "The Building of Bremo," *Virginia Magazine of History and Biography* 57 (1949): 5.

4. Randall M. Miller, ed., *"Dear Master": Letters of a Slave Family* (Ithaca, N.Y.: Cornell University Press, 1978), p. 25.

5. Lewis Cecil Gray, *History of Agriculture in the Southern United States to 1860* (Washington, D.C.: Carnegie Institution, 1933), 1:540.

6. Wells, "Eighteenth-Century Landscape of Virginia's Northern Neck," p. 4235.

7. The cultural antecedents for this practice may be found in the English countryside; see R. W. Brunskill, *Vernacular Architecture of the Lake Counties* (London: Faber and Faber, 1974), pp. 78–79.

8. Ulrich B. Phillips, ed., *Plantation and Frontier, 1649–1863* (New York: Burt Franklin, 1969), 1:252.

9. Cited in James C. Bonner, "Plantation Architecture of the Lower South on the Eve of the Civil War," *Journal of Southern History* 11 (1945): 373.

10. Norman R. Yetman, ed., *Life Under the "Peculiar Institution": Selections from the Slave Narrative Collection* (New York: Holt, Rinehart, and Winston, 1970), p. 9.

11. George P. Rawick, Jay Hillegas, and Ken Lawrence, eds., *The American Slave: A Composite Autobiography*, supp. ser. 1 (Westport, Conn.: Greenwood Press, 1977), 9:1857.

12. Yetman, *Life Under the "Peculiar Institution,"* p. 70.

13. Cited in Bonner, "Plantation Architecture of the Lower South," p. 373.

14. Quoted in Drury Blake Alexander, *Texas Homes of the Nineteenth Century* (Austin: University of Texas Press, 1966), p. 15.

15. Weymouth T. Jordan, *Hugh Davis and His Alabama Plantation* (1948; reprint, Westport, Conn.: Greenwood Press, 1974), p. 33.

16. Bonner, "Plantation Architecture of the Lower South," p. 371.

17. For more on granaries, see Bernard L. Herman, *Architecture and Rural Life in Central Delaware, 1700–1900* (Knoxville: University of Tennessee Press, 1987), pp. 70–73, 200–206.

18. Fred B. Kniffen, "Folk Housing: Key to Diffusion," in Dell Upton and John Michael Vlach, eds., *Common Places: Readings in American Vernacular Architecture* (Athens: University of Georgia Press, 1986), p. 17; see also Henry Glassie, "The Pennsylvania Barn in the South, Part 1," *Pennsylvania Folklife* 15, no. 2 (1965): 12–19.

19. Quoted in Bonner, "Plantation Architecture of the Lower South," p. 373.

20. Kniffen, "Folk Housing," p. 18; Henry Glassie, *Pattern in the Material Folk Culture of the Eastern United States* (Philadelphia: University of Pennsylvania Press, 1968), pp. 89–91; see also Howard Wight Marshall, *Folk Architecture in Little Dixie: Regional Culture in Missouri* (Columbia:

University of Missouri Press, 1981), pp. 78–81 for further discussion and illustration of the varieties of log barns in the Old South.

21. Charles H. Dornbusch and John K. Heyl, *Pennsylvania German Barns* (Allentown, Pa.: Pennsylvania German Folklore Society, 1958), pp. 25–27; Henry Glassie, "The Pennsylvania Barn in the South, Part 2," *Pennsylvania Folklife* 15, no. 4 (1966): 13.

22. See Herman, *Architecture and Rural Life in Central Delaware*, p. 214; Richard Rawson, *Old Barn Plans* (New York: Mayflower Books, 1979), p. 65.

23. Henry Glassie, "Eighteenth-Century Cultural Process in Delaware Valley Folk Building," in Upton and Vlach, *Common Places*, pp. 415–19.

24. See Jay Edwards, "French," in Dell Upton, ed., *America's Architectural Roots: Ethnic Groups That Built America* (Washington, D.C.: Preservation Press, 1986), pp. 62–67; Joseph Stany-Gauthier, *Le Maison Paysannes de Vielles Provinces de France* (Paris: Librairie Ch. Massin, 1944), p. 191; Max-André Brier and Pierre Brunet, *L'architecture Rurale Française: Normandie* (Paris: Berger-Levrault, 1984), pp. 214–15.

25. Margaret Davis Cate, *Early Days of Coastal Georgia* (St. Simons Island, Ga.: Fort Frederic Association, 1955), p. 65.

26. E. Merton Coulter, ed., *Georgia's Disputed Ruins* (Chapel Hill: University of North Carolina Press, 1937), pp. 128–31.

27. Malcolm Bell, Jr., *Major Butler's Legacy: Five Generations of a Slaveholding Family* (Athens: University of Georgia Press, 1987), p. 220.

28. T. H. Breen, "Horses and Gentlemen: The Cultural Significance of Gambling among the Gentry of Virginia," *William and Mary Quarterly* 34 (1977): 241.

29. Edmund Kirke, *Among the Pines* (New York: Carleton, 1862), p. 144.

30. Quoted in Virginia Meynard, *The Venturers: The Hampton, Harrison, and Earle Families of Virginia, South Carolina, and Texas* (Easley, S.C.: Southern History Press, 1981), p. 161.

31. Yetman, *Life under the "Peculiar Institution,"* p. 242.

32. Samuel Gaillard Stoney, *Plantations of the Carolina Low Country* (Charleston: South Carolina Art Association, 1955), pp. 63–64.

33. For other plans of horse barns, see William Radford, David Loveless, and Joan Loveless, *Practical Plans for Barns, Carriage Houses, Stables, and Other Country Buildings* (Stockbridge, Mass.: Berkshire Traveller Press, 1978), pp. 52–57.

34. Robert B. Lamb, *The Mule in Southern Agriculture* (Berkeley: University of California Press, 1963), p. 33.

35. Quoted in ibid., p. 26.

36. D. A. Tompkins, *Cotton and Cotton Oil* (Charlotte, N.C.: privately printed, 1901), 1:53; for more on mules, see Patti Carr Black, *Mules and Mississippi* (Jackson: Mississippi Department of Archives and History, 1981).

37. Yetman, *Life Under the "Peculiar Institution,"* p. 196.

CHAPTER EIGHT

1. Rhys Isaac, *The Transformation of Virginia, 1740–1790* (Chapel Hill: University of North Carolina Press, 1982), p. 27.

2. Nannie May Tilley, *The Bright Tobacco Industry, 1860–1929* (Chapel Hill: University of North Carolina Press, 1948), pp. 87–88. For an example of a nineteenth-century tobacco prize from Tracy's Landing in Calvert County, Maryland, see Orlando Ridout, "The Chesapeake Farm Building Survey," in Camille Wells, ed., *Perspectives in Vernacular Architecture* (Annapolis, Md.: Vernacular Architecture Forum, 1982), p. 141.

3. Lewis Cecil Gray, *History of Agriculture in the Southern United States to 1860* (Washington, D.C.: Carnegie Institution, 1933), 2:705.

4. George P. Rawick, Jay Hillegas, and Ken Lawrence, eds., *The American Slave: A Composite Autobiography*, supp. ser. 1 (Westport, Conn.: Greenwood Press, 1977), 9: 1439.

5. For an example of a cotton press outfitted with protective roofs, see Frances Benjamin Johnston, *The Early Architecture of North Carolina* (Chapel Hill: University of North Carolina Press, 1941), pp. 9, 11. This press, now located in Tarboro, North Carolina, originally stood on the Norfleet plantation in Edgecombe County.

6. Norman R. Yetman, ed., *Life Under the "Peculiar Institution": Selections from the Slave Narrative Collection* (New York: Holt, Rinehart, and Winston, 1970), pp. 40–41.

7. Frances Anne Kemble, *Journal of a Residence on a Georgian Plantation in 1838–1839* [1863], edited by John A. Scott (Athens: University of Georgia Press, 1984), p. 43.

8. Charles S. Aiken, "The Evolution of Cotton Ginning in the Southeastern United States," *Geographical Review* 63 (1973): 200–201.

9. Rawick, Hillegas, and Lawrence, *The American Slave*, supp. ser. 1, 6:259.

10. Ibid., 6:258–59.

11. Charles Joyner, *Down by the Riverside: A South Carolina Slave Community* (Urbana: University of Illinois Press, 1984), p. 48; see also Kemble, *Journal of a Residence on a Georgian Plantation*, pp. 109–10; "Sketches of the South Santee," in *American Monthly Magazine* (1836), reprinted in Eugene L. Schwaab, ed., *Travels in the Old South Selected from the Periodicals of the Time* (Lexington: University Press of Kentucky, 1973), 1:14, 16; and the painting by Alice Ravenel Huger Smith entitled *The Threshing Floor*, in the collection of the Gibbes Museum of Art, Charleston, South Carolina, reproduced as the frontispiece of *Folklife Annual 88–89* (Washington, D.C.: Library of Congress, 1989).

12. J. Harold Easterby, Jr., ed., *The South Carolina Rice Plantation as Revealed in the Papers of Robert F. W. Allston* (Chicago: University of Chicago Press, 1945), pp. 40, 321, 327; Herbert Anthony Keller, ed., *Solon Robinson: Pioneer and Agriculturist* (Indianapolis: Indiana Historical Bureau, 1936), 2:366.

13. Kemble, *Journal of a Residence on a Georgian Plantation*, p. 54.

14. Julia Floyd Smith, *Slavery and Rice Culture in Low Country Georgia, 1750–1860* (Knoxville: University of Tennessee Press, 1985), p. 35.

15. Quoted in Joyner, *Down by the Riverside*, p. 49.

16. Frederick Law Olmsted, *The Cotton Kingdom: A Traveller's Observations on Cotton and Slavery in the American Slave States*, edited by Arthur Schlesinger (New York: Alfred A. Knopf, 1953), p. 186.

17. Ibid., pp. 186–87.

18. David Doar, *Rice and Rice Planting in the South Carolina Low Country* (Charleston: The Charleston Museum, 1936), pp. 30–31.

19. Advertisement for the sale of Bellegrove, Donaldsonville, Iberville Parish, Louisiana, ca. 1867–68, The Historic New Orleans Collection Museum/Research Center, acc. no. 1970.13.1.

20. Quoted in J. Carlyle Sitterson, *Sugar Country: The Cane Sugar Industry in the South, 1753–1950* (Lexington: University Press of Kentucky, 1953), p. 47.

21. Ibid., p. 135.

22. Abner S. Strobel, "The Old Plantations and the Owners of Brazoria County, Texas," in T. L. Smith, Jr., ed., *History of Brazoria County, Texas* (Houston: n.p., 1958[?]), pp. 50–51. See also Allen A. Platter, "Educational, Social, and Economic Characteristics of the Plantation Culture of Brazoria County, Texas," Ph.D. diss., University of Houston, 1961, pp. 205–7.

Because the overwhelming majority of slaves in Texas were brought there from other regions of the United States, the slaves at Chenango were a very special group. How the other slaves in Brazoria County, who often were as many as six generations removed from their African origins, may have regarded the 170 Africans at Chenango is not known. But there may have been significant cultural differences that made the Chenango community an ethnic island within the county's larger black population—at least until word of emancipation reached Texas in 1865. See John Michael Vlach, "Black Craft Traditions in Texas: An Interpretation of Nineteenth-Century Skills," in John Michael Vlach, *By the Work of Their Hands: Studies in Afro-American Folklife* (Charlottesville: University Press of Virginia, 1991), pp. 95–96; Randolph B. Campbell, *An Empire for Slavery: The Peculiar Institution in Texas, 1821–1865* (Baton Rouge: Louisiana State University Press, 1989), p. 46.

**CHAPTER NINE**

1. William Kauffman Scarborough, *The Overseer: Plantation Management in the Old South* (1966; reprint, Athens: University of Georgia Press, 1984), p. 10.

2. Eugene D. Genovese, *Roll, Jordan, Roll: The World the Slaves Made* (New York: Random House, 1972), p. 21.

3. See the map of Hampton plantation in Frances Anne Kemble, *Journal of a Residence on a Georgian Plantation in 1838–1839* [1863], edited by John A. Scott (Athens: University of Georgia Press, 1984), p. 198.

4. See the map in John Solomon Otto, "Status Differences and the Archaeological Record—a Comparison of Planter, Overseer, and Slave Sites from Cannon's Point Plantation (1799–1861), St. Simon's Island," Ph.D. diss., University of Florida, 1975, p. 23.

5. Frederick Law Olmsted, *The Cotton Kingdom: A Traveller's Observations on Cotton and Slavery in the American Slave States*, edited by Arthur Schlesinger (New York: Alfred A. Knopf, 1953), p. 429.

6. A. Lawrence Kocher and Howard Dearstyne, *Shadows in Silver: A Record of Virginia, 1850–1900, in Contemporary Photographs Taken by George and Huestis Cook with Additions from the Cook Collection* (New York: Charles Scribner's Sons, 1954), pp. 108–9.

7. Robert Wormley Carter Diary, copy in the research library at Colonial Williamsburg, Williamsburg, Virginia.

8. J. F. D. Smyth, *Travels through the Interior Parts of America* (London: Wilane, 1789), 2:381–82.

9. Camille Wells, "The Eighteenth-Century Landscape of Virginia's Northern Neck," *Northern Neck of Virginia Historical Magazine* 37 (1987): 4236–38.

10. John Spencer Bassett, *The Southern Plantation Overseer as Revealed in His Letters* (Northampton, Mass.: Smith College, 1925), p. 262.

11. Scarborough, *The Overseer*, p. 11.

12. James O. Breeden, ed., *Advice among Masters: The Ideal in Slave Management in the Old South* (Westport, Conn.: Greenwood Press, 1980), p. 295.

13. Scarborough, *The Overseer*, p. 11.

14. James C. Bonner, "Profile of a Late Ante-Bellum Plantation," *American Historical Review* 44 (1949): 674.

15. Norman R. Yetman, ed., *Life Under the "Peculiar Institution": Selections from the Slave Narrative Collection* (New York: Holt, Rinehart, and Winston, 1970), p. 52.

16. Mechal Sobel, *The World They Made Together: Black and White Values in Eighteenth-Century Virginia* (Princeton, N.J.: Princeton University Press, 1987), p. 113, indicates that George Washington also provided the overseer at his Union Farm quarter with a one-room cabin that had a loft.

17. Catherine W. Bishir, *North Carolina Architecture* (Chapel Hill: University of North Carolina Press, 1990), p. 149.

18. George P. Rawick, ed., *The American Slave: A Composite Autobiography* (Westport, Conn.: Greenwood Press, 1972), 12 (pt. 1): 241.

19. Otto, "Status Differences and the Archaeological Record," pp. 113–15.

20. Kemble, *Journal of a Residence on a Georgian Plantation*, p. 64.

21. Genovese, *Roll, Jordan, Roll*, p. 366.

22. Cited in ibid., pp. 381–82.

23. William L. Van Deburg, *The Slave Drivers: Black Agricultural Labor Supervisors in the Antebellum South* (Westport, Conn.: Greenwood Press, 1979), p. 16; see also Kemble, *Journal of a Residence on a Georgian Plantation*, p. 79.

24. Van Deburg, *Slave Drivers*, p. 16.

**CHAPTER TEN**

1. Alfred H. Conrad and John R. Meyer, "Economics of Slavery in the Ante-Bellum South," in Harold D. Woodman, ed., *Slavery and the Southern Economy: Sources and Readings* (New York: Harcourt, Brace and World, 1966), p. 71.

2. Quoted in James O. Breeden, ed., *Advice among Masters: The Ideal in Slave Management in the Old South* (Westport, Conn.: Greenwood Press, 1980), pp. 163–64.

3. Eugene D. Genovese, *Roll, Jordan Roll: The World the Slaves Made* (New York: Random House, 1972), pp. 50–51.

4. George P. Rawick, Jay Hillegas, and Ken Lawrence, eds., *The American Slave: A Composite Autobiography*, supp. ser. 1 (Westport, Conn.: Greenwood Press, 1977), 1: 113–14.

5. Norman R. Yetman, ed., *Life Under the "Peculiar Institution": Selections from the Slave Narrative Collection* (New York: Holt, Rinehart, and Winston, 1970), p. 124.

6. Ibid. p. 104.

7. Charles Joyner, *Down by the Riverside: A South Carolina Slave Community* (Urbana: University of Illinois Press, 1984), pp. 35–37.

8. Quoted in Breeden, *Advice among Masters*, p. 164.

9. Frederick Law Olmsted, *The Cotton Kingdom: A Traveller's Observations on Cotton and Slavery in the American Slave States*, edited by Arthur Schlesinger (New York: Alfred A. Knopf, 1953), p. 181.

10. J. Harold Easterby, Jr., ed., *The South Carolina Rice Plantation as Revealed in the Papers of Robert F. W. Allston* (Chicago: University of Chicago Press, 1945), p. 448.

11. Herbert Anthony Keller, ed., *Solon Robinson: Pioneer and Agriculturist* (Indianapolis: Indiana Historical Bureau, 1936), 2:367.

12. Frances Anne Kemble, *Journal of a Residence on a Georgian Plantation in 1838–1839* [1863], edited by John A. Scott (Athens: University of Georgia Press, 1984), pp. 69–70.

13. Quoted in Julia Floyd Smith, *Slavery and Rice Culture in Low Country Georgia, 1750–1860* (Knoxville: University of Tennessee Press, 1985), p. 133.

14. Genovese, *Roll, Jordan, Roll*, pp. 202–9.

15. Yetman, *Life Under the "Peculiar Institution,"* pp. 12–13.

16. Quoted in Breeden, *Advice among Masters*, p. 236.

17. Drew Gilpin Faust, "Culture, Conflict, and Community: The Meaning of Power on an Ante-bellum Plantation," *Journal of Social History* 14, no. 1 (1980): 85.

18. Yetman, *Life Under the "Peculiar Institution,"* p. 337.

19. Albert J. Raboteau, *Slave Religion: The "Invisible Institution" in the Antebellum South* (New York: Oxford University Press, 1978), p. 155.

20. Quoted in Breeden, *Advice among Masters*, p. 234.

21. Smith, *Slavery and Rice Culture in Low Country Georgia*, p. 159; see also Erskine Clarke, *Wrestlin' Jacob: A Portrait of Religion in the Old South* (Atlanta, Ga.: John Knox Press, 1979), p. 61.

22. George C. Rogers, Jr., *The History of Georgetown County, South Carolina* (Columbia: University of South Carolina Press, 1970), p. 283.

23. This building compares closely with Georgia "praise houses." See Smith, *Slavery and Rice Culture in Low Country Georgia*, p. 160; for an example from Liberty County; Savannah Unit, Georgia Writers' Project, *Drums and Shadows: Survival Studies among the Georgia Coastal Negroes* (1940; reprint, Athens: University of Georgia Press, 1986), plate 18A, for an example from Sapelo Island, McIntosh County. For a glimpse of another slave chapel from South Carolina, which shows a short steeple extending from one of the buildings within a slave village, see the photograph of Friendfield plantation, Georgetown County, in Joyner, *Down by the Riverside*, facing p. 127.

24. Mary Boykin Chesnut, *A Diary from Dixie*, quoted in Raboteau, *Slave Religion*, pp. 221–22.

25. Quoted in Faust, "Culture, Conflict and Community," p. 85.

## CHAPTER ELEVEN

1. Letitia Burwell, *A Girl's Life in Virginia before the War* (New York: Frederick A. Stokes, 1895), p. 8.

2. Frederick Law Olmsted, *The Cotton Kingdom: A Traveller's Observations on Cotton and Slavery in the American Slave States*, edited by Arthur Schlesinger (New York: Alfred A. Knopf, 1953), p. 31.

3. Gerald W. Mullin, *Flight and Rebellion: Slave Resistance in Eighteenth-Century Virginia* (New York: Oxford University Press, 1972), p. 51; Cary Carson, "Doing History with Material Culture," in Ian M. G. Quimby, ed., *Material Culture and the Study of American Life* (New York: W. W. Norton, 1978), p. 53.; Fraser D. Neiman, "Domestic Architecture at the Clifts Plantation: The Social Context of Early Virginia Building," in Dell Upton and John Michael Vlach, eds., *Common Places: Readings in American Vernacular Architecture* (Athens: University of Georgia Press, 1986), p. 297.

4. Nieman, "Domestic Architecture at the Clifts Plantation," p. 308.

5. On the development of slavery in Virginia, see Edmund S. Morgan, *American Slavery, American Freedom: The Ordeal of Colonial Virginia* (New York: W. W. Norton, 1975), chap. 15.

6. Durand de Dauphine, *A Huguenot Exile in Virginia, or Voyages of a Frenchman Exiled for His Religion*, translated and edited by Gilbert Chinard (1687; reprint, New York: Press of the Pioneers, 1934), p. 120; see also Cary Carson, "The 'Virginia House' in Maryland," *Maryland Historical Society Magazine* 69 (1974): 185–96.

7. John Michael Vlach, "Afro-American Domestic Artifacts in Eighteenth-Century Virginia," *Material Culture* 19 (1987): 8.

8. Edward Kimber, "Observations in Several Voyages and Travels in America in the Year 1736," *William and Mary Quarterly*, 1st ser., vol. 15 (1906–7): 148.

9. On the earliest slave housing in South Carolina, see Leland Ferguson, *Uncommon Ground: Archaeology and Early African America, 1650–1800* (Washington, D.C.: Smithsonian Institution Press, 1992), pp. xxiii–xxxi, 63–82. On the colonial settlement of South Carolina, see Peter H. Wood, *Black Majority: Negroes in Colonial South Carolina*

*from 1670 through the Stono Rebellion* (New York: W. W. Norton, 1974), esp. chap. 5.

10. Olmsted, *Cotton Kingdom*, pp. 81, 161, 290.

11. Norman R. Yetman, ed., *Life Under the "Peculiar Institution": Selections from the Slave Narrative Collection* (New York: Holt, Rinehart, and Winston, 1970), pp. 168, 265, 124, 304.

12. For a similar house from Louisa County, Virginia, attributed to the mid-eighteenth century, see Henry Glassie, *Folk Housing in Middle Virginia: A Structural Analysis of Historic Artifacts* (Knoxville: University of Tennessee Press, 1975), pp. 84–85, 125, 126.

13. Joseph Ball to Joseph Chinn, April 23, 1754, Joseph Ball Letterbooks, Manuscript Division, Library of Congress. See also John Michael Vlach, "Afro-American Housing in Virginia's Landscape of Slavery," in John Michael Vlach, *By the Work of Their Hands: Studies in Afro-American Folklife* (Charlottesville: University Press of Virginia, 1991), p. 218.

14. James O. Breeden, ed., *Advice among Masters: The Ideal in Slave Management in the Old South* (Westport, Conn.: Greenwood Press, 1980), pp. 130, 137.

15. Yetman, *Life Under the "Peculiar Institution,"* p. 336.

16. George P. Rawick, ed., *The American Slave: A Composite Autobiography* (Westport, Conn.: Greenwood Press, 1972), 16 (Maryland section): 6, 26.

17. Dell Upton, "Vernacular Domestic Architecture in Eighteenth-Century Virginia," in Dell Upton and John Michael Vlach, eds., *Common Places: Readings in American Vernacular Architecture* (Athens: University of Georgia Press, 1986), p. 317.

18. Quoted in Julia Floyd Smith, *Slavery and Rice Culture in Low Country Georgia, 1750–1860* (Knoxville: University of Tennessee Press, 1985), p. 122.

19. Henry Glassie, *Pattern in the Material Folk Culture of the Eastern United States* (Philadelphia: University of Pennsylvania Press, 1968), pp. 78–79, 82–83, 102–6.

20. Olmsted, *Cotton Kingdom*, p. 42.

21. John Roles, *Inside Views of Slavery on Southern Plantations* (New York: John A. Gray and Green, 1864), p. 9.

22. Rawick, *The American Slave*, 4 (pt. 1): 55, 5 (pt. 3): 253; Yetman, *Life Under the "Peculiar Institution,"* p. 15.

23. Anne King Gregorie, *History of Sumter County, South Carolina* (Sumter, S.C.: Library Board of Sumter County, 1954), pp. 131, 144. See Janie Revill, *Sumter District* (Columbia, S.C.: State Printing Co., 1968), pp. 16–17 and the map between pages 28 and 29, for a discussion of the early development of the Singleton plantation.

24. Rawick, *The American Slave*, 2 (pt. 1): 104.

25. Ibid., 3 (pt. 2): 152.

26. John W. Cocke, "Remarks on Hedges, Bene Plant, and Pisé Buildings," *The American Farmer* 3, no. 20 (1821): 157.

27. Glassie, *Pattern in the Material Folk Culture*, pp. 89, 94–98.

28. Rawick, *The American Slave*, 16 (Ohio section): 50.

29. See Glassie, *Pattern in the Material Folk Culture*, p. 95, for examples of dogtrot house plans with doors in the passage.

30. Fred B. Kniffen, "Folk Housing: Key to Diffusion," in Dell Upton and John Michael Vlach, eds., *Common Places: Readings in American Vernacular Architecture* (Athens: University of Georgia Press, 1986), pp. 18–19. Square and rectangular units are also the basic house design elements along the coasts of West and Central Africa, indicating that slave housing in the United States may retain African as well as Euro-derived features of form.

31. Breeden, *Advice among Masters*, p. 114.

32. J. Harold Easterby, Jr., ed., *The South Carolina Rice Plantation as Revealed in the Papers of Robert F. W. Allston* (Chicago: University of Chicago Press, 1945), p. 348.

33. Herbert Anthony Keller, ed., *Solon Robinson: Pioneer and Agriculturist* (Indianapolis: Indiana Historical Bureau, 1936), 2:367.

34. Olmsted, *Cotton Kingdom*, p. 184.

35. Ibid., p. 249.

36. Frances Anne Kemble, *Journal of a Residence on a Georgian Plantation in 1838–1839* [1863], edited by John A. Scott (Athens: University of Georgia Press, 1984), pp. 67–68.

37. Glassie, *Pattern in the Material Folk Culture*, pp. 118–21; see also Jay Edwards, *Louisiana's Remarkable French Vernacular Architecture* (Baton Rouge: Department of Geography and Anthropology, Louisiana State University, 1988), pp. 2–11.

38. Jay Edwards, "French," in Dell Upton, ed., *America's Architectural Roots: Ethnic Groups That Built America* (Washington, D.C.: Preservation Press, 1986), p. 64.

39. George P. Rawick, Jay Hillegas, and Ken Lawrence, eds. *The American Slave: A Composite Autobiography*, supp. ser. 1 (Westport, Conn.: Greenwood Press, 1977), 8: 1037.

40. Breeden, *Advice among Masters*, pp. 124, 120.

41. Ibid., pp. 121, 128–29.

42. Ibid., p. 130.

43. Ibid., p. 121.

44. Cited in Ulrich B. Phillips, *Life and Labor in the Old South* (Boston: Little, Brown, 1929), pp. 333–34.

45. Olmsted, *Cotton Kingdom*, p. 160.

46. Alabama planter James Tait of Wilcox County actually intended to build a slave barracks in 1839. His written

specifications called for a brick structure three hundred feet long and eighteen feet wide, with walls eight feet high. Rooms were to be partitioned off at fifteen-foot intervals. Because of a slump in the price of cotton, the structure was never built (see Phillips, *Life and Labor in the Old South,* p. 281).

47. For examples of West Indian slave barracks, see William Chapman, "Slave Villages in the Danish West Indies: Changes of the Late Eighteenth and Early Nineteenth Centuries," in Thomas Carter and Bernard L. Herman, eds., *Perspectives in Vernacular Architecture IV* (Columbia: University of Missouri Press, 1991), p. 115.

48. Savannah Unit, Georgia Writers' Project, *Drums and Shadows: Survival Studies among the Georgia Coastal Negroes* (1940; reprint, Athens: University of Georgia Press, 1986), p. 179. See also John Michael Vlach, *The Afro-American Tradition in Decorative Arts* (Cleveland: Cleveland Museum of Art, 1978), p. 136, for an example of another African-inspired house built by a slave in Edgefield County, South Carolina.

49. Yetman, *Life Under the "Peculiar Institution,"* p. 291.

50. See Susan Denyer, *African Traditional Architecture: An Historical and Geographical Perspective* (New York: Africana Publishing Co., 1978), pp. 138–39; John Michael Vlach, "Sources of the Shotgun House: Antecedents for Afro-American Architecture," Ph.D. diss., Indiana University, 1975, 1:147–54.

51. Jean Cuvelier, *Relations sur le Congo du Père Laurent de Lucques (1700–1717),* quoted in Georges Balandier, *Daily Life in the Kingdom of Kongo from the Sixteenth to the Eighteenth Century* (New York: Pantheon Books, 1965), p. 141.

52. Peter Wood, *Black Majority: Negroes in Colonial South Carolina from 1670 through the Stono Rebellion* (New York: W. W. Norton, 1974), pp. 340–41; Philip D. Curtin, *The Atlantic Slave Trade: A Census* (Madison: University of Wisconsin Press, 1969), p. 157.

53. Vlach, *The Afro-American Tradition in Decorative Arts,* pp. 124–28.

54. Rawick, *The American Slave,* 2 (pt. 1): 173–74.

55. Rawick, Hillegas, and Lawrence, *The American Slave,* supp. ser. 1, 1:88.

56. Ibid., 11:129.

57. Ibid., supp. ser. 2, 7 (pt. 6): 2776.

58. Roderick A. McDonald, "Goods and Chattels: The Economy of Slaves on Sugar Plantations in Jamaica and Louisiana," Ph.D. diss., University of Kansas, 1981, p. 291.

59. Rawick, Hillegas, and Lawrence, *The American Slave,* supp. ser. 1, 4:644.

60. Olmsted, *Cotton Kingdom,* p. 185.

61. Eugene L. Schwaab, ed., *Travels in the Old South Selected from the Periodicals of the Times* (Lexington: University Press of Kentucky, 1973), 2:499.

62. Rawick, Hillegas, and Lawrence, *The American Slave,* supp. ser. 1, 8:866.

63. Breeden, *Advice among Masters,* pp. 266–75.

64. Eugene D. Genovese, *Roll, Jordan, Roll: The World the Slaves Made* (New York: Random House, 1972), p. 537.

65. Rawick, *The American Slave,* 4 (pt. 2): 157.

66. Rawick, Hillegas, and Lawrence, *The American Slave,* supp. ser. 1, 1:40.

67. "A Very Stern Discipline: An Interview with Ralph Ellison," *Harper's Magazine,* May 1967, p. 84.

**CHAPTER TWELVE**

1. John H. Scarff, "'Hampton,' Baltimore County, Maryland," *Maryland Historical Magazine* 43 (1948): 100.

2. Neal A. Brooks and Eric G. Ruckel, *A History of Baltimore County* (Towson, Md.: Friends of Towson Library, 1979), p. 226.

3. For further discussion of the Hampton outbuildings, see Lynne Dakin Hastings, *A Guidebook to Hampton National Historic Site* (Towson, Md.: Historic Hampton, Inc., 1986), pp. 63–69.

4. See Dawn F. Thomas, *The Green Spring Valley: Its History and Heritage* (Baltimore: Maryland Historical Society, 1978), pp. 217, 219, 285, and 373.

5. For stone construction in the mid-Atlantic region, see Scott T. Swank, *Arts of the Pennsylvania Germans* (New York: W. W. Norton, 1983), pp. 22–32.

6. George P. Rawick, ed., *The American Slave: A Composite Autobiography* (Westport, Conn.: Greenwood Press, 1972), 15 (pt. 2): 364.

7. Herman Ginther, *Captain Staunton's River* (Richmond, Va.: Dietz Press, 1968), pp. 17–18; Robert D. Lancaster, *Historic Virginia Homes and Churches* (Spartanburg, S.C.: Reprint Co., 1973), pp. 422–23.

8. For more on the I-house, see Fred B. Kniffen, "Folk Housing: Key to Diffusion," in Dell Upton and John Michael Vlach, eds., *Common Places: Readings in American Vernacular Architecture* (Athens: University of Georgia Press, 1986), pp. 7–10; and Henry Glassie, *Pattern in the Material Folk Culture of the Eastern United States* (Philadelphia: University of Pennsylvania Press, 1968), pp. 64–67.

9. Frederick Law Olmsted, *The Cotton Kingdom: A Traveller's Observations on Cotton and Slavery in the American Slave States,* edited by Arthur Schlesinger (New York: Alfred A. Knopf, 1953), p. 42.

10. Basil Hall, *Travels in North America in the Years 1827–1828,* quoted in Katharine M. Jones, *The Plantation*

*South* (Indianapolis, Ind.: Bobbs-Merrill, 1957), p. 101.

11. Charles Joyner, *Down by the Riverside: A South Carolina Slave Community* (Urbana: University of Illinois Press, 1984), p. 19.

12. Olmsted, *Cotton Kingdom*, p. 181.

13. Julia Floyd Smith, *Slavery and Rice Culture in Low Country Georgia, 1750–1860* (Knoxville: University of Tennessee Press, 1985), p. 101.

14. Charles H. Fairbanks, "The Kingsley Slave Cabins in Duval County, Florida," *Conference on Historic Site Archaeology Papers* 7 (1968): 67.

15. Philip S. May, "Zephaniah Kingsley, Nonconformist (1765–1843)," *Florida Historical Quarterly* 23 (1945): 154, 158.

16. Ulrich B. Phillips, *Life and Labor in the Old South* (Boston: Little, Brown, 1929), pp. 94–95; idem, *American Negro Slavery* (New York: D. Appleton, 1918), p. 212.

17. For an example of how much of the market planters could control, see Randolph B. Campbell, "Harrison County: A Study of Plantation Economics," in LeRoy Johnson, Jr., ed., *Texana II: Cultural Heritage of the Plantation South* (Austin: Texas Historical Commission, 1984), pp. 8–12.

18. Rawick, *The American Slave*, 6 (pt. 1): 385.

19. George P. Rawick, Jay Hillegas, and Ken Lawrence, eds., *The American Slave: A Composite Autobiography*, supp. ser. 1 (Westport, Conn.: Greenwood Press, 1977), 9: 1857.

20. Glassie, *Pattern in the Material Folk Culture*, pp. 89, 94–96.

21. For the contents of slave cabins, see John Michael Vlach, "Afro-American Domestic Artifacts in Eighteenth-Century Virginia," *Material Culture* 19 (1987): 3–24.

22. A similar pattern of land use is found in Edgefield County, South Carolina, the leading cotton-producing county in the state during the first half of the nineteenth century. See Orville Vernon Burton, *In My Father's House Are Many Mansions: Family and Community in Edgefield, South Carolina* (Chapel Hill: University of North Carolina Press, 1985), pp. 36–38.

23. J. Carlyle Sitterson, *Sugar Country: The Cane Sugar Industry in the South, 1753–1950* (Lexington: University Press of Kentucky, 1953), p. 45.

24. Cited in ibid., pp. 46–47.

25. John W. Blassingame, *The Slave Community: Plantation Life in the Antebellum South* (New York: Oxford University Press, 1972), p. 159.

26. John B. Rehder, "Sugar Plantation Settlements of Southern Louisiana: A Cultural Geography," Ph.D. diss., Louisiana State University, 1971, pp. 89, 98–99, 100–103.

27. Terry G. Jordan, "The Imprint of the Upper and Lower South on Mid-Nineteenth-Century Texas," *Annals of the Association of American Geographers* 57 (1967): 667–90.

28. George W. Tyler, *The History of Bell County* (San Antonio, Tex.: Naylor Co., 1936), p. 166.

29. Glassie, *Pattern in the Material Folk Culture*, pp. 103–6.

30. For the testimony of a slave cowboy from Texas, see Norman R. Yetman, ed., *Life Under the "Peculiar Institution": Selections from the Slave Narrative Collection* (New York: Holt, Rinehart, and Winston, 1970), pp. 50–52.

31. John B. Boles, *Black Southerners, 1619–1869* (Lexington: University Press of Kentucky, 1983), p. 77.

## CHAPTER THIRTEEN

1. Quoted in James Oakes, *Slavery and Freedom: An Interpretation of the Old South* (New York: Alfred A. Knopf, 1990), pp. 139–40.

2. James O. Breeden, ed., *Advice among Masters: The Ideal in Slave Management in the Old South* (Westport, Conn.: Greenwood Press, 1980), p. 55; capitals used in the original.

3. Dell Upton, "White and Black Landscapes in Eighteenth-Century Virginia," *Places* 2, no. 2 (1985): 69.

4. Frederick Douglass, *Life and Times of Frederick Douglass: His Early Life as a Slave, His Escape from Bondage, and His Complete History* (1892; reprint, New York: Collier Books, 1962), p. 40; emphasis in the original.

5. Kenneth M. Stampp, *The Peculiar Institution: Slavery in the Ante-bellum South* (New York: Random House, 1956), chap. 3, esp. pp. 90–91.

6. Drew Gilpin Faust, "Culture, Conflict, and Community: The Meaning of Power on an Antebellum Plantation," *Journal of Social History* 14, no. 1 (1980): 83.

7. John Blassingame, *The Slave Community: Plantation Life in the Antebellum South*, (New York: Oxford University Press, 1972), p. 180.

8. Faust, "Culture, Conflict, and Community," p. 93.

9. Leslie Howard Owens, *This Species of Property: Slave Life and Culture in the Old South* (New York: Oxford University Press, 1976), p. 224.

10. Leon Litwack, *Been in the Storm So Long: The Aftermath of Slavery* (New York: Alfred A. Knopf, 1979), p. 387. See also Sidney W. Mintz and Richard Price, *An Anthropological Approach to the Afro-American Past: A Caribbean Perspective* (Philadelphia: Institute for the Study of Human Issues, 1976), p. 20.

11. See Paul D. Escott, *Slavery Remembered: A Record of Twentieth-Century Slave Narratives* (Chapel Hill: University of North Carolina Press, 1979), pp. 72–73, 83–84, for discussions of slaves who hid in the woods near planta-

tions. For descriptions of slaves who became maroons, see George P. Rawick, ed., *The American Slave: A Composite Autobiography* (Westport, Conn.: Greenwood Press, 1972), 12 (pt. 1): 292; and Charles L. Perdue, Jr., Thomas E. Barden, and Robert K. Phillips, *Weevils in the Wheat: Interviews with Virginia Ex-Slaves* (Charlottesville: University Press of Virginia, 1976), pp. 209–10.

12. Douglass, *Life and Times of Frederick Douglass*, p. 39.

13. Quoted in James Oakes, *The Ruling Race: A History of American Slaveholders* (New York: Alfred A. Knopf, 1982), p. 185.

14. "Letters to the Jefferson Family," in John W. Blassingame, ed., *Slave Testimony: Two Centuries of Letters, Speeches, Interviews, and Autobiographies* (Baton Rouge: Louisiana State University Press, 1977), p. 17.

15. On black slaveowners, see Michael P. Johnson and James L. Roark, *Black Masters: A Free Family of Color in the Old South* (New York: W. W. Norton, 1984); David O. Whitten, *Andrew Durnford: A Black Sugar Planter in Antebellum Louisiana* (Baton Rouge: Louisiana State University Press, 1981).

16. Quoted in Oakes, *Ruling Race*, p. 190.

17. Rawick, *The American Slave*, 2 (pt. 2): 139.

18. Litwack, *Been in the Storm So Long*, p. 158.

19. Escott, *Slavery Remembered*, p. 93.

20. Quoted in Oakes, *Ruling Race*, p. 187.

21. C. W. Harper, "Black Aristocrats: Domestic Servants on the Antebellum Plantation," *Phylon* 46 (June 1985): 131; Rawick, *The American Slave*, 9 (pt. 3): 121.

22. Rawick, *The American Slave*, 4 (pt. 1): 261.

23. Quoted in Lynne Fauley Emery, *Black Dance in the United States from 1690 to 1970* (Palo Alto, Calif.: National Press Books, 1972), p. 112.

24. Oakes, *Slavery and Freedom*, p. 147.

25. Raymond A. Bauer and Alice H. Bauer, "Day to Day Resistance to Slavery," *Journal of Negro History* 27 (1942): 388–419.

26. James C. Scott, *Weapons of the Weak: Everyday Forms of Peasant Resistance* (New Haven, Conn.: Yale University Press, 1985), p. 34.

27. Douglass, *Life and Times of Frederick Douglass*, p. 52.

# Index

Page numbers in *italic* type refer to illustrations.